# GO FIGURE

# GO FIGURE

## My Wacky Journey
## From Outlaw to Leading Citizen

RICK CARLE

Carle Publishing
706 N. 20th St.
Fort Dodge, Ia. 50501

**GO FIGURE! My Wacky Journey From Outlaw To Leading Citizen**

ISBN: 978-0-9834615-2-4 Print
ISBN: 978-0-9834615-1-7 eBook

Edited by Cliff Carle
Cover photo by Aaron Will
Highway Patrolman illustration by Jeff Carle

# Table of Contents

**Chapter 1**      3
AS IT WAS IN THE BEGINNING

**Chapter 2**      11
YOUNGEST (AND DEAREST?)

**Chapter 3**      23
SLOW GETAWAYS

**Chapter 4**      35
VALUES ADDED

**Chapter 5**      43
SCHOOLIN' AND FOOLIN'

**Chapter 6**      55
GRANDFATHER'S WORK FARM

**Chapter 7**      67
GROCERY STORE FUN GALORE

**Chapter 8**      77
FIRE

**Chapter 9**      91
LAST CHANCE AT FIRST LOVE

**Chapter 10**      101
I FOUGHT THE LAW ... AND IT WAS A TIE

**Chapter 11**      115
IT'S A BUST

**Chapter 12**      125
COLLEGE CRAZIES

**Chapter 13**      147
JUNIOR ENTREPRENEUR

**Chapter 14**      157
DEALIN' AND WHEELIN'

**Chapter 15**      173
DOCTORING ME UP

**Chapter 16**      181
EX – CUSE ME!

**Chapter 17**      203
AFTER DIVORCE: THE FUN FRONTIER

**Chapter 18**      221
WORKING OVER TIME

**Chapter 19**      249
FRIENDS, ACQUAINTENCES & PEOPLE I'D LIKE TO FORGET

**Chapter 20**      275
DAD

**Chapter 21**      287
WHO KNEW?

**Chapter 22**      291
LIGHTNING STRIKES TWICE

**Chapter 23**      295
IT'S BEEN A GOODYEAR

**Chapter 24**      307
PARTING THOUGHTS

# AUTHOR DISCLAIMER

While I'm calling this a memoir, unlike James Frey (*A Million Little Pieces*) and Greg Mortenson (*Three Cups of Tea*), I'm letting you know right out of the gate that this book is not entirely factual and comes with a self-protective disclaimer. All illegal events described herein, and the unlawful acts perpetrated by myself and my co-conspirators are *mostly* true. Some have been exaggerated for effect or humor, and in each case I expect this to be obvious.

The names of all my partners in crime have been changed to protect the guilty… oops, I meant to say to protect them and their families. As far as I know, almost all of them have changed their outlaw ways, and have turned their lives around as I did; thus they deserve to be left alone. Certain other names of totally innocent people have been changed as well for a variety of reasons; the most popular being: "upon request".

On other specifics such as exact dates, dollar amounts, types and quantities of drugs, and other criminal details, I plead the fifth. If ever called to task by the authorities, I will vehemently deny everything, proclaim this is a work of fiction, and evoke the Mark Twain Mandate: *"Never let the truth get in the way of a good story."*

## Chapter 1

# AS IT WAS IN THE BEGINNING

I had a flashback this morning while driving to work: I saw myself back in the good ol' days, coming home from Colorado with a trunk full of illegal drugs. Marijuana, amphetamines, Quaaludes, LSD, cocaine, you name it. And I was filled with absolute wonder: *How can I possibly be walking this good earth today a free man?* But I'm getting ahead of myself.

My story begins on February 14th, a cold, blistery, winter day back in 1924 on the plains of Nebraska. It was the day my mother, Elinor M. Carlberg, was born. I thought it was worth noting because without Mom I wouldn't have been born. Plus, I don't know anyone else whose birthday is also Valentine's Day. I've always felt sorry for people who have a birthday on a holiday. They have to split their one special day—and they're really screwed if it's December 25th. They get the same number of presents, but one says "Happy Birthday" on it.

To this day Mom has never told me her middle name. Her story is, "I've never liked it, my mom was going for Jayne, but my older sister came up with my middle name." Mom went on to explain, "When my sister, my best friend Phyllis, and I lived in California after high school, we had a mean old neighbor with bright red hair, who was uglier than a mud fence. She had the same name."

My guess is that her sister and Phyllis made fun of Mom's middle name by reminding her of that old bat. Mom has a small frame; she's very smart, sometimes stubborn, and honest as the day is long. In fact, if she was put on a horse with a noose around her neck, and given the choice to lie, or have the horse swatted on the butt, she'd say, "Slap the horse." This is why I've always had a hard time telling a lie …okay, sometimes I make an exception.

Mom is somewhat of a prudish woman, which I think came from being raised in the 30s and 40s by strict parents. When I was a kid, my parents told my brothers and me stories of when they were young: "In the dead of winter, we had to get up before dawn to milk thirty cows," they'd say, "and then we had to walk two miles to school uphill, both ways … carrying our younger brothers and sisters!"

We knew they were exaggerating for effect, but later in life I realized that what they were trying to tell us was they had to work hard even before they went to school, and that growing up back then wasn't cake. They'd always remind me of that whenever I complained about how tough I thought my life was. I often used that line on my kids whenever they complained that life wasn't fair. Instead of milking cows, I told them that starting at 4:00 AM, I delivered over 100 newspapers before school. My fabrication had the same effect on them as it did me: "Yeah right!"

My dad, Louis David Carle, was born in Yankton, South

Dakota. His birth certificate somehow disappeared, and with eight other kids to keep tabs on, his parents lost track of the day he was born. They decided to say it was May 21; the same day as his dad's birthday. He was medium sized, but a very strong man, as I found out later in my teens. Perhaps his most defining feature was his perennial butch haircut.

The summer I turned nine, I cried and cried because I wanted a butch cut like all my friends were getting. Mom, who doubled as the family barber, and was an expert in the "bowl cut", warned me, "Your hair is too thin and you are too light skinned. Believe me, Rick, you will burn."

I wouldn't relent and she finally gave in. After my first day in the sun, I felt like smoke was coming off my head; even with Noxzema plastered all over it. That was my hell week. From then on, I learned to always heed Mom's advice…except when I didn't. Yeah, I know, that makes no sense.

Dad was a proud Navy man who had traveled around the world several times. He told us stories of other Navy men who had jumped into the ocean to cool off and go for a swim, only to be attacked by sharks. I know if I'd been on the ship, I wouldn't have jumped in for anything. After seeing the movie *Jaws*, it took me almost a year to feel comfortable just taking a bath.

The story Dad liked to tell over and over was that he was on one of the ships that took the Marines to Iwo Jima, where the famous picture of the four Marines raising the flag was taken. He harrumphed, "The Marines got all the credit, but they couldn't walk on water. They weren't Jesus. It was the Navy who got the Marines over there."

It is said that opposites attract. Whoever coined that phrase must have met my parents. Dad smoked three packs of Salem menthol cigarettes a day, routinely drank vodka 7's, cussed a lot, and got his point across with a belt. He'd also spend money on things that he never used, or that didn't make sense. Dad had a garage full of almost every tool ever made, and they always looked brand-new. In some cases, he had duplicates of the same one. For example, he'd forget he already had a Dual Function Scriber Guage, and dash to the hardware store to buy a new one. It was a good thing the Home Shopping Network wasn't on TV back then.

Mom, on the other hand, has never smoked. I think wine has touched her lips twice in her lifetime. To my knowledge she has never uttered a cuss word. She occasionally gave us a swat on the butt with her hand. And she's very tight with her money. I liked to say, "Mom can turn a dime into a quarter." Their differences must have been one of the reasons they got along all the years they were married. It was good that Mom controlled the checkbook at home and in the businesses. Dad either bought all of his tools behind Mom's back, or was a good enough salesman to convince her that he desperately needed them. Mom was a good reality check for Dad.

They met at a roller skating rink in Pender, Nebraska. It was the only form of entertainment back then if you don't count pig, chicken, and sheep judging at the county fair. After a short dating period, Dad was called up to join the service. He was stationed at Treasure Island in San Francisco, California. Soon after WWII started, Mom, her sister Dorothy, and best friend Phyllis drove from Nebraska in a beat-up 1938 Pontiac sedan that Dorothy had bought just days before the trip. Amazingly the three women traveled by themselves and were lucky they didn't have car problems along the way. None of them were mechanically inclined to do any repairs if needed. They ended up in Eagle Rock, California to do their part for the war effort. All three worked in a box factory that was converted over to make guns, bullets, bombs, and radar equipment.

Dad must've gotten lonely on board the ship because he called back to Nebraska to talk to Mom. Her parents told him, "She is out in Los Angeles." After some effort, he was able to locate her, and they started up their relationship again.

When the war ended, Dad went to work for Orrie Rodeffer, a friend who he met in the Navy. Orrie's uncle owned a large cement company in California. Within a year, the uncle decided to retire, and sold the company to Orrie.

Orrie wasn't sure he could run the company by himself and said, "Lou, I'd like you to be my partner."

By this time, Mom had moved back to her parents' home in Nebraska. Dad told Orrie, "Thanks for the offer, but I'm going after Elinor." Her friend Phyllis, was smart enough to stay and marry Orrie. Even with all the hot bikini-wearing babes in California, Dad couldn't get his mind off Elinor.

Back in the cold, wind-driven, nothing-to-do plains of Nebraska they got married. When I was older, Dad informed me, "Orrie became a huge success. His company built several of the freeways in California, and some of the driveways in Beverly Hills. But he's most famous for building many of the first indoor racquetball courts." The man is a mega-millionaire and my mom's best friend is his wife. What in the hell were my parents thinking? They could've had a double wedding out in L.A! I could've grown up on the beach, been a knarly surfer dude. I had the long blond hair look down.

Whenever we had tough financial times, I'd remind my parents of Orrie's company. They never liked hearing it, but I enjoyed rubbing it in. The moral of this story is when opportunity knocks, open the frickin' door!

By the time I was born on the fourth of June in 1955, both of my grandmothers had already passed away. I've always said, "That is why I was never spoiled as a child." I'm sure my older brothers will disagree with that statement. As a toddler, my hair was so whitish-blond, the joke was you needed sunglasses to look at me. Now, can somebody tell me why blond kids are unmercifully called a "toe-head"?

Being the youngest of four brothers, I was always referred to as "the baby of the family." Even as I got older, people didn't let up. What a pain—literally. At family reunions, my aunts came over to me, put a lobster-claw clamp on one of my cheeks, and say, "Aren't you so cute, the baby of the family."

"Hello!" as I held up my driver's license.

I don't know if it was because of my parents' strict upbringing, or just the times back in the 50s and 60s, but I don't remember getting many hugs or being told, "I love you." I know they did love me, it just wasn't ever said out loud. Maybe they didn't hear it from their parents either, but they inadvertently passed the trait on to me. I have a difficult time telling my kids and grandkids how I feel about them. I do love them very much and they know that I do, but I don't say it as much as I should. My daughter, Katie, is really helping me to say it more. I've learned to tell Mom that I love her when I finish talking to her on the phone. I think most of the time it takes her by surprise. I am glad that when Dad was suffering with cancer in 1989, I told him that I loved him every day when I talked to him on the phone. It was bad enough that he lived so many miles away, so I used the telephone to reach out and touch him.

So now I don't have to go through the rest of my life wishing that I had gotten over myself. Life is tough enough without that dark cloud hanging over your head. I strongly suggest telling those you love how you feel every time you see them, or talk to them. You never know when that day will come when they are gone. Otherwise, you'll go through life with your head hung low, kicking the can down the road of life, and wishing you'd taken that opportunity.

For myself, I've realized the best way to achieve this is not to go around being too full of myself. My older brothers did their part to help me keep my ego in check. I'll bet you can't imagine some of the sick things they did to me when I was young.

*Elinor Carlberg, my mom, 1924, six months old*

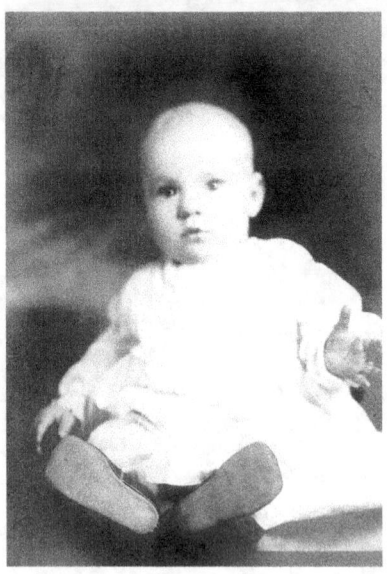

*Louis David Carle, my dad, 1924, five months old*

## Chapter 2

# YOUNGEST (AND DEAREST?)

B eing the youngest had an equal number of advantages and disadvantages. Whenever we had a babysitter, for some reason I can't remember, us kids chased each other around the house like a bunch of pint-sized maniacs. Inevitable accidents happened, but I could always blame things that got broken on my older brothers, since my parents couldn't believe that little ol' innocent me could get into trouble. I'd tell on my big brothers and the parents always took my side. I loved it!

But Rodney, Cliff, and Jeff were forever on the lookout for ingenious ways to get even with me. They knew that I loved to drink 7-Up soda. One day they took grease from a frying pan, mixed it with cold water, and put the mixture in an empty 7-Up bottle (They were dark green in those days, which camouflaged the brown grease). My loving brothers pretended to pop the cap, then handed it to me to drink. I should've thought something was up since they rarely did anything nice for me. Instead, I trusted them and took a big swallow. Seconds later, my face matched the color of the 7-Up bottle. I was sick for the rest of the day, while they enjoyed a good laugh.

One time, another trick they pulled was giving me a bite of bitter Baking Chocolate and telling me it was Hershey's. This is one of those "Don't Try This At Home" stunts. Take my word: if you ever need to make yourself vomit for any reason, after grease and water, unsweetened Baking Chocolate is your next best bet.

While Mom and Dad were at work my bro's made me do the dishes, the laundry, vacuum the floors, fold the clothes, etc. (I never realized that later in life after getting married, then divorced, that I'd be glad I had mastered all of those chores.)

They'd gang up on me: "You tell Mom or Dad and we'll beat the crap out of you."

"But it's not fair that I have to do all of the work," I protested.

"Tough, and you better do it right, so we don't get into trouble."

"And if I don't…"

"Just try it and see what happens to you."

They had put the fear of God in me, so I did *all* the chores that were supposed to be equally shared, and never told our parents until I was in my twenties. They were very upset to hear about it, but by then my bro's had long ago moved out.

In our three-bedroom house in Lyons, Nebraska, we had one of those old-fashioned clothes chutes that you threw clothes in from the upstairs and they ended up down in the basement. The wooden clothes box downstairs was approximately four feet wide by three feet tall. It had a hinged lid so it could be opened to get the clothes out.

My brother, Cliff, the second oldest, got some weird satisfaction out of putting me, and my next oldest brother, Jeff, in the box.

He'd then close the lid and sit on it so we couldn't do a thing until he was damn good and ready to let us out. It was dark, scary, and crowded in there.

We'd yell, "Let us out! Please let us out!"

Cliff just sat on the lid and cackled with sadistic glee while waiting for us to say the magic words...

We had an aunt who was grossly overweight, had dark moles on her face, and always wanted you to kiss her on the cheek when she came to visit. While I'd never kissed a horned toad, I couldn't imagine it'd be much different. Her name was Ethel. Between us brothers, when you'd had enough torture, or the pain was too great, you never said, "I give!" If you were put in a full nelson, a choke hold, being sat on, or in some kind of an inescapable situation, in order to get out of it, you had to say, "I love Aunt Ethel!"

So, we'd be held against our will in the clothes box prison until we said the embarrassing words. We didn't want to give in, so we'd cry and cry, hoping Cliff had a soft side.

But Cliff just laughed louder and said, "You know what to say if you want out..."

Finally, after we couldn't take it anymore, begrudgingly we'd holler, "I love Aunt Ethel!" Then, and only then, did Cliff let us out.

Cliff never knew what kind of lasting effect being boxed in would have on us. To this day, Jeff will not get on an elevator. It doesn't matter if he has to go up to the top floor of a 30-story building—he will always take the stairs. In 1987, my kids and I visited Jeff in Lincoln, Nebraska. They wanted to go to the top of the Capital Building for the panoramic view of the city. The antiquated elevator fit five people max. Jeff adamantly refused to go up with us.

Myself, I still have a hard time with elevators as well. I get in them and have to look down at my feet while I quietly pray to

God, "Please don't let the elevator freeze, and please let the doors be well-oiled and working properly." I'm sweating bullets until the door mercifully opens.

When I went to work for Goodyear, they sent me to school in Ohio. I was booked on the fifth floor of the hotel. My training lasted four weeks. On the third day, I was riding the elevator up to my room. All of a sudden, the elevator stopped in between the second and third floors. I immediately got visions of my childhood in the clothes box and began freaking out. I desperately wanted to ring the emergency button and yell, "I love Aunt Ethel!" but that wouldn't have helped; Cliff wasn't there.

Thank God there was someone else in the elevator with me who knew what to do. He somehow got the inner doors open. Then we banged on the outer doors with our fists until someone on the outside heard us, and pried them open. They grabbed our arms and helped us climb out of the elevator. I made a beeline for the front desk and demanded they move me to the ground floor. But the hotel was completely books up for the training. So every day, three or four times a day, it was up and down five flights of stairs for me.

Something else that freaks me out today is getting in an MRI X-ray machine. As I am conveyored into the device I feel my arms and shoulders being squeezed very tightly. I look upward and all I see is a white tomb that is inches from my face. I feel like I'm in a cylindrical casket.

The first time I went in for an MRI the nursed asked me, "Are you claustrophobic?"

I said, "I could write a book about it."

"You'll have these headphones on so you can listen to music, and we'll be able to talk to each other." She handed them to me with an encouraging smile.

"How long will it take?" I inquired as bomb-size sweat droplets poured down my forehead.

"Only about twenty minutes."

Let me tell you twenty minutes seems like twenty hours when you're freaking out. After ten minutes I could feel my heart racing like Secretariat at the Kentucky Derby, and yelled out, "You have to get me out of here! I can't take this anymore!"

The nurse said sweetly, "We're almost done, Mr. Carle. Surely you can hold on for just a few more minutes."

"No!" This time I screamed. "Get me outta here!"

She showed mercy and hit the eject button and the machine slowly slid me out. I went from flat on my back to standing across the room in what must have been record time.

The nurse jumped back and gasped, "I'm sorry, Mr. Carle, but we didn't get all the pictures we need. You're going to have to go back in."

"Yeah right," I said over my shoulder, already out the door, "Maybe tomorrow."

Ten years later, I was scheduled to have another MRI. I told my nurse about the last experience.

She offered, "How about we give you a little sedative? That'll help you."

Let me tell you, "little" was the operative word because my heart was racing just as fast as the first time. I don't know how, but this time I was able to weather the twenty minutes, but I was a pathetic wreck when they brought me out.

The third and last time I was scheduled for an MRI, the nurse came up with the idea to put a cloth towel over my eyes before they sent me in. That worked much better. When I looked up it was pitch dark and I pretended I was home in bed at midnight.

I still don't like the closeness I feel with my arms and shoulders, but I can now last the twenty minutes without yelling for them to get me out, or impulsively blurting out, "I love Aunt Ethel."

I even had a hard time whenever I took my kids camping. We'd sleep in pup tents and when I woke up in the middle of the night, I felt like I couldn't breathe. I'd have to vacate the tent and walk around the campgrounds, taking deep breaths before I could go back inside, and try again to fall asleep. My kids never knew about this. I've never told them, but one time I had to sleep with my head just outside the tent. As much as I tried, and even with the thought of a bear mistaking my noggin for a midnight snack, I could not go back inside. I'd like to take this time in the book to thank Cliff for messing me up for life.

At one of our family reunions, the subject of the clothes box came up. Mom could not believe that the story we were telling was true.

"Clifford, how could you have done that?" she exclaimed. Cliff just sat on the couch chuckling to himself. Jeff and I can also laugh about it today as long as we aren't on an elevator. I felt sorry for Mom...she believed she was a bad parent for not knowing about and putting a stop to it. There were a lot of cruel and unusual things she found out that day she didn't know about while we were growing up...

***

Dad often told us, "As long as you are under my roof, you will do as I say." And if any one of us ever wanted to challenge this rule, we had the option to go down to the basement with him and put on the boxing gloves. "If you win," he promised us, "you can do as you please. But if I win, you do as I say."

When I was fourteen, I grew tired of having to be home by nine o'clock at night. My older brothers were able to stay out later and I wanted too as well. So, I grew some balls and decided to take Dad on.

"Let's go, Dad. I'm ready," I said, sticking out my chest.

"Are you sure?"

"I know I can beat you."

Dad just chuckled as he walked down to the basement and put on the boxing gloves. I cockily slammed mine together to let him know he was going down.

"You ready?" Dad said calmly.

"You bet I am."

I put my left boxing glove up to protect my face. Before I could float like a butterfly, and sting like a bee with my right hand, the fight was over with only one punch. Dad smacked my left glove, which ricocheted into my face. The power of his punch was so strong that I flew into the cement wall, six feet away, with the right side of my face, and I was down and out. I remember seeing stars and hearing Howard Cosell say, "Down goes Carle, down goes Carle," then counting to ten. Minutes later I had a welt on the right side of my face the size of a golf ball. I wish I'd known ahead of time that Dad was a boxer in the Navy. For some reason, *that* never came up during his war stories. Now that I think about it, anytime I wanted to challenge his rules, it was always settled with a boxing match; not arm wrestling or finger jousting. He knew he'd always win. Talk about putting the thumb on the scale!

The next day I had to go to school and explain to my friends, the teachers and the principal, what had happened to me.

"My Dad hit me!" I sighed.

Now, back in those days, there weren't any child protective services, so no police or social worker came to our door, or anything like it, to get Dad in trouble. Once I explained what had happened, and that I was stupid for not putting both hands up to protect my face, everybody thought it was funny.

I didn't challenge Dad again until I was sixteen. It was Prom Night; three of my friends and I didn't have dates. We decided to drive around, do some illegal drinking, and play Mailbox Baseball. For those of you not familiar with this Midwestern game, I'll explain. You drive around the countryside half drunk with your windows down. As you go by a farmer's mailbox, you hang a baseball bat out the open window and swing. Usually, it does some decent damage to the mailbox because the car is moving at least twenty miles per hour. And you get your frustrations out at the same time. More Midwestern fun!

My curfew for the evening was midnight. By the time any of us checked our watches it was one in the morning.

I knew I'd be in trouble and announced, "I gotta go home, it's after twelve."

One of my concerned friends explained it to me: "You're already late, so you might as well stay out a little longer and have some more fun." It must have been peer pressure (or beer pressure) that made me say, "That makes sense to me."

I got home at four in the morning. I figured I'd just sneak in the back door, head straight to my room, and nobody'd be none the wiser. I was proud of myself for being so quiet considering that I'd had a lot to drink. Wouldn't you know it —my parents were waiting up for me in the living room. Before I had a chance to make up a dumb excuse, Dad had knocked me to the floor. At that point the yelling began. Dad must not have liked my lame explanation because he kind of lost it and started kicking me.

Mom, lovely Mom, yelled, "Lou, don't kick him in the face!"

I was thinking, *Face? How about the rest of me? As in don't kick me any-damn-where!*

I want to tell you, until I graduated and left for college, if Dad yelled, "Jump," my immediate response was, "Is this high enough?" I probably could've been a star high jumper in track my senior year. I only would've needed Dad standing behind me.

*** 

My parents and I were watching TV one Saturday night; I think it was *The Lawrence Welk Show*. They rarely missed it. He was like a musical god to them. I couldn't stand the show. They played really old people's style of music and there was a lot of dorky-looking dancing going on. We also had to watch *The Ed Sullivan Show* every Sunday night. I think the only time I enjoyed Sullivan was the night The Beatles were on, singing *I Wanna To Hold Your Hand*. That was the one night my parents hated the show. They couldn't understand why all the girls were screaming. They must've thought, *Nobody ever screams like that on the 'The Lawrence Welk Show.'* All of a sudden there was a loud bang down in the basement. It sounded like a gun had just gone off.

"Oh my God, what was that?" Mom screamed. She thought one of my brothers had been shot. I've never seen my parents run so fast. When we all got downstairs, there stood Rodney and Cliff. They had these huge surprised and scared faces. The "just got caught with their hands in the cookie jar" kind of look. Or your expression when your girlfriend says, "I'm pregnant!"

We could see that neither one of them were injured or bleeding.

"What the hell happened?" Dad barked.

Rodney, with a dopey grin on his face, said, "Uh…we were just tossing a shotgun shell back and forth to each other and it hit the basement floor. The shell just went off."

Here's what really happened: Cliff had earlier emptied all the BBs out of the shotgun shell. The dufus wondered what would happen if he took a hammer and a nail and pounded on the primer. Duh? Rodney held the shell while Cliff took aim and… KABLOOEY! Then they were too embarrassed at their stupidity to tell Mom and Dad the truth.

My parents were glad that nobody was hurt; but then I saw the belt coming off. And Dad's face had that look…the "Justice is mine" look. I thought, *Am I glad I was upstairs, because I'm really gonna enjoy this.* There were a few things I really liked to do while growing up; going to the zoo in Omaha, kissing a girl that first time, getting a bike for Christmas; but having a front row seat while watching my older brothers getting a lickin' was at the top of my list. My brothers had to go up the stairs while getting their butts whipped with the belt. Now, in our house skipping steps was not allowed, it was one at a time. That afforded Dad as many swings as he thought necessary for them to learn their lesson. Meanwhile, I'm laughing and thinking to myself, *Batter up!*

I don't know where I came up with the idea that I could walk on water, but I discovered at a very early age that it's easier to sink than to float.

*(L to R) Jeff, Cliff, Dad, Rodney, and me June 1960*

# Chapter 3

## SLOW GETAWAYS

My parents were really into taking family vacations. Each summer we went to places like The Badlands in South Dakota, The Royal Gorge in Colorado, and fishing for Northern Pike and Walleye in Minnesota. We weren't rich, but not dirt poor either. So, I guess that leaves middle class. With three older brothers there was no elbow room left in the back seat. Therefore, being the youngest, I had to sit in the front seat of our 1956 Chevy station wagon, in between our parents. My older brothers in the back seat played "last touch," a game where they try to be the last one to tag the other. Then the other retaliates and tags back. The game goes on some time between forever and when Dad screams, "Knock it off already!" You then try to do it nonchalantly, so you can still get away with it, and claim the victory.

The parents tried to keep us entertained by playing the alphabet game while we were riding for miles and miles in the car: You looked for billboards along the highway; the game begins by someone finding a word that starts with "A". When you saw the sign, you had to yell out "A", then say the word to prove it. We were so competitive, that wasn't good enough for our family; you also had to have someone else see the word on the sign to verify it. Of course, fights erupted when two of us saw the word at the same time. Mom couldn't play—she had to be the referee and determine who saw it first. The game usually stalled out when we got to the letter "Q". You could go a hundred miles and never find a sign with a word that started with "Q". So, we evolved the rules to include license plates of cars that we'd meet or pass to keep the game going.

Mom continually pointed out the lovely, breathtaking scenery along the way. But my older brothers couldn't care less about purple mountains majesty or fruited plains. They were only interested in the answer to an age-old question. Like all kids on a long, boring drive, they kept badgering Dad with, "Are we there yet?" My brothers asked it over and over until they drove Dad batty! He'd warn them, "Don't make me stop the car and come back there!" We'd just snicker under our breaths so he couldn't hear us.

Even though Dad could get real mean when he lost his temper, I never considered him a child abuser; more like a strict disciplinarian. My brothers and I definitely were taught right from wrong. Sometimes we were slow learners, and he'd use the belt on our behinds to get our attention, so "right" could soak in real deep. But then he'd actually say, "This is hurting me more than it is hurting you." I don't know if you have ever been hit with a belt--the pain kept us from sitting down for several hours. But I guess somehow his arm hurt more from swinging the belt--like that rotator-cuff thing baseball pitchers get…yeah right!

**\*\*\***

Before I was born, the family was living in West Point, Nebraska. Dad left for work and told my older brothers, "You boys play in the *yard*. I don't want to catch you in the street—or else." My brothers must have thought with Dad at work, how could he catch them? Like most curious boys they wanted to test the waters of the forbidden street. But one of Dad's jobs at the market where he worked was to deliver groceries to elderly customers who weren't able to come to the store. On the way back, he'd swing by the house to check on the boys; and once in a while he'd catch them where they weren't supposed to be. Dad stopped the car, jumped out, and paddled my brothers right on the spot, ordering them, "Get back in the yard where I told you to stay." One of the neighbors thought Dad was being too mean, but Dad explained to him, "I'd rather spank them so they stay in the yard than have them get run over by a car."

Back in those days "time-outs" hadn't been invented yet--like kids today get when they misbehave. With four of us kids to deal with, Dad didn't have time for "time-outs," instead it was batter-up.

I remember developing pretty good reaction reflexes there in the front seat while we traveled on vacation. When Dad had enough with my brothers' antics, he took his right arm and swung it into the back seat, usually getting one or two of them. I had to guess when the swing was coming, so I could duck, or I'd get clipped by the hit that was intended for the misbehaving brothers.

When I was finally old enough to sit in the back seat, but still too young to pack my own suitcase, Mom did it for me. I guess I was too dumb to figure out which shorts, underwear, socks, shirts and shoes were needed. But I was just smart enough to figure out the seating strategy. I'd be out in the car a good half hour before we left. I'd sit in the seat directly behind Dad, then lock the door. As my brothers come out to the car one-by-one, they'd try to open the door. Obviously, they couldn't.

They'd knock on the window and yell, "Open the door and slide over!" But I'd just sit there shaking my head back and forth. They knocked harder as if I was deaf, and demanded that I move over. I may have been the youngest, but I was no fool. I knew this spot was the safest one in the entire car, being out of Dad's reach. Plus, I got to enjoy seeing my older brothers get smacked. I thought it was God's way of evening it up for the mean things they did to me.

**✳✳✳**

When I was five, we went to Pikes Peak in Colorado--one of the highest mountains in the United States at over 14,000 feet. Behind our station wagon, Dad pulled a pop-up camper. Do you remember those smelly, hot, no-room campers that slept three comfortably…if you were lucky? At last count, we had six… over-crowding to the max!

In 1960, the means to get up the mountain was just a narrow gravel road. Mom suggested leaving the camper at the bottom. Since Dads know everything, we headed up the mountain, hauling the camper along behind.

As we went around the winding curves to the top, we looked out the right-side windows, and it felt like the car was going to careen off the side of the mountain. *Real Midwestern Excitement!* When we'd meet another car, both of us had to move over the best we could so the cars didn't scrape each other, or tear off the side mirrors.

By the time we got to the top, the car was shaking and making a loud thumping noise. Dad got out, and discovered we had a flat tire. As you can imagine, the back of the car was full of luggage. That is also where the spare tire and jack was kept. Dad had to unload the entire luggage first. He finally got the jack out, and began jacking up the car, but it wouldn't move—not even an inch. Dad realized this was because the camper was hooked to the back of the car. As he unhooked the camper, Mom said, "You should have listened to me, and left it at the bottom." That was advice Dad did not need at that particular moment. Nor was that the end of the lesson.

After Dad got the tire changed, we took in the spectacular view from the top of the mountain. Just like in the song, "You could see forever…and ever." Security fences were unheard of back then, and Mom later told me, "You headed right for the end of the cliff." I guess I thought the view of forever and ever would be better from the very edge. Besides, kids don't have any fear when they are that young. Lucky for me, my oldest brother, Rodney, dashed over and grabbed me right before I would've tumbled and bounced off all the rocks on the way to the bottom of the mountain. This was my first of many near misses with death. Apparently, I have more lives than a gunnysack full of cats…as you'll see later.

On the way down the mountain, the other side of the car had the scary view. About halfway down, an awful smell of something burning wafted in through the windows. Dad stopped the car and discovered that the brakes were bright red, and hot enough to fry proverbial eggs on. I guess when you have to use them all the way down you can really burn them up, especially if you're pulling a camper. We had to stop several times to let the brakes cool off.

One of the times while we were waiting, steam began pouring out from under the car's hood. Kee-riste! Now, the damn radiator had overheated. Poor Dad, he couldn't catch a break that day. The rest of the way down, besides having to let the brakes cool off, he also had to keep putting water in the radiator. Unlike the cars of today where you simply fill a plastic reservoir tank; back then, each time you had to unscrew the burning hot cap with a handkerchief, while trying to dodge the scorching water that was erupting like a volcano.

We finally got to the bottom, after what felt like a week later, and Mom couldn't resist: "This wouldn't have happened if you'd left the camper down here." I watched the steam rolling off Dad's head as I hid behind him, quietly snickering.

✱✱✱

We took several vacations to Ten Mile Lake at Bemidji, Minnesota. For those of you who've never been there, it is the home of Paul Bunyan and his ox, Blue. They have a huge statue of them that stands over fifty feet tall. I guess the Bemidji citizens hoped to bamboozle gullible tourists into believing the legend was true.

We went fishing on the lake, which got its name for; you guessed it, being ten miles long. TML was also four miles wide. The cabins were located on the west side of the lake. I found out when I was ten years old how long it takes to get across the lake in a rental boat. While everyone else slept in, Dad and I were up at dawn and motored over to the east side because, "The biggest Northern Pikes are hiding in the reeds over there," he claimed.

"Okay," I said.

"When we get there, we'll troll along the edges of the reeds."

"How long will it take to get there?"

"Not long, just sit back and be quiet."

Trust me, it takes a long time with a nine-horse motor. We finally got there and fished for the better part of the morning. There were no clouds in the sky, and the summer sun was scorching hot. Plus, we forgot to bring water along.

Around 2:00 in the afternoon, Dad sort of groaned and said, "I'm not feeling too good, we need to head over to the shore."

When we got there, Dad crawled out of the boat and lay down under a shade tree. After a while on shore, Dad realized he was having a heat stroke.

"Take the boat and go get help," he said feebly.

Just the day before, Dad had shown me one time how to run the boat motor.

"It's a long way back to the cabin, Dad." As panic set in, I didn't know what was vibrating more, my knees, or my teeth.

"I can't drive the boat, so you have to. And bring back some water." Dad could see I was scared. "On the way back just keep looking at these big trees on the shoreline, and you'll find your way here."

Lucky for me, the trees were tall enough to see from the cabin. I guided the boat back to the other side, got help, water, and probably saved his life.

I've always thought that this was payback from when I was six years old. The entire family and Grandpa Carle went fishing at a gravel pit in West Point, Nebraska. For those who did not grow up in the Midwest, a gravel pit is a 50+ foot deep manmade excavation of stones or rock that has filled up with water and somehow became stocked with bass, crappie, and bullheads. Unlike a lake, it doesn't get deep gradually, but instantly—picture a giant cup—which is important to know for what happened next. It was early spring, and the ice had just melted. Fearless me walked out on a log to fish because I was getting my line caught on snags from the shore. Within a short time, I slipped and fell in.

I was later told that Mom ran to the edge of the water, and could hear my grandpa yelling, "Elinor, don't jump in after him, the water is too cold." Obviously, I must not have been grandpa's favorite. Simultaneously, Dad, with his clothes and shoes still on, was already in the water. Being an ex-Navy man, he had training in water rescue. You never know how things you learn early on in your life may come in handy later on. Fortunately for me, Dad was taught how to be an expert swimmer, as opposed to how to shoot a 50-caliber antiaircraft gun.

With the woolen winter jacket from Montgomery Ward I had on, I was sinking like an anchor. Deeper and deeper I went. The water was so murky I couldn't see a thing. The scariest part was when I found myself thinking, *What if no one saw me slip off the log? Oh my God, I'm going to drown!* But Dad was frantically flailing his arms back and forth in the brown water until he found me, then kicked his legs like mad to bring us both to the surface, and pulled me out of the freezing water. We were both soaked to the bone and shivering like bunnies. Since it was a day trip, there were no extra clothes along. Never mind I could-a been a goner; for weeks my loving brothers blamed me for putting an instant end to the fishing.

I could never figure out why we spent so many vacations at Ten Mile Lake. The fishing wasn't that great and there wasn't a lot for us kids to do. It could've been that the bar in the steak house was a "bring your own bottle" kind of establishment, and Dad liked his vodka.

Right outside of the bar one night, we witnessed a big fight. This guy was getting the crap beat out of him. Blood was running out his nose and from a cut above his right eye. Finally out of the blue, he begged the other guy, "Wait a minute," ran to his car, grabbed his boots with silver tips, pulled them on, and ran back. After that, he was winning the fight. He must've been thinking of Nancy Sinatra's song with a little twist: "These boots are made for kicking…and they'll kick the crap right out of you." He did more girly kicking than punching, but it was effective. The other guy ended up all bloody and worn out. As for me, I had never seen a good beating like that before. Pretty cool as long as it isn't you.

When I got older, I found out the real reason we kept going to the lake: My parents had spent their honeymoon there. I don't know if they originally went there because they liked fishing, or if they just drove until they got tired and decided it was as good a place as any to stop. In any event, Ten Mile Lake ended up being their honeymoon haven. So, on those particular trips, Mom and Dad sent us boys out to fish, while they reenacted their honeymoon.

When I was twelve, I got sick about two weeks before we were going to head up to the lake. The doctor told Mom, "He just has a virus, it will pass."

"We're going on vacation in less than two weeks," Mom worried, "will Rick be okay to go?"

"It will run its course and he should be just fine," the doctor assured Mom.

On the way to the lake, I broke out with spots all over my face. Turned out I had chicken pocks. I spent the entire week in the cabin out of the sun. The few minutes a day I was allowed out, it was with Dad's big ol' sunglasses on. I felt bad for Mom because she stayed in the cabin with me while the rest of them went fishing. It was just like Mom to give up her fun to take care of one of her sons. She always put her concern for us before herself.

✳✳✳

Every time we went on vacation, Mom had to go look for rocks. It didn't matter if we were in Minnesota, Colorado, or South Dakota, for her it was a full-on rock hunting expedition. When Mom found one that was "just right"—and just right for what I couldn't begin to tell you—no matter how big, or small it was, she'd yell at one of us boys to come get it and put in the trunk of the car, so she could keep looking without losing her place along whatever hillside she was scouring. I'm not kidding, by the time we were headed back home the rear bumper of the car was dragging on the highway shooting sparks. It had to be a hilarious sight to see. Cars passed us and pointed at our backend like we didn't know about the light show we were putting on.

✳✳✳

Twelve years old had few highlights. Besides the chickenpox, earlier that spring I also had the mumps. Both of my cheeks swelled up like grapefruits. I was out of school for weeks while I got over them. In December, I was having pain in my chest about where the heart is located. My parents took me to the nearby Oakland, Nebraska hospital to have me checked out.

The "country" doctor looked me over and announced, "Don't worry, if it was serious, I'd have Rick transferred to Omaha."

The next morning, I was in an ambulance heading for St. Joseph's Hospital in Omaha. I was freaking out; my heart was hurting even more, and I had difficulty breathing. It was probably all psychological, but I was too young to understand the difference. At St. Joseph's I had five doctors checking me out.

After a long conference, they informed my parents, "We think Rick has a heart murmur. We need to keep him here a few days to run some more tests."

One of the tests was a heart catheterization. I was put in a room that was colder than the winter air outside. They prepped me, then the doctor cut open my right arm where it bends, and inserted in a cable with a camera on the end of it. The cable went all the way from my elbow to inside my heart. Then I was injected with a dye, which had a terrible burning sensation. I didn't know what to think. I was getting hot flashes except that I was too young for menopause.

As I lay on the table, the doctor directed my attention to one of the TVs that were located in the room. Wow! I was able to see the inside of my heart. I thought that was really cool until it was time to pull the cable out. By then the Novocain had started to wear off.

The doctor gave me two choices: "I can give you another shot of Novocain to deaden the area, or I can pull real fast."

I never have liked needles so I said, "Pull fast."

Man, I wished I had gotten the shot. The pain was so bad three nurses had to hold me down so the doctor could finish the job.

All I knew was being twelve really sucked and I couldn't wait to turn thirteen. Even though twelve was a particularly bad year for me, as you will see, I had many more rough lessons to learn.

*(top to bottom) Rodney, Cliff, Jeff, and me on a Triceratops,
at Dinosaur Park, Colorado, July 1958*

# Chapter 4

## VALUES ADDED

Growing up in Nebraska--or most parts of the Midwest--you were taught good American values: To be polite, not to steal, right from wrong, respect others, and treat people the way you 'd want to be treated by them. I did my best, but I had some ... let's say, weak moments. Like at the bowling alley with my friends. I was thirteen at the time. Ah, the teens, where you are starting to know just about everything--at least you think you do! In your mind, you feel you're so smart that you'll never get caught when you break the rules, or the law.

My friends, Tom, Alan, and I came up with a plan to steal cigarettes at the bowling alley. One of us distracted Harry, the owner, who was hard of hearing, overweight, and approaching 70. The designated distracter lured Harry away from the checkout counter where the cigarettes and cigars were kept by asking him questions about the bowling balls, or buying a bag of chips, which were at the concession counter across the way. The others reached behind the counter and took as many packs as we could rapidly stuff into our jacket pockets before he looked back at us. After we left, we ran along the railroad tracks until we were a half mile away, and smoked up what we'd stolen. We thought we were so cool!

One time, my best friend, Tom, stole a package of Spark Plug Chewing Tobacco.

I was completely shocked. "Tom, why the hell did you take chaw?"

"I was in a hurry and just grabbed what I could," he defended himself.

Being virgins with chewing tobacco, we weren't exactly sure how to do it, and nobody wanted to go back to the bowling alley and ask Harry for instructions. So, we opened up the package and all of us took turns biting off a sizable chunk. I found out the hard way that you don't want to swallow any of the juice when I started puking my guts out. "Chew, spit, *do not swallow*," would've been good advice to know up front. It was the first and last time in my life that I have ever chewed tobacco. Too bad I didn't have the same experience a few years later, the first time I tried "recreational drugs".

The bowling alley had a row of pinball machines. I loved to play and I got good enough to keep getting free replays. I could go all day...a *Pinball Wizard* who could see and hear. The only problem was; you had to have money in order to *start* playing them. Being a happy-go-lucky, no work--no worries kid, I had to ask my parents for the money, and most of the time the answer was "No." Or there was some kind of a work trade off (cleaning the attic or garage/mowing the front, side, and back yards) I wasn't keen on.

So, I came up with a brilliant idea: Rather than working for money—why not just write a check from Dad's grocery store? All I had to do was learn how to forge his name on the checks. I went to my room, closed the door, and practiced his signature on a piece of paper until I was confident I had it down pat. I went to his office, swiped a few blanks out of the back of Dad's checkbook, and headed for the bowling alley. I thought to myself, *This is easy money!* I played pinball for days. I was on a Bally high.

Then one day, Dad said in *that* tone of voice, "Rick, come to my office."

"Yes, Dad, what do you want?" I looked left and right, trying not to make eye contact.

Now, Dad had a way of asking questions he already had the answer for, to see if you'd spill the beans first, and incriminate yourself. I always thought that you never wanted to admit to anything until you were absolutely sure that Dad wasn't bluffing, and already knew the truth. And the truth usually hurt.

I followed Dad into the office where he casually asked, "Have you been to the bowling alley lately?"

"No," as I wiped the sweat off my brow.

"Are you sure?" he pressed, just a little.

I played dumb: "Not that I can remember." Besides, I figured that being vague was not really lying.

"Last chance." Dad slammed his hand on the desk. "I want to hear the truth!"

Once again, I went with vague: "I don't really remember."

Next thing I knew he's reaching into his desk drawer and pulling out some checks that were written to the bowling alley. At that moment I couldn't even swallow my own saliva. I needed a drink of water, but I knew Dad wasn't going to let me leave the office to get one. I turned white as a sheet in a snow storm—at that point I knew I'd just been busted.

Dad leaned forward right into my face. "Do you realize that what you have done is breaking the law? This is called forgery. You can go to jail for this. If it wasn't for me, you'd be in jail right now."

He was very believable on the jail subject. I didn't know that you can't put a thirteen-year-old away for forgery. But he had me believing that it could easily be done; and if I ever did it again, he'd let them haul me away. This soaked in real deep. Of all the crimes I committed after that, forgery was not among them.

I ended up grounded for weeks, which I conceded was better than the belt. I'd never been in jail before, so I didn't know what that was like; but being grounded sucked and was probably not too different, because it was summertime.

I later found out the reason I got caught wasn't because of the forged signature. That had passed muster. Since I didn't have my own checking account, I had no idea that the written checks were returned at the end of the month. Brain-child me had written the checks for $3.00. I thought that since Dad went bowling every week, he had to write checks to pay for it. I didn't know that Dad had never written a check for $3.00 in his entire life. It never occurred to me to write the checks for a larger amount. Besides $3.00 lasted The Wizard all day playing pinball, and I could even get a Royal Crown Cola and a Bit-O-Honey candy bar. I just wrote the checks for what I needed to cover the day. And if I did need more money, no problem; scratch off another three-dollar check.

\*\*\*

One summer day that same year, my friends and I had gone to baseball practice in the morning, then swimming in the afternoon.

Dad was my baseball coach. If any of you have been taught a sport by your dad, I'm sure you'll agree that he was harder on you than the other players. Dad's expectations were ratcheted too high for me to live up to. On top of that, he didn't have any patience with me.

I played every position except catcher while Dad was trying to find a spot where I could excel. I even tried pitching, but when you walk six batters in a row you find yourself sitting on the bench real fast. Right field ended up to be my spot, since there weren't many left-handed batters back then. Of course, with no action, it got completely boring just standing there in the outfield. Dad would catch me looking around, not paying attention, or even sitting down in the grass a couple of times.

I could hear his voice all the way from the dugout: "Rick! Dammit, pay attention!"

Then I got chewed out when I came in from the field, and again in the car on the way home. I wasn't one of those kids who got better by ass-chewing. I did better with the back-patting style of coaching. Dad didn't understand that, so there was not a father-son baseball legacy in Lyons.

In those days, there wasn't a bat boy. Who knows, I might have been good at that. Instead, by the end of my baseball career I was a star bench warmer.

*** 

Lyons had the largest public swimming pool in northeast Nebraska. Our pool opened on Memorial Day. My friends and I had a contest to see who could be the first one in the pool. The winner got bragging rights for the entire year. Once inside the gate, you had to *walk* as fast as you could to the deep end, because the posted sign, *No Running!* got you whistled, then sidelined, by the lifeguard.

There was no time to put a toe in to test the water. It was a complete dive into the usually arctic temperature pool. Once in, you had to pretend the water was just fine so you could sucker your buddies into hopping right in behind you.

On Thursdays, two bus loads of Indians arrived to go swimming. Lyons was just fifteen miles from the Walthill, Winnebago, and Macy Indian tribes. They had their own tribal rules and laws. We were never allowed to hunt or fish on their land; and they had their own Indian police who were exceptionally vigilant with law enforcement.

In the early seventies, Bob Devaney, Head Coach of the Nebraska Cornhuskers, who had just won back-to-back national college football championships, was speeding down Highway 77 and passed through the Indian reservation. Bob was going over 100 mph in a 55 mph speed zone. It took a while for the Indian police in their 1962 Ford Crown Vic to catch Bob in his 1972 Cadillac and get him to pull over.

The Indian patrolman asked Mr. Devaney, "Do you know how fast you were going?"

Bob smiled up at him and said, "Do you know who I am?" Bob went on to detail his fame and exemplary football record expecting it'd make a big impression.

"Nope, never heard of you," the patrolman shrugged as he handed Bob the ticket.

I guess when you lived on an Indian reservation, watching the Big Red on Saturday afternoon wasn't the same priority as it was for about 99% of other Nebraskans.

When the sixty or so Indians came to swim, it overcrowded the pool. Occasionally, a fight broke out—until the lifeguard blew his whistle and yelled, "Everyone one out of the pool...ten-minute recess!" Most of the time, I'd just leave the pool when the Indian buses arrived. It wasn't worth the hassle. In my adult years, I've come to realize that I was being very small minded. The Indians had every right to swim in the PUBLIC pool--as well as the right to keep us off their PRIVATE land.

After swimming that particular day, Tom announced he'd heard that there was a body on display at Phillips Funeral Home. None of us had ever seen a dead body before. We were feeling the same excitement like the boys in the movie *Stand By Me*, so we decided it'd be cool to sneak into the funeral home and have a look.

Everything was going as planned until Mr. Phillips, a six-foot-five man, with a deep, mortifying voice, came up behind us. "What are you boys doing?"

I wanted to say, "Just shitting my pants," but when I opened my mouth nothing came out. Mr. Phillips made us stand in front of the casket looking at the body for about twenty minutes, but it seemed like hours. I guess that was our punishment. It was so weird staring at this lady whose face didn't look real because of all the caked-on makeup. And I knew that any moment her eyes were going to pop open and make me jump out of my Keds.

That experience has affected me to this day. I avoid going to wakes unless I knew the dead person real well, and I feel that I have to go. Then I just give my condolences to the family, and walk by the casket with my eyes closed, hoping nobody notices.

After we had served out our sentence, Mr. Phillips said, "I hope you boys have learned a lesson."

All we could do was stand there sheepishly and shake our heads yes.

As we were walking out, he explained, "I know who you boys are and your parents."

I had practically forgotten about it up until Dad got home. At supper, he calmly asked, "Rick, did anything interesting happen to you today?"

Once again, I could tell it was one of those questions to see if I'd spill the beans.

I, of course, said, "No, nothing exciting happened today." In my mind, I was telling the truth because the experience was far from exciting...it was freakin' scary.

"Are you sure?" Dad said more definitively.

"Yes," I committed to my white lie.

"I got a call this afternoon ... from Mr. Philips ..."

I couldn't believe that I got busted again and looked away from Dad.

"He said you paid a visit to the funeral home today ... is that true?"

"Yes, I did." I peeked to try and gauge the level of Dad's anger.

"Why did you lie to me?"

"You asked if I had done anything 'exciting' today, and it wasn't exciting, so I didn't think I was lying."

"Don't try to bullshit me." His hand clipped the back of my head. "You knew you were lying. Go to your room, you're grounded."

In my defense, I don't know if I acted the way I did as a rebellion against my parents, or because in a small town of around 900 people, there's not enough things for kids to do; so you are left to find your own moral compass. And mine did not always point true north. Okay, so I had been a bad boy all summer, but it was nothing compared to the trouble I got into once school started.

## Chapter 5

# SCHOOLIN' AND FOOLIN'

I was one of ten students in my class who went all thirteen years at Lyons Public School. It was not easy for me to get away with anything in school. Unfortunately for me, Superintendent Dan Brown's secretary was my mom. Just imagine getting into trouble and having to walk by your mom's desk to get to the superintendant's office. The whole time that I am getting yelled at, Mom can hear every word from her desk. After the butt chewing was over, I had to leave the same way I came in. I wasn't bothered by what the superintendent said anywhere near what I knew Mom was about to say.

"Wait until your Dad gets home and hears what you did."

Like she had to remind me. The rest of the day I couldn't concentrate on school work. I had beads of sweat running down the side of my face while thinking about what Dad was going to do to me. Would it be the belt? Or some kind of tortuous restriction on my freedom?

When I was in sixth grade, a few of my closest friends and I were outside the school enjoying recess. Out of seemingly nowhere, Carole, a female classmate, who was an early bloomer, came up to us and asked, "Do you boys want to see my breasts?" Can you imagine what was going through our minds? No girl had ever asked us that question before. We rapidly nodded our heads with a smile from ear to ear. Carole had a shirt on that zipped down the front and today she wasn't wearing a bra. Of all the girls in my class, Carole was the most developed, and very proud of that. Also, I'm guessing a bit of an exhibitionist streak.

Before that day, the only breasts I had seen were in men's magazines like *Rogue* and *Nugget* that I'd found in my parents' bedroom. Dad kept them under the *Popular Mechanics* magazines in a night stand by his side of the bed. While Dad was at work, I went into the bedroom and checked out a couple of the magazines. The women were generally a bit overweight and always had their hands placed strategically over the best parts. After a quick peek, I made sure to put the mags right back exactly the way I found them.

So, my friends and I were gazing at the real McCoys, when all of a sudden, I felt a finger tapping me on my back. My first thought was: *Leave me alone, you'll get your turn when I am done.* Being my first time, I was in no hurry to give up my spot. Besides, I wanted to take my time to ingrain this vison into my memory bank. Then I felt the finger tap me even harder. I turned around and to my surprise it was Mr. Smith the school principal.

"What are you boys doing?"

It should have been obvious; four boys with their tongues hanging out and drool running down their chins. But for some reason, people in authority always have to ask the stupid, or obvious question. All I could think was, *Holy shit I am in trouble!* I thought about running, but I had seen the principle run down students before. He was as fast as a cheetah chasing after a scared rabbit. I opened my mouth but nothing came out. When you don't know what to say, sometimes silence is the best defense.

Mr. Smith pointed us boys in the direction of the office, and said to Carole, "I will deal with you later!"

In my mind, this was the worst thing that I had done so far. I couldn't imagine what the punishment would be for this. Then the realization came to me that I was going to have to go past Mom's desk and into the superintendant's office. How would I ever explain this one? I also knew that Mom was going to hear every word. The principal marched us right to the superintendent's office and told him what had happened.

Mr. Brown was in utter astonishment when he asked us, "What were you thinking, looking down a girl's shirt?"

"It was all Carole's idea," I quickly shifted the blame.

"What do you mean it was Carole's idea?" Mr. Brown said in disbelief.

"She came up to us and asked if we wanted to see her breasts. She then zipped down her shirt and we took an innocent look." My cohorts were wide-eyed frozen with fear, so I guess I was unofficially elected the spokesperson for the group.

"Do you boys see anything wrong with what you have done?"

I thought the only thing I saw were two breasts, and there was nothing wrong with them; they both were a very nice size with rosy nipples on 'em, but I couldn't tell him that.

"Yes sir, we shouldn't have looked," I answered instead.

"Well, I hope you boys have learned a lesson."

"Yes sir, we have."

The lesson I learned was: The next time I look at a girl's breasts, make sure that I'm not on school grounds.

Now, get this: When I walked past her desk, there was Mom, head down, making busy work, as if she hadn't heard a word of the conversation that just took place in her boss's office. And at home that night, to my surprise the subject didn't come up. She never told Dad about it. I guess her lifelong discomfort with talking about sex trumped her desire to punish me.

Until I moved out of the house, I can't ever remember hearing Mom and Dad talk about sex. In fact, sex was a strictly taboo subject in the Carle household. We couldn't even say words like "pregnant" or "contraception" …and, God forbid, "intercourse". Plus, we never got "the birds and the bees" lecture. I can't help but wonder if our family had been more open, maybe I wouldn't have gotten in trouble, or got *someone* in trouble; but that's a story for later.

**\*\*\***

The reason we moved to Lyons was Dad got hired to work in a grocery store as a butcher for Ed McMonnie. Ed pronounced his last name "Mc-Money." When you have it, flaunt it. When Ed decided to retire, Dad was given the opportunity to buy the store from him. Dad was able to get a loan from the bank and soon he was a proud business owner. Dad was also a fireman. The Lyons Fire Department was made up of all volunteers. Each of them had a special phone in their house or business that rang when a fire call came in.

The week before July 4th, my brothers were playing with firecrackers. Did you notice that I did not include myself in this? Always blame it on them.

One popular firecracker was called a Pop Bottle Rocket. It had a long stem that you placed in an empty…say 7-Up bottle. When lit, it took off like a missile and then blew up about 30 feet in the air.

One of the rockets landed on the wood shingles of our garage before it exploded. The explosion sparked a fire in the shingles but my brothers were able to quickly put the fire out with the garden hose.

Lucky for them, the burn spot was on the neighbor's side of the garage: the old widow Mrs. Louella. They were so proud of themselves; that they got away with it; and probably Dad would never see the burn area—or at least not for several months, after the heat was off, so to speak. What my bro's hadn't counted on was that Mrs. Louella saw the smoke—after all it was on her side—and dialed the fire department. She stood in front of her house waiting for the fire trucks to come so she could show them where the fire was (or had been).

When the call came in, Dad answered the phone at the store, only to find out that the fire was at *his* house. Dad did not drive to the fire department to ride on one of the water trucks. He got in his car and drove right to the house. By the time Dad, and minutes later the fire department, got to our house, my brothers, the junior firemen, were still trying to put the garden hose away. Now you'd think that they'd receive badges for their gallant effort, but Dad did not pass out badges. He handed out discipline.

Every Fourth of July we had a spectacular display in our backyard, with Skyrockets, Roman Candles, and Whistling Moon Travelers. Dad bought at least a hundred dollars worth of fireworks each year. Our punishment for the garage incident was *no fireworks*, only those wimpy sparklers. Yes, the punishment was meant for us, but I know it was secretly hard on Dad as well… because he really got a bang, 'scuse the pun, out of lighting those rockets.

**\*\*\***

Ther paper delivery business was a long-held tradition in my family. All of my brothers before me had a paper route. I wanted extra spending money, and the check forging plan was no longer an option, I decided to follow in their footsteps. I didn't realize you sometimes had to deliver papers in the pitch dark of early morning and in all kinds of bad weather. Plus, the route had to be completed before I went to school. If you complained about the snow or rain, you were reminded of the old story of what my parents did before they went to school. None of their stories ever made delivering the papers any easier, but I realized that bitching did not get me anywhere except late for school.

When I first started the route, I had to use a list, so I knew who in town got the paper. One morning, I couldn't find my list and decided, *No problem, I cand do it by memory.* That day, people who were not subscribers got the paper and those who were supposed to get them didn't. My parents told me the phone was ringing off the hook with upset customers, who apparently relied on corn, sorghum, and livestock news to make it through their day. I soon jettisoned the paper route and went to work in Dad's grocery store.

**\*\*\***

Another family tradition was going out for high school football. The problem was, none of the Carle boys had any bulk or weight. We were all built like twigs.

Now, on all football teams you need players, and you need someone to sit on the bench to keep it warm for the starters when they come off the field. The State of Nebraska is known for the great football team called the Cornhuskers, but in Lyons, the Carle brothers were famous as the "best bench warmers in the town". My brothers were very proud, and stayed up late perfecting their trade by sitting on a bench in our back porch. Then they passed the job on to me. I was the last bench warmer in the family, and I wanted to be the best of all the Carles. Who knows, maybe I could even get a plaque? It'd read: "Hear sits Rick Carle. The best bench warmer in Lyons Public School history." After I graduated, I don't know how the starters handled coming off the field to a cold place to sit down.

Later in life, when Cliff was asked by his new Los Angeles friends what position he played in high school, his answer was, "I played right bench. And I was the best. In four years no opposing player ever got by me and into the stands."

Never considered "starter" material, during football drills I was placed on the "practice squad". This meant my assignment was to hold a dummy. Then the first string three-hundred-pound lineman would practice their blocking and tackling by running full speed and hitting the dummy. I began to feel that there was a dummy holding a dummy. After scrimmage was over, I'd find myself buried in the ground while still holding on to it, and a three-hundred-pound lineman on top of me. Lucky him: He got two dummies with one shot.

One time during football practice, Coach Ashby heard a rumor that several players had attended a keg party the night before. Coach asked to see a show of hands of those who were there. Of course, no one fessed up.

Coach Ashby said, "Well, if nobody wants to admit they were there, I guess we'll find out the hard way. Start running around the football field until I tell you to stop."

Several of the guilty players tried to be troopers, but it was not long before they were puking their guts out. The coach knew that with the eighty-degree afternoon, it wouldn't take long to get his answer. I was fortunate enough not to have been at the party. But I have a weak stomach, and seeing others upchuck made me follow suit. So, the coach presumed I had been there also.

Freshman initiation was a treat. The seniors felt they had a moral obligation to break in the rookies on the football team. The most common practical joke was to put cow manure in your helmet, so when you put it on you'd either gag…or in my case, start barfing. Another trick was to put a salve called "Heat" in your jock strap. You'd be all suited up—pads and all—and it didn't take long before the puppies started heating up and you felt like they were on fire. Trust me, you could not get undressed and to the shower fast enough to put the flames out. Of course, the seniors lolled around in the locker room, waiting to see the reaction; then laughed until their stomachs hurt. I guess there was humor in it if you were on the right side of the prank…come *my* senior year.

**\*\*\***

I went out for track my junior year. Hurdles and pole vault were my events. I was average at both. Just before summer vacation there was a track meet with five of the surrounding towns.

Coach Ashby came over to me and said, "Rick, I need you to run the 440 race today. Bill's mom just told me he's sick and can't be here."

"But coach, I've never run that race before," I protested.

He put a hand on my shoulder and reassured me, "Rick, you'll be fine. Just do your best. That's all I ask."

"Okay, Coach." I immediately tried to come up with a strategy for how I was going to *win* —not just do my "best". After a few minutes a lightbulb went off in my head: *I will jog the first half of the race and when I reach the 220 mark I'll turn on the after-burners and fly by all of the other runners to victory!*

The race was announced over the loud speakers, and the runners were told to get ready. I took my place at the starting line and looked around at the parents, grandparents, and students from the five towns in the bleachers, all abuzz about the race. I thought to myself, *They must be excited to watch the new 440 champion, Rick Carle!*

*BANG!* The starting gun went off, and I began my jog, as planned. I kept my head down so I wouldn't have any distractions. When I got to the 220 mark, I could feel the heat from the fire —my after-burners were lighting up! I lifted my head and looked to the left just in time to see the rest of the runners crossing the finish line. I had to run the last half of the race all by myself in front of the huge crowd. I also noticed that no one was clapping for me. I was so embarrassed that I could have kept on running all the way home. This being my first time, I had no idea the 440 race was an all-out sprint.

I was never asked to run it again, and you will not find my name in any track and field record books in the state of Nebraska.

\*\*\*

I went out for basketball because the b-ball team needed bench warmers also. One game, as usual, I was on the bench; the coach looked down the row of players and yelled, "Carle, get in there!"

I think he put me in because there were only seconds left on the clock, and he must have wanted me to gain some game-time experience. I'm not sure what a player can learn with ten seconds left. Besides, what could go wrong in ten seconds?

I jumped up, checked in at the scorer's table, and ran onto the court. My team was ahead by two points and the other team had a player at the free throw line shooting two free shots. He made the first one. Our coach immediately called time out.

"If he makes the second shot, just throw the ball in and run the clock out," the coach instructed us. "The game will be tied and it will go into overtime. And for heaven's sake DO NOT FOUL!"

The player shot the second free throw and missed. I must have blacked out, because the next thing I remember the ref was blowing his whistle. I thought, *Who'd be stupid enough to cause a foul?* Besides, the coach just told us not to. As I turned around, I saw the ref pointing at me. Somehow, I must've bumped into the opponent standing next to me as he was going for the rebound. The kid at the free-throw line got two more shots, made them both, and time ran out. We ... rather I, lost the game.

The team went into the locker room after the game. The coach was so mad he lifted up the table you sat on to get taped up by the trainer, and slammed it to the floor, breaking it in half.

"Carle! What in the hell were you thinking?" he screamed.

"I don't remember fouling the guy."

"Well you sure the hell did, and you lost us the game."

I did not get to play in another game the rest of the year. I was back to the Carle family tradition of bench warming. The next year, I quit the team, and went out for intramural basketball. I got to show what I could do if I was given a chance to play more than ten seconds. I averaged twenty points a game.

**\*\*\***

Speaking of basketball, Mom told me a story about an event that happened before I was born. Dad, Mom (with baby Jeff in her arms) and my two older brothers, Rodney and Cliff, were at a high school basketball game. Now, Dad did not like the way the refs were calling the game. Dad never yelled when everybody else did. He'd wait until it got real quiet, then he'd yell names at the refs. His favorite was calling them "striped monkeys".

This particular game, Dad was going overboard. When Dad saw a ref doing a makeup call on our team for an earlier call he'd missed, perpetrated on the visiting team, he laid it on heavy.

Finally, the ref stopped play, pointed to Dad in the bleachers, and shouted, "This game will not continue until *that* man is gone from the building!"

Dad called his bluff and refused to leave. But it was obvious the ref meant what he said.

The school principal came over and said, "Lou, you are right. It was a bad call, but for the kids' sake, would you please leave so they can finish the game?"

Dad, Mom and baby, and my brothers had to get up and walk down the bleachers in order to leave. The entire crowd watched them as they silently made their way to the bottom. When they got to the exit doorway, Dad turned around and bowed to the crowd. He got a standing ovation.

When I was older, and heard the story, I asked Dad, "Why did you always yell when the crowd was quiet?"

Dad said, "The refs can't hear me when everybody else is yelling."

"Makes sense, I guess, but you got thrown out of a game."

"I never liked basketball, anyway."

Dad always had the last word.

I always thought Dad was tough on us, but my grandpa, Mom's dad, taught me what strict really was. I think it was because of his upbringing, but he often made us do things that just did not make sense to me.

## Chapter 6

# GRANDFATHER'S WORK FARM

Almost every Sunday, we had to go to Grandpa Carlberg's house in Pender, Nebraska. It was a twenty-mile drive that felt like two hundred. He was Mom's dad. We were told that at one time in his life he was a Nebraska State Senator. I wasn't sure whether or not to believe it. But I took a trip to the Capitol Building in Lincoln, Nebraska when I was older. Lo and behold, on the framed photo for the 1941-1945 Assembly, there was a young-looking Roy B. Carlberg representing Thurston County. When I knew him, he was the oldest living abstractor in the state.

Grandpa believed that if you put food on your plate, you will eat it. One Sunday lunch, I put him to a test of wills. My eyes were bigger than my stomach. I put three heaping scoops of mashed potatoes and gravy on my plate beside a big chicken breast. He was shaking his head as I greedily filled up my plate. He knew deep down that I was too small of a boy to eat that much food. I ate the chicken but could not finish the potatoes.

Grandpa Carlberg did not use the psychological ploy of telling you, "Eat your food, people in Africa are starving." His method was you stayed at the table until you ate *all* the food on your plate. By three in the afternoon, I was still at the table; the gravy was cold and gooey, and I was not going to eat it.

He kept coming into the kitchen to check on me; it was a Mexican standoff. Finally, when Grandpa was in the living room, Mom grabbed the plate and told me, "Go outside and play." I never found out the story she told Grandpa when he discovered I had won the "war of wills".

Besides being a bonded abstractor, Grandpa Carlberg was a lawyer. As an abstractor, you write up the deeds when people buy land; and being a lawyer came in handy when legal problems surfaced. He also operated a dairy farm during the 1930s. It put food on the table during The Depression years. Nobody had money to buy land or afford legal fees.

Grandpa had 30 cows that were milked every morning and evening. Mom and her siblings had a milk route that was run every day. They put the containers of milk in a large wagon and pulled it behind them.

While I was writing this I asked Mom, "Did you ever have a horse pull the wagon?"

She started laughing. "Heck no, *we* were the horse."

In the winter when the snow was too deep for a wagon, they used a sled. I can't help but chuckle when I hear someone practically boast that they are "lactose intolerant!" As a kid, Mom drank enough lactose for three lifetimes. "There was no such thing as 'lactose intolerant' during The Depression," Mom commented. "Nobody could afford to be."

Roy B owned acres and acres of land on the outskirts of Pender surrounded by wire fences. We went to his house each weekend because he always had something for us to do. He was the task master and there was never a shortage of work to be done.

Whenever he'd sell off some land, to make room for a hospital, a football field, or a new housing project, we had to move the fence. That meant digging holes with the old-fashioned post hole digger, turning it one direction and then back to the other side, lift it up, and dump out the dirt. Take out the old posts and move them to the new holes that we just dug. Unhook the wire, put it around the posts, then stretch it tight so the dwindling herd of cows didn't get out. I can't tell you how frustrating it was maintaining a fence for one old bossy that Grandpa just couldn't seem to part with, for sentimental value.

On another side of town, he owned some land that bordered a creek. On both sides were at least a couple hundred walnut trees. We had to cut most of them down and haul them out. Later on, he took some of the trees to a man in town who had a woodworking shop, and had tables and chairs made out of them. For helping, Grandpa gave me and my brothers each a table and chair set. He also sent them to all of my cousins in other states who did not help, but reaped the benefit all the same.

Having lived through The Depression, Grandpa learned not to waste *anything*. We had to help him tear down a rickety old barn that if the wind blew hard enough, he wouldn't need our help.

Before we got started, Grandpa instructed us: "I do not want any boards broke and save all the nails."

I thought, *You've got to be kidding me? The boards are as old as Grandpa and the nails are rustier than the metal on the Titanic at the bottom of the ocean.*

As we tore the barn down, you should've seen the look on Grandpa's face whenever he heard a board crack. His head spun around like Linda Blair in *The Exorcist,* and you got the look that burnt right through you. The barn slowly came down, the mostly rotten boards were stacked, and the rusty nails were put in Mason jars. What his plans were for them had me stumped. Maybe to build another rickety barn for his great grandkids to tear down someday.

In the open field, behind where the barn had stood, my brothers and I played Army, or Cowboys and Indians. We tried to make the games as authentic as possible. For example, when we played Army we used loaded BB guns, and shot the BBs at each other. The only rule was you had to shoot below the neck —like we were that good of shots. I always wore a thick parka, just to be safe. But one time, Cliff shot me right in the leg and left a bruise mark lasting for days. It hurt like hell, but you couldn't let him know that.

When playing Cowboys and Indians, real bows and arrows were used, but we removed the pointed tips…well, most of the time…

Jeff thought he was hiding well enough behind a mound of dirt when all of a sudden, we heard him scream, "Dammit, I've been hit! And I'm bleeding!"

By the time the rest of us got there, we found him with an arrow (oops, someone must've forgotten to remove that tip!) that had landed in his butt. He was not hurt that badly—the arrow didn't go in very deep, so the rest of us got to have a great big laugh. Sorry, but with us kids, the injury had to be real severe if you wanted sympathy. I remember an ol' Midwestern saying: "You're okay—just get up and walk it off."

I sometimes wonder how all of us kids escaped serious injury using real ammunition. Danny, one of our neighbors, wasn't so lucky. He and his brother Joe were playing a similar game in their barn using .22 caliber rifles. The objective was to come as close as possible without hitting each other. As the saying goes, Danny zigged when he should have zagged, and took a hollow-point square between the eyes. Poor Joe…what he had to live with every day. But the family soon relocated to another town. Everybody knew it was a mercy move, for Joe's sake.

When I was six, Jeff and I were horsing around with a football in Grandpa's breezeway. Mom told us several times to quit running or someone might get hurt. As usual, we didn't listen. Jeff tossed the football, I ran to catch it, and the next thing I knew I was crashing though the 2' x 4' glass window in the door. I had cut my right arm bad enough that I needed twenty stitches. Lucky for me the hospital was only a few blocks away. But you gotta give me credit for one thing. Even with the glass shattering and raining down on me, I caught the football.

That reminds me of another story Mom told me, about how daring (or dumb) I was. In the late fifties, we had one of those old-fashioned washing machines that had the automatic double ringer on it so you could put the clothes through and squeeze ninety percent of the water out before you hung them out to dry on the clothes line.

I was only four at the time, and I had crawled up on a box so I could turn on the automatic ringer when Mom wasn't looking. After it was running, I put my fingers close to the ringer and then I'd pull them back. I must have been tempting the ringer to try and grab my fingers. Well, one time the ringer won. Not only did my fingers go into it, but it continued to drag my entire arm. Thank God, it jammed and shut off when it got to my shoulder.

Mom turned around, saw my arm deep in the ringer, and panicked. Luckily, Mom was able to somehow jack the rollers apart, but not before my arm swelled up like a Macy's Thanksgiving Day balloon. I'm surprised the hospital didn't keep a bed on reserve just for me.

\*\*\*

It was a Turkey Day tradition to drive over to my Aunt Clara's outside Wakefield, Nebraska for the big festivities. The meals were absolutely fantastic, and there was so much food it could have fed a Marine Corp.

Aunt Clara lived in an old farmhouse without the modern facilities that I was used to. The house was heated by burning corn cobs in an old black cast iron stove. At least three times a day, someone had to go outside with a bucket to fetch a load of cobs to keep the fire going. One of our cousins ventured too close to the stove, and got burned. He now has a scar in the shape of the letter R on his leg. The manufacturer of the stove was Round Oaks.

When you had to go to the bathroom, you carried the toilet seat with you to the outhouse. The seat was kept inside so it stayed warm. It was so cold outside, the last thing you wanted was your warm, sweaty butt to become ice-welded to the seat while you did your business.

One Thanksgiving, after eating, my cousins, brothers, and I went out to play Army. I was running for cover while holding a stick in my hand as my gun. I slipped on some ice and the stick jabbed me in my right eye. I was in extreme pain. I couldn't see out of my one eye. I cried all the way back to the house.

"Let me take a look," Mom said after I told her what happened.

"It hurts, and I can't see!" I cried.

Blood had covered my eye temporarily blinding it. I was rushed to the doctor, and had to wear a patch over my eye for two weeks. I went from the army soldier to Rick the pirate, aye-aye mateys.

***

Mom's three siblings all lived on the West Coast, so when they came to visit it was a big deal. They always stayed at Grandpa's house. After lunch, they cleared the table and played poker. All the siblings had nickels, dimes, and quarters in front of them. Mom only played with pennies. I think it upset the rest of them because when Mom won a hand, nobody had pennies to pay her.

As a youngster, I wanted to play cards with the adults, but they just smiled and suggested I go play with my toys. Finally, after whining most of the afternoon, they let me play a match game with playing cards. You put all the cards face down on a table. Taking turns you had to match a six with a six, a five with a five, and so on until all the cards were matched up. I won the first time that we played. They all thought it was beginner's luck. Until we played another game and I won that one also.

I always prided myself that I had a great memory and could beat them. I think that when you are young, your mind has a better ability to retain mental images—in this case where the cards were—than later on as an adult. But whatever the case may be, that day I was undefeated.

***

During World War II, my Uncle Robert, a First Lieutenant, was flying a B17 (the Flying Fortress) airplane from London to France. His plane was shot down; he was captured and taken to a German prisoner of war camp. It was Stalag Luft III. If you haven't heard of that camp, it's in the book, *The Great Escape*, later made into a movie staring Steve McQueen. My uncle and the other prisoners dug tunnels 30 feet below the ground and two square feet in size. The prisoners had baggy pants that they filled with the dirt and sand. As they walked across the exercise yard, they'd let the dirt/sand mixture out and spread it on the ground. They had to quit digging during the winter because with the snow there was no place to put the dirt-sand where it wouldn't be noticed by the German guards.

In March of 1944, of the 600 prisoners in the camp, the 200 that helped dig the tunnels planned an escape. hey were separated into two groups; the first 100 were those who could speak German. My uncle was in the second group of 100 prisoners. The first group got to the end of the tunnel, and realized that they hadn't dug it far enough. The tunnel came out by a guard tower, 30 yards short of the woods.

The prisoners had to wait a few days until there was a moonless night, then crawl the 30 yards to the woods. Only 76 men escaped that night. Before the others could get away the Germans found the tunnel. Of the 76 who got out, 50 were caught and summarily executed by the Gestapo.

Uncle Robert spent almost three years in that prison. After the war, he was inspired by his experiences in the war to become a doctor. I never heard him talk about his day-to-day life in the camp; I'm sure it was something he tried to forget. I could only imagine his nightmares of torture and suffering that he'd witnessed. Uncle Robert practiced his profession in Seattle, Washington until his death in 1989.

*** 

Mom's other brother was Duane. At 5' 4" he was the runt of the family. Uncle Duane had the gift of gab; he could talk to anyone about anything. He loved horses and Grandpa often found him at the sale barn chatting with the salesmen, rather than doing his chores.

One day, Grandpa had business in Omaha, and took Duane with him. Grandpa dropped Duane off at Aksarben race track. (If you're wondering how a race track got such a weird name, spell it backwards). By the time Grandpa returned to pick Duane up, he had talked his way into a job there. Duane used his small size to his advantage and became a jockey. Duane had to add lead weights in his saddle so he could pass the 110-pound minimum.

Duane joined a Florida circuit where he raced until he'd put on too much weight. The fat jockey lost by a gut to fast food. Duane so loved the sport, but claimed he was spending more time in the sauna than racing. Too bad they couldn't have put helium in his saddle.

At the same time, he was having his weight problem, the war broke out and Duane enlisted. He traveled to Italy and Africa with a group of soldiers who were hunting down Rommel. They were not successful, but during the mission, Duane had a grenade that blew up near him and left a piece of shrapnel near his heart. It was too close for the Army doctors to operate. He lived the rest of his life with that reminder of the war.

After the war, Uncle Duane went to work in California for a lock company. He started out on the ground floor, but after thirty years he'd worked himself up to senior VP.

I remember Uncle Duane commenting that at the lock company there was a woman who'd worked on the assembly line for twenty years, where she put the same five pieces in the locks as they went by her. Duane said she was the happiest employee he ever had.

One day, he asked her, "Why are you always smiling?"

She said, "Because I have a job where I don't have to think."

\*\*\*

Mom's older sister Dorothy was my favorite aunt. She'd always let me get away with things.

Mom tried to get me to behave, and Aunt Dorothy interjected, "Loosen up, Elinor, let the boy have some fun."

I enjoyed hearing that because I couldn't talk back to Mom. I'm sure Mom did not like the parenting advice, but she let it slide because she also knew that Aunt Dorothy was only visiting for a week, and after she left, Mom was back in control.

Dorothy lived in Simi, California with her son Jimmy, and his wife, Tammy, until her recent death. Even though I didn't see her a lot, I still miss her.

\*\*\*

Grandpa Carle was very strict and ruled with an iron foot. His punishment for his kids was a swift kick to the butt. Maybe that's the reason Dad was so strict with us.

Grandpa Carle was a butcher for over thirty years at a Super Saver grocery store in West Point, Nebraska. That must have been where Dad got the desire to become a butcher himself (like father, like son).

Dad was the fifth child out of nine born to Grandpa Carle. There were six girls and three boys in the family, of which five of them joined the service during World War II. Dad's older sister, Grace enlisted in the Marines and served until she retired. Aunt Grace was a Sgt. Major at that time, the highest rank a woman could attain in the Marines. Back then they didn't allow women to become generals.

Dad was closest to his younger brother Dewey. One time Dewey was getting beat up by the school bully and Dad ran over to break up the fight. The bully wouldn't stop until Dad picked up a brick and smacked it across his head, knocking him out. After that incident Dad and Dewey were almost inseparable.

The two of them loved tomatoes. They'd sit in the garden and eat them right off the vine. Anticipation must have gotten the best of them when they decided they couldn't wait for the tomatoes to ripen and stuffed themselves with green ones. Both of them were sick for two whole days. To this day, Dad has never eaten another tomato. I guess the idea of frying them never crossed their minds.

Dad's other brother, Eugene Carle, lived in Los Angeles, California, and worked as a cartoon animator for Hanna Barbara. He drew the Flintstones: Fred, Wilma, Barney and Betty. I recently watched old reruns of the cartoon and saw his name in the credits at the end of the show listed under "animators". As a kid, I thought that was so cool, my classmates thought I was lying when I said that my uncle drew the Flintstones.

In exasperation, I asked Dad, "Could you please call Uncle Eugene and have him send me some pictures of the Flintstones with his signature on them so my friends will believe me?"

"I'll see what I can do," Dad said.

Dad made that call, and within a couple of weeks I had my pictures. I took them to school and during "Show and Tell" I blew all the other kids out of the water...Pretty Miss Popular, Karen Lipinski, with pictures of her cute new cocker spaniel puppy... ha! You lose.

## Chapter 7

## GROCERY STORE FUN GALORE

When your Dad owns a grocery store and has four sons, he expects you to work there. I know some of you will remember back when grocery stores gave out S & H Green Stamps along with your purchase along with the complementary books to paste them in; and then you could redeem the stamps for various household items. We had one elderly lady, Gertrude Swanson, who filled up her book and tried to redeem it for cigarettes. She was on food stamps and knew that she couldn't use them for cigs, so she tried the Green Stamps. Didn't work. But I felt sorry for Mrs. Swanson and slipped a pack of Chesterfields in her bag whenever the checkout lady wasn't looking.

I started out at the bottom of the barrel in Lou's Market as the grocery bagger. "Basically," Dad told me, "all you have to remember is put the heavy items on the bottom and the lighter items on top."

But the very next day he cussed me out: "Dammit, Rick! Never put the eggs on the bottom!"

So, what do you do? Because a carton of eggs always crushed a loaf of Wonder Bread???

The big difference today from back then is the number of bags you get. I was always taught to fill 'em up. Nowadays it seems like it's somehow illegal to put more than three to four items in the bag. I guess the stores today want you to feel like you are getting a lot of bags for your money. We held the belief that you get a lot of items for your money, not bags.

After I bagged the customer's groceries, it was also my job to carry them out to their car, while the customer signed the receipt (remember grocery store charge accounts?) and put them in the back seat. Our competitor in the grocery business was right across the street, so our customers were also his. It irritated Dad when certain customers, on Saturday (our busiest day), shopped both stores and only bought the specials (loss leaders).

For the most part, Dad and the competition, Bill Jones, got along. But there were times when Bill absolutely frustrated Dad. For example, they'd agree to put like items in the weekly ads; four loaves of bread for a dollar. When the ads came out, Bill had switched his ad to *five* loaves of bread for a dollar. Dad came home and cursed Bill under his breath all through supper. I was too young to understand why he was so upset over one loaf of bread. But now I see it was a matter of trust and honesty.

I got even with Bill Jones's Grocery Store bread scam. Whenever I carried groceries out to one of our customer's car and saw Jone's grocery bags in the trunk, I'd grab a loaf of Jones's bread and squeeze it like an accordion, then put it back inside the bag. I pictured the customer in their kitchen merrily putting away their groceries and coming upon the smashed loaf of bread in the Bill's bag; then saying to themselves, "This is the last time

I shop at Jones's! It's Lou's Market only from now on." Like that was going to happen.

As I got older, I graduated into the produce department. I was so excited because I was moving up the corporate ladder.

The first day in produce, Dad said, "Rick, come over here. You are going to learn how to sack potatoes."

I thought, *This is so cool. I'm no longer the grocery bagger, I'm the big-time sackin' potatoes guy.* Little did I know what that entailed. Dad pointed to what looked like a horse trough. He'd dumped in a couple hundred-pound bags of potatoes.

Dad gave me the instructions: "I want you to put the potatoes in these plastic bags, place them on the scale, weigh them to five pounds, then put a twist tie around the bag. You might have to take out a bigger one and replace it with a smaller potato to get the weight to come out. When you get done, I'll dump two more hundred-pound bags and you need to weigh those out to ten pounders."

"This will be fun," I replied.

Little did I know that in each hundred-pound bag, there are several rotten potatoes. The squishiness and the smell would make someone with a weak stomach lose their lunch.

"When you find a rotten one, throw it away," Dad instructed. "Then take this wet rag and wipe off the potatoes that are next to the bad one."

Trust me; the horrible smell was also on the good ones. I later found out that other produce like lettuce, apples, tomatoes, etc. also go bad. Turned out the main job of the produce boy was to clean up rotten messes. At this point in my new career, bagging groceries was looking not so bad after all. But I had my pride, so I hung in there, no matter how ridiculous I looked with nose plugs on.

During the middle of July, for about two straight weeks, an old school bus pulled up in front of the store. The door opened and out trudged friends of mine who had dried mud all the way up to their waists, carrying their water jugs and lunch boxes. You could see on their faces that they'd literally been worn down and almost worked to death. These poor suckers, I mean dear friends, had been detasseling corn: You get up before the butt crack of dawn, walk through a mile-long, mile-wide muddy cornfield, and pull the tassels off the female plant. This is done so it won't pollinate itself. The procedure results in a hybrid seed corn that can be planted the following year. It was always done early in the day because the heat of the summer afternoon almost suffocated you in the cornfield. While watching them wearily buying tomorrow's lunch meat and potato chips, I'd go up to Dad and thank him for making me work in the air-conditioned grocery store.

One other time that I ended up being very thankful for my grocery job was on a snowy winter day. My best friend, Tom, and some other school kids stopped by the store and did their best to entice me: "Rick, we're going to Oakland to throw snowballs at cars. You wana go along? It's gonna be fun!"

Oakland was a town six miles from Lyons, and our #1 sports rival in basketball and football.

"Damn, I can't, I have to work," I answered sadly. "No way will Dad let me take off on a Saturday. It's our busiest day."

"Okay, but it is your loss," Tom said breezily.

They drove away, three of them in the cab of the pickup, and Tom and two Benson brothers in the pickup bed. On the way home, on a county road, Brian, the driver of the pickup, ran a stop sign and was broadsided by a cement truck at fifty miles per hour. Those in the front of the truck were thrown around and sustained minor injuries. Tom and the two brothers were literally catapulted out of the truck bed. Tom's body flew almost one hundred feet, but that is not what killed him —he actually landed in soft dirt in the middle of a bean field. But a forty-pound cement cinder block that was in the back end of the pickup, followed Tom's body, and came to rest on his head. What are the odds of that happening?

When the ambulance got there, they had no idea who Tom was; he was unrecognizable. The two brothers, nine and eleven, had died on impact. Had I gotten my way, I would've went with them and been in the back of the pickup with my buddy Tom. No two ways about it, I'd also be dead. All I can say is, "Thank you, Dad!"

Tom and I did everything together so I felt like I had lost a twin brother. I was devastated and in disbelief the day of his funeral. I no longer had my best buddy. I felt lost. Practically every day I went to Tom's house or he came to mine to hang out—those days were over, just like that.

We built a pole vault stanchion out of wood in Tom's backyard. We had nails every few inches up the poles so we could move the bamboo crossbar higher as we successfully made the previous height. In the front we'd made a chute to plant the pole before lift off. We tried many items for the pole; sticks broke, brooms weren't long enough, eventually we found a long metal pipe in Dad's garage that we hoped he wouldn't miss. We had even dragged out of Tom's house an old pee-stained mattress to land on. Tom and I had dreams we were going to make it to the Summer Olympics one day.

Tom and I did get on the school track 400-yard relay team and had won a trophy for second place in a district meet. I was so angry after the funeral that I threw the trophy across my bedroom, hitting the wall, and smashing it into pieces.

\*\*\*

When I was fifteen, once again I moved up the corp ladder, this time to the meat department. I always thought that was the best job in the grocery business. Dad and my brother Cliff were the meatcutters at the store.

By this time, I'd let bygones be, and I had grown close to Cliff. He taught me how to drive his VW. I learned to drive a stick shift before an automatic. At first, the car herked and jerked, until I got the hang of letting out the clutch with the left foot and giving it gas with the right. I think the main reason he taught me to drive was for his convenience, though.

In the cold, snowy, Nebraska winters, Cliff trapped beavers and muskrats. He set traps along the river banks and had to walk about a mile, from one end to the other, checking his traps. He didn't want to have to walk all the way back, so he taught me how to drive the VW and I'd be waiting for him at the far end. Of course, I didn't piece this together until I was much older. I thought he was being a good older brother and maybe trying to make up for the clothes chute episode. Could I have been more stupid?

One day at work Cliff said, "I have something in the back of Curt's car I want you to see." Curt was a trapping buddy of Cliff's. We walked out to his car where Curt was waiting. They stood back as I opened the back of the station wagon. To my surprise, there were five beavers staring at me with their mouths open and teeth showing. I jumped back at least five feet. I think I even peed my pants. Cliff and Curt burst out laughing. The beavers were dead, but looked very alive to me. They had caught the beavers earlier in the day, and staged them to look like they were going to jump out at me. Once again, Cliff got a laugh at my expense.

Working in the meat department of Lou's Market was cool because all the salesmen came back there and told Dad jokes, so they could loosen him up in order to sell him something. When it came to running a business, Dad was smart in some areas, and naïve in others. Dad's secret nickname amongst the salesmen was "Lou-easy." It seemed like he'd buy practically anything; a good example was a large "tree" that you put bananas on.

The slick salesman explained to Dad, "With this tree, your sales of bananas will double."

I never knew if banana sales went through the roof, but my brothers and I chuckled every time we walked by the tree, festooned with a hundred brown, overripe bananas.

While standing behind the meat counter, Cliff and I played a game we called "Who Am I?" We'd do an imitation of one of our customers, and then the other had to guess who it was. It passed the time while we cut the meat off the bones to make hamburger, or cut up chickens and packaged them. Out of the corner of his eye, Cliff would spot a customer headed our way and quickly do an imitation of her. When the lady walked up to place her meat order, I'd make the connection and burst out laughing—right in the lady's face. Man, did Cliff have a warped mind.

I always wanted to operate the band-saw, but Dad told me I was too young. So one day, when Dad and Cliff were on a break, I started up the saw, determined to prove Dad wrong. Of all the things I decided to experiment on, I chose ham hocks. They are made up mostly of bone and grease. As I started cutting the ham hock it twisted on me. The next thing I know, my right index finger had been cut by the blade. It was deep enough to require stitches. I was too terrified to tell Dad because I knew I was wrong for not listening to him. And I'd be banned from the saw for life. I decided to just stop the bleeding by putting a tight Band-Aid on my finger. We got little nicks from the sharp knives all the time, so I was never questioned. Thanks to my fear of Dad, today my right index finger has a noticeable curve in it.

While growing up you never know what kind of a treasure trove you can have right under your nose. n At the front of the grocery store we had a special rack for comic books. All of them came in plastic sheaths. We had Action and Marvel books like *Superman, Spiderman, Batman, Archie,* and *Josie & the Pussycats* to name a few. Back then they cost fifteen cents each. At the end of every three-month quarter, it was my job to take the ones that didn't sell and toss them in the Dumpster to make room for the new issues. I've been told that today those plastic-encased comics would be worth a fortune. If only I knew then what…

Sometimes it hurts to think about how I could have been a millionaire twice in my life. First, growing up as the son of the co-owner of a booming cement company in Southern California. Second, when I had saved and sold all of those valuable comic books. Well…I can dream, can't I?

**\*\*\***

One day, out of the blue, Cliff's girlfriend, Deanna, came into the meat department, grabbed my arm, and led me into the meat cooler.

She turned and asked me, "Do you want to see my breasts?"

I don't know what it is about girls wanting to show me their breasts! The first thought that came into my head was my earlier experience with this situation…not a good outcome. But I figured by going into the cooler, the chance of the principal tapping me on the shoulder was remote. Even so, I was so embarrassed and surprised that a girl six years older had made me that offer, that I declined. I later found out that Cliff had put her up to it, and I wanted a second chance for a peek; but it never happened. I guess the moral to that story is, "Opportunity to see knockers is only once."

*** 

Growing up in Lyons, Nebraska there wasn't much to do, but we did have a movie theatre. It was right next to Phillips Funeral Home and owned by the Thoenes. I have since learned that the author Nicholas Sparks married their daughter. What a small world. The theatre had a balcony on both sides of the projection room. My buddies and I tried to get our girlfriends up there to make out and then brag about what base we got to —or didn't, but said we did. Most the time we just got slapped in the face.

Right across the street from the grocery store, on the corner, was the Lyons pool hall. My friends, brothers, and I all learned to play pool and billiards.

One of the games we played on the pool table was Golf. You have to shoot your ball into the first hole and continue around the table in a consecutive order till you sank your ball in the last hole. Five or six other players are trying to do the same thing. There was a blackboard on the wall to keep score. If you missed your ball, scratched the cue ball, or hit someone else's ball by mistake, you got an X. When the game ended, you counted up your X's and paid the winner five cents for each one. The biggest loser also had to pay the owner of the pool hall a penny for each minute of the game. It wasn't a cash cow by any means, but it passed the time.

The pool hall's front door was all glass. When Dad couldn't find any of his sons working at the store, he'd first head over to the pool hall. He never realized that we could always see him coming—there weren't many men walking Main Street wearing a white apron. We'd hide behind the pool table when he came in.

"Have you seen my boys?" he'd call out.

"No we haven't, Mr. Carle," our friends fibbed for us.

"Well, if you happen to see them, tell 'em to get back to the store-- and I don't mean 'maybe'."

Dad left and continued on down the street looking for us. We'd light out the back door of the pool hall, and sneak in the side door of the store.

When he got back, he'd ask us, "Where in the hell have you been? I've been looking all over for you."

I answered, "You shoulda checked the bathroom. I was probably in there." I know he didn't believe me, but at least I was back at the store working, which was what Dad wanted all along.

I was always surprised that Dad didn't search the pool hall more thoroughly when he came in, or that he believed our friends when they lied for us. Then again, he might have known all along that we were in there and just gave us an opportunity to do what was right. And right was to get our butts back to the store.

I learned the hard way to appreciate what you have; like your job, best friend, and family; you never know when the day might come that you no longer have them.

## Chapter 8

# FIRE

We ate a lot of steaks and roasts. To some people, who rarely get to eat steaks, that'd be great, but the excess of anything can get old. Dad took meat from the case when it turned brown because the customers wouldn't buy it. Most people don't know how tender and good aged beef is compared to fresh bright red meat.

After I graduated, I moved to Iowa to go to college. One of my first jobs was in a meat locker. It was a job that I could easily do, but was very boring—the guy I worked with didn't know the "Who Am I" game?

Most of the time, I had to cut stag beef off the bone. This was an older cow that didn't have much fat in it, and was very tough. Grocery stores mixed it in the grinder with excess fat to make hamburger.

I took a beef tenderloin from the stag, hung it in the cooler for a few weeks to age it, and make it tender enough to eat. The outside of the loin was as black as a Goodyear Tire. I cut off the black portion, sliced the rest it into two-inch thick steaks and grilled them. My friends thought it was the best steaks they'd ever eaten, and I have never told them what it was, until now.

Most of the time, the steaks I ate growing up were well done. It wasn't because that was the way I liked them. Mom had the meal ready before six thirty. My brothers and I always had to be home right after the town's six o'clock whistle blew. It didn't matter what you were doing or where you were at, when we heard the siren we made like Ferris Bueller, running to beat his parents to their house. Then we had to get cleaned up and sitting at the dinner table by 6:15. Our dad did not get the same memo.

We gathered around the table waiting for Dad to get home. After Dad closed the store at 6:00, he started to drink his vodka and forgot about the time. There were many evenings when Dad got home around seven-thirty. Mom was furious; the meat was overcooked and dry as a tumbleweed blowing across the prairie... which suited Dad just fine. Having to look at raw meat all day, the more well done his steaks were, the better!

One time Mom glared at Dad and said, "Where have you been? We've been waiting supper for you."

"I had to work on the cooling unit to the meat case. I'm not that hungry anyway," Dad slurred.

"You've been drinking!" she accused him.

"I only had a couple," he said, holding up three fingers.

That broke the tension and Mom threw up her hands in exasperation. "Just sit down and eat!"

That was one of the few times I ever saw Mom get mad at Dad. It seemed like they never fought and always got along so well, except when Dad drank too much and lost all sense of time and responsibility. I'm sure he was only trying to relax and forget about the stressful day he'd had; but we were the ones who suffered by having to eat carbonized meat for supper.

**\*\*\***

There is a fine art of having just enough meat packaged up so the case doesn't look empty, versus so much that it doesn't all get bought by customers. Sometimes, too much meat turned brown in the meat case and we couldn't eat it fast enough. When this happened, Dad filled up boxes and put them in the freezer. At the end of the month he took the frozen meat up to the Indian reservation's hospital and gave it to them at no charge. Most times he asked me to ride along with him. This gave me the opportunity to see Indians on the reservation, rather than at the swimming pool. We drove down Main Street to get to the hospital. I remember seeing a couple Indians flat on their backs in front of a building.

I asked Dad, "Why are the Indians lying on the ground? Are they dead?"

"No, they are not dead," he explained, "that is the bar they're are in front of. The Indians had too much fire water and they're are sleeping it off on the ground."

Before I was old enough to drink, I didn't understand how the Indians, or anyone for that matter, could keep drinking until they just passed out. I knew that Dad drank, and there were times that I might have seen him drunk, but he never drank so much that he sank into his socks on the ground. Once I was of age, I found out the hard way how it happens.

**\*\*\***

On Friday, June 4, 1971, on my birthday, it was raining elephants and rhinos, with thunder as loud as cannons, and lightning that lit up the entire sky like a fireworks show. I didn't know that this day was going to end up being one of my worst birthdays ever. At four in the morning the fire phone rang at the house. Dad jumped up out of bed to answer it and froze when he heard where the fire was.

While making his rounds, the town cop, Bob Richardson, was driving by Lou's Market when suddenly the front windows blew out, nearly missing his patrol car. The blast threw glass a block away.

Dad hung up the phone and yelled, "The store was hit by lightning and is on fire!"

"Oh my God!" Mom screamed.

Dad threw on some clothes and was out the door. Dad's yelling woke the rest of us up. We got dressed and headed up to the store. By the time we got there, flames were shooting up to the sky. It was an incredible sight to see…if only it wasn't my parents' store.

To Mom's complete shock, Dad made a mad dash into the burning building.

Mom yelled, "Lou! What are you doing? Come back!"

But by then Dad was already inside. Flames were everywhere and burning boards fell to the floor as Dad continued on his mission. He came out a couple of minutes later juggling a hot metal box in his hands.

"The accounts receivable box…" Dad explained to Mom.

"Are you crazy?" Mom shook her hands at him. " You could have been killed."

"I had to get the receivables. This is the most valuable thing in the store right now. We lose them and we have no recourse to get the money our customers owe us."

"You could've let one of the firemen with the fireproof suits get it."

"There was no time. Besides they wouldn't have known where we kept it."

If you remember, people charged their groceries for a month at a time, then paid when they received a bill in the mail from Mom. Dad later sent letters to the people in town with a statement in it, asking for the money they owed us. Some of the people were absolutely appalled that Dad was asking for the money. Can you imagine that? They assumed Dad's insurance company took care of the loss including what they owed. Unfortunately, Dad's insurance policy paid the depreciated value of the fixtures, shelving, and coolers. When the final tabulation was done, Dad only had enough coverage for half of what it'd cost to rebuild.

On Thursday there was a thriving store on the corner, and by Monday, after the bulldozer was through, there was an empty lot. What a difference four days can make in your life.

I was standing next to Mom while the store was in flames. She had tears running down her face and she kept saying, "Why? Why Lord?"

I couldn't imagine what was going through her mind as she watched our store burn to the ground. I know I was having visions of the bus letting the detasslers out, and seeing myself as one of them in the near future.

✳✳✳

This was the second huge blow in her life. The first happened six years earlier. I was in the fourth grade. The principal, Mr. Smith, came to my classroom and whispered something in my teacher's ear. Her unmasked reaction told the class that something really bad must have happened. We were holding our collective breaths.

Mr. Smith then slowly turned, looked right at me, and announced in a sad voice, "Rick, will you please come with me." I thought, *Thirty-seven other kids to choose from and it had to be ME he wants.*

It never is good news when the principal pulls you out of class. He's not going to take you aside and say you won some kind of an award. I was thinking, *Now what could I have done to get in trouble this time?* I followed him into the his office and saw my parents in the room. My first thought was, *I am really in trouble for the school to call my dad here. What the hell did I do?* But as hard as I tried, I just couldn't remember any recent stunt I'd pulled.

Then as I looked at my parents, I could see they were crying. I had never seen Dad cry before so I knew something big was up.

Dad motioned and said, "Sit down, we need to talk to you."

Mom was barely able to say the words: "Rodney is gone."

At first, I did not know what she meant by "gone". Where did he go and when was he coming back?

They were silent on the drive home; then sat me, Jeff, and Cliff down in the living room and explained, "Rodney and some classmates were picking sweet corn to make money for Senior Sneak Day. They thought everyone was in the station wagon and took off. But Rodney was still in the field and ran after the car. He jumped on the open tailgate just as the driver shifted to another gear. That threw Rodney up in the air and he landed on his head. He died from his injuries."

Cliff had a real hard time with Rodney's death. A few days earlier they were having one of their typical brotherly fights. They didn't swing fists at each other; it was always more of a violent shoving match. This time the argument got real verbal, with a lot more name calling than usual.

At one point Cliff said to Rodney, "I wish you were dead."

Two days later Cliff got his wish. But it was one of those wishes you never wanted to come true. Cliff was absolutely crushed. He wasn't able to tell Rodney he was sorry. It changed Cliff in a way I can't really describe, except to say he started to go inward and at times was hard to reach.

There was too much of an age difference between Rodney, the oldest, and myself, the youngest, for me to have many memories of him. Although, he was the one who kept me from walking off of Pikes Peak. It saddens me that I didn't get the opportunity to know Rodney better, and have an understanding of who he was as a person. I once asked myself, *"What would I say to Rodney if I had one final minute with him?"*

"I love you, Rodney, and I miss you. I wish we could have had more time together. Sometimes I think about all of the things I could have learned from you. I don't know why God took you away from us before you had a chance to make something of your life. I don't think that it was fair. On the other hand, the doctor said if you had survived the accident, you would've been in a vegetable state for the rest of your life. And that I think would be more unfair. So, I guess it was a blessing God took you. By the way, I never had the chance to say, thank you for saving my life on Pikes Peak. You will always be with me in my heart."

***

After the fire, my parents weren't sure what they were going to do. Everything that was left in the store that didn't burn had smoke and water damage, and had to be either removed or buried. The decision was made to bulldoze and bury everything.

My parents decided to clear their heads by taking a trip to California.

Dad put out feelers to us boys, "We are going to *drive* to California, do any of you want to go along?"

Dad didn't do a very good job at selling the trip. I think secretly they were hoping we'd do a Nancy Regan and *just say no*. Us boys never faired well riding peaceably in the car, and Nebraska to California was a long trip. It was summertime, none of us were in school; I'd just turned sixteen and was old enough to be by myself. I wanted to go since I'd never been to California, but I also wanted to stay.

I eventually made my decision, and told Mom and Dad, "I'm not going. I'll be okay. Cliff and Jeff will take care of me."

The deciding factor was I'd just started up with a new girlfriend and didn't want to leave her.

It must've taken a long time for my parents to make up their minds about what they were going to do with their lives. They were gone for well over a month. In the meantime, my brothers and I had a five-week nonstop party. During that time, I saw things I'd never seen before. Cliff's friends brought their girlfriends over and took showers together. Apparently, the water was better at our house than theirs. Or maybe it was they didn't have to worry about their parents walking in on them...duh!

When I woke up in the morning the house had a funny herbal smell to it, and the records were stuck together with peanut butter. If you're trying to figure out the connection—you've never gotten seriously stoned. For those who have been high, you know exactly how the peanut butter gets on the records.

I came out of my bedroom and there'd been a slumber party. I had to step over guys and girls in the dining and living rooms to get to the kitchen. Thinking back, I'm sure it wasn't all fun and games for Cliff. He had to make sure none of his stoned and drunk friends broke anything during the perpetual party.

About two weeks into the bacchanal the phone rang. I picked up and it was Mom.

"How is everything going?" she asked sweetly.

"Good," I said. There was a lot of static on the phone.

"It's hard to hear you with all the crackling," I said.

"It might be because I'm calling from Hawaii."

I may have barely squeaked by in geography class at school, but I'd learned enough to know that Hawaii is not part of California.

"What are you doing there? You said you were going to Los Angeles!"

"Your Dad decided to surprise me."

Now I know why Dad wasn't too persuasive in asking us to go with. When he made the reservations, he must've known that we'd want to stay at home. That took some big balls to keep the secret not only from Mom, but from all of us. At this point in the conversation, I wished I could turn back the clock and change my mind. It probably would've been my only chance to ever go to Hawaii. It is almost fifty years later and I still haven't seen the Hawaiian Islands.

"I'd have gone with if I'd known you were going there!" I whined.

"I'm sorry, but I didn't know either," Mom said defensively. "Listen, I can't stay on the line much longer, so can I talk to Cliff?"

I handed the phone to Cliff and left the room very pissed off.

The party lasted until the day before they were scheduled to come home. That day was spent vacuuming up the butts and roaches, scrubbing the food and drink splattered walls, doing four and a-half week's worth of dishes--and making sure everything was back to where it was before they left. I did most of the cleaning since I had the most experience in that department.

Cliff was worried about the neighbors. They were all older people and we were sure they probably saw a lot of things they'd never seen before: like a constant parade of teenagers coming and going through our front door. Cliff's choice was either to go around to each of the neighbors and ask them to keep quiet, or he had to tell our parents about the parties. He must've learned from earlier experiences with Dad, similar to mine, that it's better to come clean than to wait for the evidence to bite you in the ass.

Rather than "Welcome home!" when Mom and Dad walked in the door, the first words out of Cliff's mouth were, "While you were gone, we had a *little* party here."

Now, I'm not sure what *you'd* call it, but a five-week free-for-all is not exactly a small party.

Cliff performed his best nonchalant shrug and said, "The neighbors might exaggerate about the party, but nothing really happened."

As far as Mom and Dad could see, the house was clean and everything was in its place. Lucky for Cliff that Glade Air Freshener was around in the seventies. He should've sent them an engraved "Thank You!" for getting rid of the marijuana smell in the house.

Over the next few weeks, our parents never said anything, so the white lie of the teeny party was our secret.

I worked up the courage a few years later and asked Mom, "Did any of the neighbors ever say anything to you about the parties?"

"No, not a word…so, what really happened?"

Me and my big mouth!

\*\*\*

My parents eventually decided to buy the local Highway Café. So Dad was now in the restaurant business. Dad got to the café early to serve the breakfast crowd and then got the lunch food ready. He'd then turn the kitchen over to his assistant, Theresa, who ended up becoming Jeff's wife.

I remember a saying Dad quoted to me one day at the café: "I never have to worry about any of the clocks being stolen here because all my employees are watching them."

I still think about that bon mot today when I'm at work and catch myself sneaking a peek.

There was time to kill in between breakfast and lunch so Dad and I headed to the golf course for a quick nine holes. I played golf almost every day with Dad during the summer. In the beginning, when I hit a bad shot, I threw my clubs. Dad never gave me a ride in the golf cart to go get my club, he made me walk. He must've figured that someday I'd get tired of walking after my clubs and stop throwing them. I wasn't that smart, and he eventually had to threaten me.

"If you throw a club one more time, I will quit bringing you along," he said in no unmistakable voice.

I never realized until recently how much Dad's discipline had soaked in. Nowadays, when I hit a terrible shot, I do not throw my golf club...I snap it in half over my knee. So much more fun. And *then* you can throw it—and walk away—with a clean conscience.

I remember a story Dad told us after he'd finished golfing one day. He had just showered at the clubhouse and as he was getting dressed, he heard two men talking. He was somewhat shocked to see that they were All Star wrestlers, and even more surprised to hear them discussing how that night's match at the county fair between the two of them was going to play out. Now, the Carle boys were big believers in TV wrestling being legit, so Dad saw his opportunity to prove to us that it's a put on. On the drive to the fair, he told us how the fight between Verne Gagne, the reigning champion, and the Mad Russian would go down—the moves, the blows, the holds, and how Gagne would win (a body slam off the ropes).

We watched the final match of the evening, and it happened exactly as Dad described it. Us kids were all silent in the car on the way home. We just couldn't believe that in reality All Star Wrestling was a staged entertainment show.

When I had kids of my own, they begged me to go see a WWF wrestling match in Des Moines, Iowa. Unlike my dad, I didn't want to spoil their illusions, and I never told them what I knew. To my kids' surprise I had purchased front row seats. And to MY surprise, all the way home they were laughing about how the wrestlers fell to the floor when they didn't even get hit that hard. "Dad," the youngest concluded, "it's such a fake!"

I took them to two more WWF matches and they still had a great time. Today, my grandkids are big fans and like I did, they think pro wrestling is for real. But I'm staying out of it.

Cliff and Jeff didn't get the hang of the game of golf. They both got so frustrated when they hit a bad shot that they never went with Dad. Cliff could hit the irons but not the woods. In his wisdom, he figured that it must be because the woods are a longer club. He went into the garage, took a hack saw, and cut the shafts of all his woods to the length of the irons. What a genius! He now could hit the woods, but the shot had no distance. He probably could've thrown the ball farther.

Today, I play golf four to five times a week. Jeff has taken up the game again and plays when he has time on weekends. Cliff plays tennis. I guess you don't have to cut down the size of your racket in order to play that game.

Cliff now lives in Los Angeles, California. At his house he has installed a basketball hoop. Besides tennis he can also shoot hoops. He has the idea that since he is a Los Angeles Lakers fan, he can play the game. I haven't played much since my high school days, except once in a while at a nearby gym with my kids. Cliff and I have always been competitive. When we get together at family reunions, we play Twenty-one, HORSE, and One-on-One. I win just about every game that we play. No brag, just fact.

It's like riding a bike; once you have it, you always have it. Besides, just because you own a basketball hoop does not automatically make you a basketball player. Note to Cliff: Stick to tennis.

## Chapter 9

# LAST CHANCE AT FIRST LOVE

At Christmastime, my brothers and I knew that all the good presents were not under the Christmas tree, but beneath our parents' bed, because they were too large to wrap. On Christmas morning, we always acted completely surprised, so Mom and Dad wouldn't find a new and more ingenious hiding place for next Xmas. There might be a Carrom Board (a pool-like game that used wooden rings in lieu of balls), or the Rock 'Em Sock 'Em Robots, where you boxed each other until one of the heads popped up. Then you had to push the head back down in order to start another round. One of our favorites was the Electric Football Game, where the players were moved up and down the field by the vibration. The players never went where you wanted them to; they all just slowly drifted off to the left sideline; but we played for hours all the same.

My brothers and I always got Dad a new tie. His closet had more ties than one man could ever wear in two lifetimes. It was ironic because Dad rarely went to church.

The only thing that Dad and the church had in common was his CB radio. He had the latest equipment, including an antenna twice as tall as the house that allowed him to talk to people all over the world.

On Sunday mornings, while the rest of the family were in church, Dad was on the CB radio being the goodwill ambassador to the world…and the churchgoing citizens of Lyons, NE. One Sunday, when the pastor was giving the sermon, over the loud speakers the famous words came right through: "Breaker, breaker, one nine, come in." It wasn't the pastor or even Jesus saying those words. That was Dad's calling card.

Of course, everyone, including the pastor, immediately recognized his voice and glared directly at our family. We couldn't sink low enough in the pews to get away from the piercing eyes.

If you are not up with CB lingo, here's how it works: You have to keep saying "Breaker, breaker, one nine, come in," until someone finally answers you.

Mom came home red in the face and told Dad, "You can no longer use the radio during church. We can hear you over the sound system!"

"On Sunday mornings," Dad pleaded his case, "the skip is just right to reach all over the world."

"That may be," Mom said, "but I can't keep making excuses for you not being in church when you're clearly just having your fun."

Dad gave in. It was either stop using the radio during those hours, or go to church.

I was raised Presbyterian. They didn't take religion as serious as the Catholics in our town. For example, in my Sunday school room, the Bible study "table" we sat around was a pool table with a plywood board placed over it. This was shortly before my best friend, Tom, was killed, and we used to get into trouble for skipping church services and playing pool. For some reason, the sound of balls hitting each other traveled all the way into the adjacent church.

"What are you boys doing?" one of the deacons asked us.

I don't mean to be a smartass, but it should have been obvious. I guess they always have to ask the question anyway.

"You boys stop that and get to church."

Also, during Sunday school, we sat around the table with the boys on one side, and the girls on the other. When the teacher was not looking, us boys took the pool balls out and passed them around, until the girls had all of them in their hands, but one. Then we rolled the last ball along the floor, until it hit the wall with a bang.

The teacher spun around and said, "Who threw that ball?"

The girls were busted! They tried to blame it on us, but they were the ones holding all the balls.

\*\*\*

Marsha Jones was the first love of my life. She had natural smooth rosy lips, ocean blue eyes, long straight blonde hair, and a beautiful smile that just melted my heart. She was the oldest daughter of Dad's rival, the five loaves of bread for a dollar guy. Dad never told me that I couldn't see Marsha since her dad was his competition. I always respected Dad for that, because for a while it was the talk of the town.

Our backyards were only 30 yards apart. I had just been given a new puppy and was so proud that I had to go right over and show Marsha. I bought a new choke chain and leash so I could take her for walks. We sat on her porch and played with the puppy for about fifteen minutes.

Marsha suggested, "Do you want to come in and have something to drink?"

"Yes, of course," I answered.

I tied the puppy with the leash to the railing on her porch and went inside. When I came back out ten minutes later, I couldn't find my new puppy. Then I saw the leash pulled tight over the railing and swaying from side to side. I thought she was struggling to get free. I went to the railing with the intent to cuss her out for trying to get away; then again, maybe she got lonely and decided to try to go back home?

When I looked over the railing…I saw her limp body swaying back and forth, her hind feet just a few inches off the ground. I had walked my dog over to Marsha's house, and now I was carrying her lifeless body back home with tears streaming down my face. It took many years before I was able to have another pet.

I took Marsha to several concerts, the first one was Three Dog Night, but the most memorable one was the Eagles. It was the early seventies, and they were playing in Omaha, Nebraska. Mom said, "If you want to really impress a girl, take her out to eat first."

"Where's a good place?" I inquired.

"The concert is at the Civic Center, isn't it?"

"Yes," I nodded.

"Close by is the Hilton Hotel, and on the nineteenth floor there's a restaurant where you can see all over Omaha. It'll be very romantic if you sit at a table by the window."

"Thanks, Mom!" and off I went to pick up Marsha.

We got to the hotel and rode the elevator to the 19th floor. You can't show fear in front of your girlfriend. I pretended that my shoes needed to be retied so I could get as close as possible to the safety the fetal position provides. Once inside the restaurant,

I asked for a table by the window. On our way to be seated, we walked by the bar in the middle of the room. Mom hadn't told me ahead of time that the bar revolves 360 degrees. Marsha and I had never seen a bar that rotated, and for her it was really cool. But I wanted to see it get out of granny gear. Also, I thought it'd really suck if you got drunk and your head was spinning. You'd have to navigate getting off, crossing your fingers that the bar and you were revolving in the same direction.

The waiter came over and handed us a menu, but recommended the buffet. I opened the menu, glanced at the prices, and thought, *The buffet sounds pretty good.* As we were getting into the line, we noticed that the band members of the Eagles were just ahead of us. How amazing is that, seeing them at supper before the concert? I've told the story over and over that I "ate dinner with the Eagles." So, I might have stretched the truth a little. We sat three tables away; but that was the same as eating with them in my book. And the rock star sexual chemistry must have transferred to me by osmosis—I could not have impressed Marsha any more than I did that night...based on what happened later in the back seat of my car.

Marsha and I were both virgins when we had our first sexual experience. We were only sixteen, and we really didn't know what we were doing. Remember, I never got that father to son talk about the birds and the bees. Over the next six months we made love several times.

Then one day in January, Marsha asked me to come over and pick her up to talk. I wasn't the smartest guy around, but I know that when a girl wants to talk it usually isn't good.

While we were cruising Main Street, Marsha turned to me and said, "I missed my period this month. What if I am pregnant? What are we going to do?"

Remember when my brothers Rodney and Cliff had the explosion with the shotgun shell? I said they had an expression on their faces like when your girlfriend says she's pregnant. Now you can see why I'm an expert on what that looks like.

I came back with, "Uhhhhhh, I don't know. Maybe if we wait a little longer you will get it?"

By the end of the following month we knew, Marsha was indeed pregnant. I guess giving it more time doesn't change fate. It seems like as I got older the trouble I got into escalated. I can guarantee you that this was worse than being caught looking down a girl's shirt.

In my small town, everybody before me who got a girl pregnant married her. When Marsha told me, I could hear the wedding bell blues playing in my head. I was in love, so I figured it was the right thing to do. I wasn't sure if we'd live at my house, or hers, until we could somehow get our own place. I was making only $140 per week.

I had to tell my parents the news. I couldn't think of a way to soften the blow, so I figured there was no beating around the bush and went right for the jugular. I asked Mom and Dad to come into the living room.

"Marsha is pregnant." I blurted out.

"How in the hell did that happen?" Dad asked.

You'd think that parents with four boys would know how it works. I wasn't sure if I was going to have a son to father talk.

"I guess we were careless. I'm sorry."

"How far along is she?" Mom wanted to know.

"I don't know."

"What are you planning to do?" Mom said unfolding her arms in a caring gesture.

"We're not sure. I'm going over to Marsha's house so we can tell her parents."

I know my parents were disappointed in me, but as I was leaving, Mom said, "If there is anything we can do, let us know."

Marsha's parents' reaction took me completely by surprise. They became incredibly mad. Her dad pointed to the door, informed me I wouldn't be seeing his daughter anymore, and ordered me to leave. Mr. and Mrs. Jones made the unilateral decision that Marsha would give the baby up for adoption. I don't know if it was because *I* was the father, or they didn't want to help raise the child, or the small-town embarrassment to them when they'd be seen pushing the baby carriage with Rick Carle's child inside of it.

We were still in high school and it would've been tough trying to raise a child at that age, but I was willing to give it a try. Regardless, neither me nor my parents were asked our opinion and we were given absolutely no say whatsoever. The Joneses totally shut us out and handled everything their own way.

When Marsha was ready to give birth, her parents took her to the same hospital I was at for my heart murmur. I didn't get a call before they left.

I remember like it was yesterday: September 27, I went to school that day, and one of Marsha's girlfriends raced up to me. "Rick, do you know Marsha is in labor?"

"No," I said in a panic, "which hospital is she at?"

"St. Joseph's Hospital in Omaha—I think room num…"

That's all I heard as I took off running to my 1968 Rambler in the parking lot. It used to be my Grandpa Carlberg's car. Grandpa never drove it over 45 mph. On the way to the hospital, it never saw below 70 mph. I am sure I blew some of the cobs out. The '68 Rambler was famous for the front seats that folded down flat all the way to the back. They'd come in handy if you were making out on Blueberry Hill. Maybe that is how Marsha got pregnant?

By the time I got to the hospital, the nurses had already given Marsha enough medication that she didn't feel anything during the delivery. That was the protocol in the 1970s when the mother was giving the baby up for adoption. If they don't feel the pain, or see the baby after the birth, that made it easier to give it up.

I walked down the hallway, and could see Marsha's parents standing outside her room. They turned and gave me a long look of shame and disbelief that I had the gall to come to the hospital. Marsha's mom walked away, but her dad blocked the doorway.

"What do you think you're you doing here?" he said with both hands on his hips. "You need to leave. Now!"

From inside the room, Marsha called out, "Dad, let Rick in."

Mr. Jones stood firm. "Your mother and I don't think he should be here."

"Well, I want to see him," Marsha insisted.

He turned and stormed down the hallway to find Mrs. Jones.

While I was in the hospital room with Marsha, a nurse came in and shocked us both when she slipped up by saying it was a girl. According the rules of adoption at that time, the parents weren't supposed to know the gender of the baby they were giving up.

Marsha and I tried to secretly remain boyfriend and girlfriend after that, but it was difficult. The experience of giving up the baby, and still having to coexist in a small town was extremely hard on us. I'd see people staring at me judgmentally as I walked down the street. I'm sure they had nothing good to say about me behind my back, or for that matter, to my face. Naïve people can be very cruel. That was one of the reasons I chose to go to college in Iowa.

After graduation, Marsha moved to Lincoln, Nebraska. She got married to a classmate of my brother Jeff, and they had two girls. To this day, I have not searched for my daughter. Maybe people will think of me as a bad person? I seriously thought about looking for her after I received a call from Jeff tin 1997 that Marsha had been sick with cancer; and on July 20, 1997 at the young age of 41, she died. I couldn't believe that she was dead. Even though I hadn't seen Marsha for years, hearing she was gone forever tore me apart. There's always a special place in your heart for your first love.

I've considered that perhaps my daughter doesn't want to be found. Or that it could upset the family she was adopted into. For example, what if, for reasons of their own, they didn't tell her she was adopted…and then I come barging in? As much as I'd love to find her, so I can end the guilt that I live with, it'd be devastating to the parents who raised her if she was never told about being adopted. I couldn't do that to them.

After Marsha died, I sent Mr. and Mrs. Jones a sympathy card. I expressed my personal feelings of sorrow, and how I imagined they must be feeling to have lost their daughter. I never received any response back from them. I guess they weren't ready to forgive—not then, and probably not ever. I was always taught by my parents that forgiveness goes both ways.

I had lost my older brother, my best friend, and now Marsha, the first love of my life. What could happen next?

## Chapter 10

# I FOUGHT THE LAW ... AND
# IT WAS A TIE

During the nonstop five-week party, I didn't partake in any of the herb smoking. Believe it, or believe it. In fact, I was chicken. But a year later, at the age of seventeen, my brother Cliff introduced me to pot. Cliff and I were hanging out a lot together. Maybe it was because of working in the meat department, or the incident with his girlfriend and her offer to expose her breasts.

Cliff had a rock band called "The British" with three of his friends. He played lead guitar. They practiced at night in our basement. Loud music is bad enough. But BAD loud music is insufferable. All the neighbors called our parents practically begging for it to stop. Mom and Dad were good about explaining that the boys have to practice in order to get good, and they'd make sure it ended at ten. Still, the Carle family never took home the "Best Neighbor Award".

It was great to sit down there and listen to them play. They actually got pretty good and went to several "Battle of the Bands" contests. They even won one or two, which got them new equipment. I don't know whose idea it was to have matching outfits and Beatle boots, but if you are going to be considered good, you had to look the part. The catch phrase on their posters was "The British Are Coming!"

Here's a fun fact about Cliff's band: The keyboard player, Doug "Duke" Erickson, in later years formed his own band. He named it "garbage" (yes, lowercase g). They became super famous with millions of fans. They tour all over the United States —and even Europe. Recently, garbage played the Hollywood Bowl; and of course Doug made sure Cliff had a backstage pass. Amazing! Who would've thought that there'd be *two* world-famous people from Lyons, Duke and me.

✳✳✳

I played drums in the school band. The downside of being a drummer was marching with a snare or bass, and in between songs, my job was to keep playing a cadence, so everybody could continue marching. Talk about no rest for the wicked.

I got a couple of my friends together and we formed a band. It was the hip thing to do at the time, and chicks digged guys in a band. Cliff taught us two songs. We practiced them until we thought we were good enough to get some local gigs…birthday parties and such. Somehow, the word got out, and we were invited to play on the Fourth of July, right before the town's fireworks were to begin.

We set up our equipment earlier in the afternoon, then agreed to meet a half hour before we were scheduled to play. I remember coming into the grounds and hearing a guitar playing. My first thought: *Hey! Some kid has gone up to our equipment and is messing around.* As I got closer, I could see Cary, our band's lead guitar player. He had hooked up his guitar to the speaker system and turned them up as loud as they could go. He was doing a bad imitation of Jimi Hendrix's *Star-Spangled Banner.* Needless to say, the crowd was not enjoying it as much as Cary was.

When I think of Cary, a funny story always comes to my mind. I went over to his house to hang out one day and when I knocked on the door, his mom, who was a large woman, opened it and told me, "Cary has to stay in his room because he's not feeling well."

"I just have to tell him something," I appealed to her. "Is it okay if I go see him for just a minute?"

"Okay," she said, stepping aside, "but I just want to warn you about his sore throat."

I'm sure Cary was hoping he wouldn't have any company that day: I opened his door and there sat Cary on his bed with one of his mom's extra-large Kotex, laced with Vicks VapoRub, wrapped around his throat. I laughed so hard then, and even now, as I can still see the mental picture. I've never let him forget that day because that is what friends are for!

When it came time for our band to play, the Master of Ceremonies told the crowd that since our group did not have a name yet, he'd give us one. He said, "Ladies and gentlemen, I present to you The Unholy Threesome."

I'm not sure he named us that because of the trouble we all got into when we were younger, or because his daughter was one of the girls who got caught with the pool balls in her hand during Sunday school and he thought it was "unholy" of us to do that.

I don't think the crowd was in favor of us playing before the fireworks. The first clue was when people in the crowd were yelling, en masse, "Get the hell off the stage! Start the fireworks."

When the crowd began tossing lit fire crackers at us, we decided that playing in a rock and roll band was not in our future.

In the late sixties and early seventies, a couple friends and I drove the 90 miles to Pershing Auditorium in Lincoln, Nebraska to see the great bands of our time. It was stadium seating, which meant the first ones in line when the gates opened got to stand in front of the stage, mere feet away from the bands. We'd get there at two in the afternoon for an eight o'clock concert. We saw Frank Zappa and the Mothers of Invention, Alice Cooper, Badfinger, Fleetwood Mac, ZZ Top, The Eagles, The Greatful Dead, The Alman Brothers, The Guess Who, Jethro Tull with Ian Anderson, Foghat with Humble Pie, Jackson Browne opening for Bonnie Raitt. And when I was at college I drove to Omaha to see Elvis. In Ames, Iowa I saw Paul McCartney and Wings at the football stadium. ZZ Top again, this time opening for Lynyrd Skynyrd. I'm sure there are some bands that I've forgotten. But what a great experience to have seen these iconic bands during their best years. Today, Fort Dodge has a concert every year with the bands from the seventies and eighties. I don't go to them, because in most cases, there is only one of the original members still playing in the band. And, after all those years of them smoking dope, the vocals don't sound anything like they used to.

**\*\*\***

Back to Cliff introducing me to pot. He took me for a ride in his car and pulled out a joint.

I said, "No thanks, I'm not interested."

Cliff came back with, "Come on, try it. What harm can it do?" Ah…the $64,000 question.

Looking back, I wish I'd gone with my first instinct and declined, but I gave in to peer pressure again. At first, I told Cliff I wasn't feeling anything. But when I began seeing orange and purple animals in the road ahead of us, I realized I was probably stoned. It was way too freaky, but what a great feeling being stoned; so of course, I began to smoke pot almost every day with my friends.

Rosalie, a town fifteen miles from Lyons, had a yearly celebration in August. It opened with a parade, followed by carnival rides, pot luck supper, a street dance, and many contests; like watermelon eating, the longest beard, and hog calling, to name a few.

At the time, I owned a 1969 full-size Ford Econoline van. Five of my friends and I decided the celebration was getting boring and we needed to change our attitudes, or altitudes, as it is known in drug lingo. The sun had just set when we drove out on a gravel road, pulled over to the shoulder, rolled up several joints, and began to smoke. After about ten minutes I thought I saw the headlights of a car approaching from behind us.

I looked out at my rear-view mirror and said, "Hey guys, a car is…"

Before I could finish my sentence, the red lights began flashing. It was the state patrol.

I heard a lot of "Oh shit!" coming from the back of the van, and "What are we gonna do now?"

Like the movie *Up In Smoke* with Cheech and Chong, the van was a fog bank. The patrolman got out of his car, came up to my window, and rapped on it with his knuckle.

"Roll down the window," he demanded.

I just looked back at him all bleary-eyed and shook my head no.

He tapped on the window harder and raised his voice: "I said, ROLL DOWN THE WINDOW!"

\*\*\*

The only other time I had a run-in with a state patrolman was the day after I got my driver's license. Mom, Jeff, and I, were going to Omaha to do some shopping.

"Please let me drive," I begged Mom.

I wanted to show how good of a driver I was. On the way to Omaha, we'd just passed through Oakland, NE, which had a steep hill right outside of town. The posted speed limit was 35 mph, but everybody went faster, because you had to ride the brakes not to. As I zoomed down the hill, I met a state patrolman coming up the hill. He immediately turned around, flashed his lights, and pulled me over. For some reason he parked his car in front of ours. I don't know if he was thinking if he pulled behind me, I'd take off. But eluding an officer and a scary car chase was not how I planned to *start out* my driving record.

He walked back to our car and said, "Can I see your driver's license, please?"

"What did I do?" I said as innocently as I could manage.

"You were speeding. Please get out of the car, and come with me."

He instructed me to get into the front passenger seat of his car. As I was sitting there, I said, "I wasn't speeding."

"You were doing 43 in a 35 zone."

"But officer, *everybody* goes faster than 35 down that hill."

"I didn't catch everybody, I caught you, and I'm going to give you a speeding ticket."

"But it isn't fair. I feel like I am being singled out."

Then the lecture began, "Son, I see you just got your license. You need to realize that a driver's license is a privilege, and this will help you see it that way."

As the lecture continued, I was getting madder and madder, but for once in my life, I was smart enough to keep my mouth shut.

The lecture droned on and on until he handed me the ticket and said, "Have a good day."

I was so mad…but I knew not to say anything, because I was thinking, *If you really want me to have a nice day, shove this ticket up your...*

I can't understand why some people say "thank you," after getting a ticket. What's there to be thankful for? And it certainly isn't what you're truly feeling. So, to let the cop know how I really felt, when I got out of his car, I slammed the door. Before I reached the back end, he was out of his side and had grabbed my arm.

"You do not slam my car door!" He said this with such force a few specks of saliva hit my face.

"I'm sorry," I said, not too convincingly.

"You go back to the door and open and close it three times the way you are supposed to close a car door."

During my door training, I got another lecture. Once he felt that I was an expert, he let me go. I was walking back to our car, and I could see Jeff was doubled over with laughter in the back seat. I am sure from his vantage point, what he'd just witnessed was hilarious.

Once I got in the car, I had to explain everything to Mom.

Her only sympathy for me was, "I hope you've learned a lesson."

*Yeah*, I thought to myself, *learn enough sign language to convincingly pretend you're deaf, and spare yourself the stupid lecture next time.*

**\*\*\***

So back to the side of the road in a van teeming with pot smoke. The officer tapped harder on the window as if being stoned makes you hard of hearing, and wanted me to open it NOW! I rolled it down, and all of the smoke in the van whooshed right into his face. (Payback for the aforementioned saliva?) If he had never gotten high before in his life, I'm sure he was getting his first buzz. He yanked open the door, looked inside the van, and saw the rest of my friends.

"Everybody out!" he ordered.

Everyone piled out and came around to my side of the van.

"Line up, put your hands on the van, and spread your legs," he instructed us.

This was my first time that I had been touched in a certain area by a male. He was feeling our pockets for pot, or any paraphernalia we might have on us. He found nothing; then began to search the van. I guess you don't need a search warrant when you get a face full of smoke, and that was considered probable cause. We just stood there looking at each other with stark fear in our eyes. We all knew we were in big trouble.

But after a thorough search of the van, all he found as evidence were some seeds in the carpet. He put them in a brown envelope and took down all of our names.

He made a sinister face. "I'm sending this envelope and your names into the state capital—there will be a record of what I found."

So, somewhere down in Lincoln, NE, there is a file containing a brown envelope with pot seeds in it, and my name attached to it. I don't know if any of you have had a similar experience, but I can tell you that it will kill a good buzz. After he drove away, we got back in the van; I reached into a secret compartment under the dashboard, and there was my bag of pot. Since the original buzz was gone, we proceeded to drive back home while firing up another one. How I wish the lesson had sunk in…

\*\*\*

As I have said, there was not a lot to do in a small town, so you had to create your own entertainment. Sometimes it was fun, and other times it could have been stupid, and got a person arrested.

One night, three of my friends and I were riding around in Bill's car. Bill was my out in the country friend. When we first became buddies, I always jumped at the chance to stay overnight at Bill's house. He couldn't believe I'd rather help him clean out the nauseating pigs' stalls for free than bag groceries at Lou's Market. But at that time, he had a car and I didn't. So, the tradeoff was I had somebody, namely Bill, to cruise up and down Main Street with on Saturday night (remember *American Graffiti*?).

One time a bunch of guys had parked their cars in the city park because they were low on gas. And after a while of shagging the drag, Bill's car was running on empty as well. The one gas station in Lyons had already closed. We decided to break the lock on the nozzle of the Midwest Co-op's gas supply. It was located on the south end of town. We filled up Bill's car then drove down Main Street, back to the park, to exchange cars.

We did this over and over, until everyone's car was full of gas. Each time we switched, the local cop saw Bill and me in a different vehicle, but he never put two and two together.

Our town cop, Bob Richardson, gave the impression he was somewhat mentally challenged—like we suspected he probably needed *instructions* to work the switch on his flashlight. One time, my brother, Cliff, was coming home from a date in the early morning hours. He noticed a fire had started in the city park. Apparently, a tree had been struck by lightning. Cliff went speeding down Main Street to get help and was pulled over by Officer Richardson.

He slowly sashayed up to Cliff's car, leaned down and said, "Alright kid, where's the fire?"

Cliff just smiled, like the Cheshire Cat, tossed a thumb over his shoulder and said, "In the park."

My friend, Bill, got home and couldn't find his billfold. He went out and searched his car, but it wasn't there. He thought maybe it fell out while he was filling up with gas and figured he'd better head back into town to make sure. It wouldn't look good with a broken lock and the incriminating evidence complete with your picture ID lying on the ground next to it. Bill owned two cars and decided to take his other one. Sure enough, right by the nozzle there it sat. He figured as long as he was there, he might as well fill 'er up. Bill's carelessness earned him an extra bonus—*two* cars full of free gasoline.

\*\*\*

In the summer of 1973, Sedalia, Missouri staged a three-day concert. It was the Woodstock of the Midwest. My friends Jeff, Kathy, Jane, and I drove there in my van. These were the same friends who were with me earlier when I got pulled over on the gravel road.

It took us five and a half hours to get there, and the line of cars was so long that it took six more hours till we got to the parking area. As we inched forward, people kept walking up and down the row of vehicles selling drugs.

We could hear people shouting, "Get your uppers, downers, LSD, speed…you name it, we got it."

All of us were shocked. We'd smoked pot, but none of us had ever seen any of these harder drugs, or had the opportunity to try them. The concert didn't start until the next day. The girls slept in the van while Jeff and me, being gentlemen, crashed on the ground next to the van. We woke up in the morning with a half-inch of dust all over us. We brushed it off, grabbed our blankets, coolers, and headed inside the fairgrounds to find a good place to watch the concert. We saw at least a hundred kids knocking down a fence and running in so they didn't have to pay. I remember thinking, *It's only fifteen dollars for all three days, why destroy a fence?* The temperature for the weekend averaged over one hundred degrees. We took one of the blankets and constructed a makeshift tent to block the hot, Death Valley-like rays of the sun.

Jeff and I wanted to take a shower. When we got to the facilities, the line was over 50 guys long. A good hour later, when my turn came, the water was just under the freezing point. No exaggeration. I saw guys in shock having to be pulled out. The paramedics thought it could have been a combination of whatever drug they were tripping on reacting to the frigid water temperature. Yeah, that and probably too freakin' stoned to be able to feel the difference between hot and cold.

The promoters were planning on 35,000 people, over 100,000 showed up. We walked around and found a barn that had fifteen faucets all lined up. It was the place where cows and pigs got water during the county fair. That was our shower for the day.

On the way back to the tent, we saw many girls who were walking around topless. That was a pleasant sight for a couple young Nebraska boys, until we saw guys who were also naked. It had to be the heat, drugs, alcohol, or a lack of caring, that inspired men to walk around completely nude.

That night, a guy tripped and fell into our tent. To make amends he offered to smoke us up with some opium he had. None of us had ever tried it before, and we were willing to give it a shot; besides we wanted to be good hosts. He hung out with us until the concert was over.

More than thirty bands performed over three days. I know I heard them, but because of the opium, I cannot remember any of them. I do remember hearing that three people overdosed on some bad LSD that was going around. Twenty years later, I wrote to the Sedalia newspaper to find out who all played there, so I could lie to my friends about all the cool bands I saw that weekend, including Lynyrd Skynyrd, Joe Walsh, Charlie Daniels, and The Marshall Tucker Band.

With temperatures so hot and long lines at the showers, the crowd decided to open up several fire hydrants. People with and without clothes were enjoying the cold water. One area had become a mud pit, which was perfect for a slide. I could not believe my eyes: topless girls took off running, hit the wet ground, and zipped along on their butts or bellies for about thirty feet; breasts a-bouncin' pretty as you please. Who needed music?

After theft became a huge problem, the local grocery put a limit on how many kids could be in the store at one time. Cars were being filled up with gas, and then off they went without paying. Some homeowners opened up their houses for people to sleep; while others woke up to their yards full of unexpected, and even unwanted, concert goers. By the third day, garbage and sanitary conditions reminded me of New York City during a city garbage strike. You didn't want to use a Port-a-Potty. The odor wafting around it burned our eyes. I'm sure the people of Sedalia were asking, "Whose brilliant idea was this?"

Just as we were leaving, the crowds got rowdy. They set a car on fire and overturned a police cruiser. I wasn't able to experience Woodstock in upstate New York, but for a Midwestern boy, "three days of so-called *peace* and music" at Sedalia was a close second.

**\*\*\***

Who'd have guessed that my hometown of Lyons, Nebraska would make it on the TV show *America's Most Wanted?* I know what you are thinking, and no, it wasn't because of me.

Our new chief of police, Greg Webb–six foot tall, blond, convivial–resided in a duplex apartment house with a single grade school teacher, Anna Anton. Officer Webb lived upstairs and she lived downstairs. He was a very likeable guy…so you probably already see where this story is going. Anyway, over time he used his wily charm on her, and they eventually started dating. A lot of this part of the story is speculation, but I'm guessing his dark side started to come out and Anna decided she wanted to break off the relationship…not what Greg had in mind.

Crime scene investigators later concluded that this is probably what happened next: Officer Webb became furious and shot her three times in his apartment, then rolled her up in a blanket, and put her in the trunk of his patrol car.

Webb thought he had the perfect place to dispose of the body up on the Indian reservation. He knew that it'd make the investigation more difficult when her naked body was found there, because only the Indians have jurisdiction.

Since he was a police officer, he made a show of helping out with the investigation, until it was getting too close to home (namely *his* home) then he ran. Four days later, Officer Webb's pickup was discovered at the Houston, Texas airport, but he was nowhere to be found.

I watched the episode on *America's Most Wanted*. The detectives used special black lights to find Anna's blood spots leading from Webb's upstairs apartment down to the front door. Officer Webb had tried to clean them up, but forensics is more effective than a rag and bleach. It was an open and shut case for CSI Lyons.

It turned out Officer Webb had disappeared down in Central America where he'd once been a Peace Corps worker. Webb successfully hid for almost five years before deciding to come back to the United States. That was his big mistake. He was living in Florida when a neighbor saw a repeat of the show and reported his whereabouts to the police. Webb was arrested and put in jail for first degree murder. It is good to know that no one is above the law, except if you work in Washington, DC. But that's another story by itself.

## Chapter 11

# IT'S A BUST

B y the time I was seventeen, my brothers, our friends, and I, were all smoking pot. A couple of my buddies, Rob and Jeff (his nickname was Skin) even tried acid. I don't remember how he got it. But one day, while Rob & Skin were tripping on LSD, Rob decided that his 1966 Chevy Impala would look really cool if it was a convertible. They took a cutting torch and lopped off the top of his car.

I asked him, "What are you going to do when winter comes?"

"I don't know," Rob shrugged and laughed it off.

I could see then that all acid did was make you come up with some stupid ideas, and that wasn't my cup of poison. No, I preferred to *inhale* my bad-idea potion.

I was always amazed that Rob knew no fear. He went to a trade school in Davenport, Iowa, which is on the east side of the state, approximately 475 miles away. After some more drug-induced customizing, Rob didn't have an operable car anymore.

After that, he hitchhiked back and forth from Lyons, Nebraska across Iowa to Davenport. One time he even hitchhiked back from Davenport with a motor for a motorcycle, he was building. Can you imagine someone stopping to pick him up and having to make room for a motor? That is something that I could not do. I've heard too many horror stories of people being picked up, and never seen again. On the other side of the coin, I have such a fear of the hitchhiking process, I won't even stop for a hitchhiker in case *they* have a weapon, steal my car, and I end butt up in a ditch somewhere.

***

One of my brother Jeff's classmates, Nick, decided to try to become a State Patrolman. When he applied for the job, they told him he was too short. I guess you have to be a certain height to hassle young kids like me while giving them speeding tickets. But they did have an "informant" program for him if he was interested. Apparently, narking on all of your friends and relatives doesn't have a height requirement.

My guess is he had an inferior complex, plus a vertically challenged phobia, and felt this job would boost his ego—in his mind it gave him the opportunity to be a Midwestern James Bond.

After some training, Nick Nark came back to Lyons and resumed farming with his dad. We all assumed he was just too stupid to pass the Patrol test. What we didn't know was that Nick was working undercover; recording shit in his journal every time he smoked with us. I suppose it's okay to smoke pot as long as you are a nark and keep detailed notes of it.

One time, while Nick Nark and I were getting high together, he asked me, "Do you know where I can buy some pot or speed?"

I nodded. "I'll ask the guy I get mine from and get back to you."

Now, at this time, I was only buying pot for myself. I went over to "Doug Dealer's" house, which was twenty miles away and in a different county. I picked up an extra ounce of pot and one hundred hits of speed, thinking I was helping out a friend.

A month later, Nick Nark approached me again: "Can I buy larger quantities of both? And do you mind if I ride along this time?"

I should've seen the writing on the wall—that this was a setup, but I grew up with this guy, and I was blind to what he was doing behind my back.

We got there and Doug Dealer was not happy that I'd brought someone along. He was smart enough to know that in order to get busted during a transaction, you need a witness. We'd always conducted business one-on-one before. I convinced him that Nick was cool. After all, he'd graduated with my brother, Jeff, and I'd known him all my life.

The first time, Nick Nark gave me the money and I paid the dealer. This time I was just the middle man while he bought four ounces of pot and one thousand hits of speed. We drove back to Lyons and for weeks I never thought anything of the deal. Although it was odd that Nick Nark never asked me again to help him buy more drugs.

One hot summer day in late July, I was in my parents' driveway, washing my van, when I heard a car pull up. A police cruiser had stopped in front of our house.

The Sheriff's Deputy, who was six-feet-five inches tall and built like a pro football linebacker, got out of his car and sauntered over to me. "Are you Rick Carle?"

"Maybe, " I said, cautiously eyeing his name patch. "So, Deputy Wesson, what's up?"

"I have a warrant for your arrest."

"What for?" I demanded in total amazement.

"Drug trafficking across county lines," the deputy replied.

I thought, *He must be crazy. I've never brought drugs across ANY line.*

"You must have the wrong guy," I said, affecting my most convincing tone of voice.

"If you are Rick Carle, living at 1289 Custer Street, you are the right guy," the deputy said nonchalantly. "You can find out the details at the courthouse. My job is to place you under arrest and take you there."

I was wearing swim trunks and no shirt. "Can I at least go inside and put on some clothes?"

He said, "Yes, but I am going in with you," as he casually rested his hand on the butt of his gun to let me know not to even think about trying any funny business.

I'm guessing Deputy Wesson must have thought I was going to try to escape out the back door. He followed me into the house and right into my bedroom. I wasn't thinking of making a run for it—he'd probably closesline me with one of his cannon-like arms.

"Can I have some privacy while I change clothes?" I asked politely.

I wasn't sure if this was going to be the second time in my life that I was going to be *violated* by an officer. Deputy Wesson stepped back into the hallway, but I could feel he was keeping me in his peripheral vision, lest I try to take a powder out the window, I suppose.

After I got dressed, he led me out to his car and put me in the back. This was my first experience in the rear seat of a patrol car. During my speeding ticket incident, I was in the front. I noticed there was a heavy metal screen between Deputy Wesson and me. This way I couldn't reach over the seat, choke the deputy until he passed out, and escape. Heck, with my luck, while making the getaway, I'd slam the door too hard anyway. I looked left and right and saw there were no door handles. Even if I wanted to, there wouldn't be a Great Escape.

After the store burned down, Mom took a job as the City Clerk.

I asked Deputy Wesson as we were driving away from my house, "Can we stop up to City Hall?"

"What for?" he said somewhat irritated.

I think he was getting tired of all my requests.

"My mom works there, and I want to tell her what's going on."

Somehow, I thought that Mom could get me out of this mess. Little did I know, Mom didn't have that kind of clout.

When you grow up in a small, *Peyton Place* kind of town, you always have the gossipers. Let me tell you, it is hard to hide from them when a sheriff's car pulls up on Main Street and he has to open the back door to let you out. The red flag goes up immediately that you've been arrested. The only good news was I didn't have handcuffs on.

We went inside and with puppy dog eyes I said to Mom, "I'm under arrest."

"What for?" Mom exclaimed, dropping the phone that was in her hand.

Before I could explain, Deputy Wesson stated, "Rick is under arrest for drug trafficking."

One of the nicest things I could've done for Mom at that particular moment was to pick her jaw up off the floor. Her youngest son, the drug dealer! She must have felt so proud at that moment.

"Where are you taking Rick?" she demanded.

"To the jail in Pender," Deputy Wesson responded.

I didn't know that one of Mom's friends was the Cumming County judge in Pender. Lucky for me, while I was being escorted there, Mom was on the phone to her friend, and found out how much my bail was going to be. Mom immediately sent Jeff with $200, saving me from a stint in county lockup. By the time the mug shots and finger printing were over, Jeff had arrived. In retrospect, maybe if I'd been put behind bars, I'd have learned a lesson and changed my ways in the future.

The papers I had to sign before I left told me when to appear in court and what my actual charges were: Three felonies and four misdemeanors for drug trafficking across county lines.

I thought that I'd go on with my life as usual until I had to appear in court. I didn't know that when you buy drugs in one county that it is another crime to bring them back to the county you live in. It didn't seem fair that I did one crime, and two counties wanted a shot at me.

Now I also had a warrant for my arrest in Burt County. Before I had to go through another ride in the back seat of a patrol car to jail without passing GO, Mom decided it'd be better if I just turned myself in—and she'd drive me there to do it.

I pleaded with her, "Mom, I can go by myself."

"No," Mom said in exasperation. "I am going to take you there, so I can pay the bail money right on the spot."

I was glad that Mom was going to keep me out of jail again, but I didn't want her to see the booking process.

The county seat for Burt County was thirty miles away in Tekamah. That gave Mom plenty of time to give me a lecture. You'd think with all the lectures I got; I would've turned out to be a professor.

We went inside; Mom explained to the clerk that we were here to turn her son in, and that she wanted to pay the bail.

"That's fine, Mrs. Carle," the clerk said. "But first we have to process him."

"Okay, but I want to go with," Mom insisted.

I pleaded with her, "Mom, why don't you just sit here in the waiting room and I'll be right back when it's over."

"No, " she said, firm and final, "I am going with you!"

As much as I wanted to, she made it clear that I couldn't talk her out of it. Mom was somewhat okay as she watched the finger printing process, but when it came to the mug shots, it was a different story. I was standing sideways for the profile shot holding the sign with my number on it. Then they told me to turn and face forward. As I did, I could see Mom's face. She was standing there with tears just billowing down her cheeks. Mom must've been thinking, *Where did things go wrong?* She'd always tried to raise us boys as good, law-abiding citizens, and somewhere along the line, she had failed as a parent; when in fact it was me who had failed her.

I mouthed the words "I'm sorry" to her.

The only other times I'd ever seen her cry like that were when Rodney had died, and when the store burned down. I couldn't believe that what I had done was causing her equal pain. I wished I could've crawled out of the courthouse and walked home.

Later, I found out that Nick Nark had evidence on twenty-seven kids in Lyons. One of them was even his first cousin. Can you believe that? I'm sure that those family reunions were somewhat different from then on.

One of my brother Rodney's classmates had just graduated from college as a lawyer and decided to move back to Lyons to start a practice. His timing was impeccable. "Allen Attorney" had just hung a shingle and automatically had twenty-seven new clients. A windfall had kerplunked into his lap.

My brother, Jeff, only had a misdemeanor for smoking with Nick Nark. Allen Attorney got his sentence thrown out on grounds of entrapment. I wasn't so lucky. Between both counties, I ended up with six Class D felonies and eight misdemeanors. I had to appear many times in the courtroom. It was there where I saw the four ounces of pot and the thousand hits of speed again.

The evidence was put in front of me and I was asked, "Did you, or did you not help purchase these drugs and then bring them from Cumming County back to Burt County?"

They had the goods and an eye witness. The days of playing stupid, like I did with my Dad, weren't going to work this time. I didn't have any defense.

I looked at my lawyer and he told me to say "Yes."

Allen Attorney was able to plea bargain and got all the misdemeanors dropped, but not the felonies. The county prosecutor fought hard for all of the charges. He was also new and wanted to make a name for himself, at my expense.

When all the smoke had cleared (no pun intended) I received one felony in each county, because it was my first offense. I had to pay a thousand dollar fine and was given a two-year probation, which I had to admit was better than jail time.

One day while I was waiting for court to begin, I ran into Doug Dealer. He'd been arrested as well and was facing two felonies for drug trafficking.

He came over to me, cocked his fist, got within inches of my face, and said, "When this is over, I am going to beat the shit out of you." He was as mad as a mosquito in a mannequin store. "Why did you bring that dirtbag to my house? Are you a nark too?"

I swore that I wasn't, as evidenced by the fact that I ended up with more felonies charges than he did.

"I was just caught up in this mess like you were," I explained to him.

I'm not sure why, but he decided to call the dogs off me, and we've never seen each other since.

Note to self: *After getting busted, breaking your Mom's heart, having to appear in court—damn luckily not thrown in jail—it'd be a good time to quit doing drugs, and never sell them again.*

[Unfortunately, I never found that memo for another twenty years.]

*My senior class picture, May 1973*

# Chapter 12

## COLLEGE CRAZIES

While the court proceedings were taking place, I applied for a job with the railroad. The job description would've had me riding a train back and forth from Fremont, Nebraska to Kansas City, Missouri for twelve hours on and twelve hours off. I wasn't sure I wanted to do that, and I also looked into attending college. The latter won out—I thought I could do better with my life having an advanced education. Years later, when I turned forty-eight, I kicked myself in the ass. I would've retired with a full pension after thirty years of working on the railroad, all the live-long day.

The Clint Eastwood movie, *Play Misty For Me,* got me thinking that being a disc jockey was my dream job. Clint portrayed a cool guy who attracted the hot chicks. So what if he almost got himself killed? I thoroughly enjoyed listening to music; getting paid for playing it made sense to me, and if bodacious babes came with the package. Not a bad perk.

In Nebraska, in order to become a DJ, you had to go to college for four years. My guidance counselor told me about a two-year program at Iowa Central Community College in Fort Dodge, Iowa. I could start my radio career much sooner if I went there.

Mom and I took a trip to check out the college and the town. Fort Dodge, a city of over 30,000 people, was a far cry from the just over 900 population town of Lyons I grew up in. I was overwhelmed and somewhat intimidated by the size of Fort Dodge, and Iowa Central had buildings spread out over many acres, unlike the one-building high school I attended; plus, I was uneasy about never having lived away from home before. But I also knew that it'd do me good to get away from Lyons where I could have just as well wore a sign around my neck emblazoned with "FELON", cuz that's how everyone looked at me. So, I decided it was time to get *into* Dodge.

While we were driving back home, a deer sprang out of the ditch and landed in our lane less than twenty yards ahead. Mom tried to swerve, but there was no time to avoid a collision. The deer flew up in the air and smashed into the windshield on my side. I can still see the deer's face as blood was spilling out its nose and mouth right in front of me.

Mom totally freaked out, knowing she'd just killed one of Bambi's parents.

"Mom! Pull over, so we can see the deer," I said, though not exactly sure why.

"No!" Mom kept her foot on the accelerator. "We are going to drive to the next town and explain what happened."

I used to hunt pheasants, but I'd never gone deer hunting. The only deer I'd ever seen were long-dead ones on the side of the road. But usually, you zip by so fast that you really can't see much. This was my opportunity to see one up close and personal; but Mom didn't share my macabre curiosity.

When we got to Danbury, Iowa, Mom stopped at the police station. She knew she needed to report the accident for her insurance company. I opted to stay in the car; I'd already seen the insides of enough police stations to last me for a long while.

**\*\*\***

Another "deer me" story: If you can't have good luck, you might as well have bad luck, and it seemed to always know where I was going and tagged along. Years later, on one of my divorce weekends with my kids, I used the Goodyear Tire company truck, without permission, to run some errands that I couldn't do with a car. Rather than take the pickup back on Sunday and exchange it for my car, I decided to drive my kids to their cousin's house out in the country. This way they could play for a while before going back to their mom's home. As we were rounding a curve on the dirt road, there was a deer standing right in front of me. Well, that deer was no match for Goodyear's ¾ ton pickup going 45 mph. After the crash, the deer had flown into the ditch. There was smoke and steam coming out the front of the pickup. The kids all thought it was pretty cool. I got out to check the truck. The impact with the deer had smashed the radiator and antifreeze was leaking all over. I knew it wouldn't start, and that I couldn't drive it the two miles to their cousin's house, so we walked there.

I explained what happened to Paul, the cousins' dad. He and I went back in his pickup to take a better look at the truck —and the deer. Neither one was a good sight to see. I called for an officer to come and make out an accident report. A state patrolman arrived in fifteen minutes. He lived just six miles away in Badger, Iowa.

While we waited for the officer, Paul went over, pulled out a mean-looking knife, and slit the deer's throat.

I was shocked. "What in the hell are you doing?"

Paul said, "If we are going to keep the meat, the deer has to be bled out."

Both Paul and I knew the State Patrolman., Cliff Caruth.

He got out of his car and eyed the truck's front. "What happened. Rick?"

I explained, "When I made the curve, the deer was standing in the middle of the road. I couldn't swerve to miss him. Cliff looked in the ditch at the deer, and saw Paul with the bloody knife in his hand.

Paul asked hopefully, "Can we keep him for the meat?"

Cliff said, "Yeah, I'll get a Department of Resources tag for you from my car, and also call for a tow truck."

At the same time, both Paul and I said, "Thanks!"

The truck was towed back to the Goodyear Tire store. I went to work early so I could be there when the manager arrived, since the pickup was in the front parking lot and would be hard to miss. I explained to my boss that it was merely a case of bad luck that I hit a deer with his Goodyear truck on a Sunday when no one was supposed to have a company truck outside of working hours. He chewed my ass out a little and wasn't interested in any deer meat. In the end, I was lucky not to have been fired, but the deer meat sure tasted good.

✱✱✱

In my teens, Dad knew a farmer in Lyons, Gene Cram, who raised greyhounds. They were trained to hunt coyotes. When there are more coyotes than *wasculwy wabbits*, or *beep-beep* roadrunners, for them to eat, the coyotes begin attacking farm animals…calves, piglets, chickens; and often pets. Coyotes especially enjoy a side of adorable sad-eyed puppy, or cute little kitten.

If you were lucky, Dad would take one of us boys along with him. Dad and the other men in their trucks surrounded the coyotes along the county roads. Then it was time to "Release the hounds!" The rule was, you could not shoot the coyotes. If you did, Gene never allowed you to take part again. Occasionally a shotgun blast was used to turn a coyote around back in the direction of the greyhounds. If the dogs didn't make the kill, then it was a good day for Wiley's kin.

I only had one bad experience while hunting. Several of my friends and my football coach, Mr. Ashby (the guy who thought the Carle boys made great bench warmers) were hunting pheasants in a milo field. Milo grows so close together that you have to walk abreast at about twenty feet apart to scare up the pheasants. You almost have to step on the birds to flush them out and get them to take wing--unless you have a dog, and we didn't.

All of a sudden, a bird flew up right between Coach Ashby and me. I raised my shotgun and as I looked down the barrel, all I could see was the coach's head. He ducked and I, on reflex, jerked the gun up in the air just as I pulled the trigger; missing both the bird and the coach's brains. We were both relieved. On one side, this could have been excessive payback for keeping me on the bench; but on the other hand, I didn't need a manslaughter on my record. Drug trafficking was enough, thank you.

\*\*\*

When I started college, I didn't know anyone there. The first week, I sat in the cafeteria at a table all by myself, feeling alone and lonely. But over time I got to know some of my fellow future disc jockeys, and we began hanging out together. In 1973, in the Iowa Central cafeteria, whites sat with whites, and blacks sat with blacks, though there were exceptions…

"Tommy Mouth", a scrawny white punk, often expressed his opinions before engaging his brain. More than once, his racist remarks got him into trouble. Cindy Franklin was Tommy Mouth's girlfriend's roommate. Cindy, a cute-as-a-button Caucasian, was dating Charlie White, one of the blacks. When Tommy visited his girlfriend in her dorm room, he'd harass Cindy relentlessly about having sex with a f[FILL-IN-THE BLANK]ing black guy.

Mouth sat in the cafeteria every day and glared at Cindy from across the room while she cozied up to her black boyfriend. But one day, he just couldn't take it anymore. Tommy slammed his fork down, marched over to Cindy, and interrupted her mid-bite. "Goddammit Cindy, why are you sitting with these Niggers?"

The entire cafeteria held their collective breath. Nobody could believe he was that stupid.

Before Cindy could tell Tommy to mind his own business, Charlie had risen to his feet and decked Tommy with one punch. *Kapow!* Lights out. Mike Tyson would've been proud of that punch. I looked around the room and it was evident that whites and blacks were united in the agreement that Tommy finally got what he deserved.

After a couple of weeks in Fort Dodge, I had to meet with my Iowa probation officer. My sentence required me to check in with him once a month for two years. His name was David Follet. I never had any reason before that day to meet a probation officer, and I was shaking in my boots. I had visions of an ex-military guy, or ex-cop, who was going to be a ball-buster and do everything by the book, like making me take unannounced piss tests, for example. Instead, Dave was a puppy dog. And lucky for me, if I couldn't always make an appointment, he was cool about it. He was just going through the motions. I think it was because he was so close to retirement that he really didn't care anymore. He was serving out his time too, and could relate.

Maybe if Dave had been stricter, my life would've taken another direction (i.e., the straight and narrow). Instead, the crowd I chose to hang with in Ft. Dodge smoked more weed than I'd ever dreamed of —like around the clock. Cheech and Chong would've fit in nicely with this crowd.

One of them, John Benson, MacGyvered a gas mask adding a six-inch glass tube in the middle of it where your mouth was, and supergluing to the other end, a two-inch marijuana bowl. While gas masks are great for not allowing noxious fumes in, they're even better for keeping pot smoke from getting out. Every morning, without exception, we'd meet in his dorm room at seven-thirty, strap on the mask, and get extremely toasted before my first class, Basic Electricity. I couldn't tell you the difference between an ohm and a resistor. And for the life of me, I also can't tell you how I ended up with a passing grade.

✳✳✳

The road to becoming a DJ was not what I had expected. Maybe it was because both of my Broadcasting instructors were Mormons. Now mind you, I have nothing against their religion. I believe everybody has a right to their own beliefs. Until college, I'd never met a Mennonite, so I didn't know drinking coffee, smoking cigarettes, or even cussing were things that they did not abide. I thought that was a shame since I did them all, plus numerous extras.

*Brother Louie* by The Stories was frequently played on other radio stations. It was a controversial song about an interracial love affair. We were forbidden to play the record on our station. I found out that our instructors were also censors. Every time new records came in, they listened to them first to determine if the song was "approved" for playing. "Number one with a bullet" on the Billboard charts meant nothing to those guys. If the song didn't pass their strict Christian guidelines it wasn't played at Iowa Central, and thrown in the Dumpster.

They also had a color-coded rating system. If a record was considered "Easy Listening" it got a green dot, if it was "Rock & Roll" a red dot. The rule was: You were not allowed to play a red dot record before four in the afternoon. For this secondary reason I chose the night shift. But the main reason was, we didn't have any supervision at night, so I could smoke pot right before I went on the air.

One evening, a so-called friend, laid some cannabinol on me before my shift. At the time I didn't know that cannabinol is a pig tranquilizer. I'm not sure what effect it has on a hog, but on a human, it makes you feel like you're rocketing out of your body into the stratosphere. Just call me Captain Space Cadet! By the time I arrived for my shift, I was higher than I'd ever been! Luckily, when you are a freshman DJ, the broadcast only goes to the college dorms.

Within a half hour of being on the air, I got a call from Sonny Thompson, one of my classmates. "Rick, what the hell is wrong with you?"

"Uh…N-Nothing," I replied, "W-Why?"

"You are spelling out the words," Sonny said with a laugh.

I guess that when I was reading a PSA (Public Service Announcement) and I came to a big word like "concentrate", I said (con...cen...tr...ate). It must've sounded pretty funny, or awful stupid. I asked if he could finish my shift and I'd trade with him. I went back to my dorm room, got into bed, closed my eyes, and tried my best to come down from the intense buzz. It lasted for over five hours, and I decided to leave cannabinol to the piggies.

I kept my word and took his place the following morning. Instinctively, as I did in the evening, I grabbed a Rock & Roll record and placed it on the turntable. I instantly found out that the instructors listened during the day.

Professor Rosser charged into the studio and yelled, "Mr. Carle! You know that you can't play a red dot record before four! Don't ever do it again!"

That morning when I first woke up, I'd asked myself, "What can be worse than a cannabinol hangover?" Well, try five hours of playing Easy Listening. I was so glad when I finished my shift and knew there was another reason I chose being on the radio in the evenings. Like Joan Jett and the Blackhearts, *I Love Rock 'N' Roll*...

✱✱✱

Weed, speed, and pig sedative weren't cheap, and damn, I had to get a part-time job. I signed on to work in a meat market right across from the city jail. Each day an officer came in and picked up 40 - 50 lbs. of hamburger to serve the prisoners. Lucky for the bad guys we sold meat, and not bread and water.

I had a long-standing tradition of not working on my birthday; and so far I *never* had. Three months into the job, I said to the owner, Bob Wingerson, who'd been a meatcutter for over thirty years, "Tomorrow is my birthday, so I'd like to take the day off."

"Not gonna happen," Bob drawled. "We got us a hunnerd prisoners need hamburger."

"You don't understand, Bob." I shook my head disbelievingly. "I have a tradition to uphold," then joked, "I may even have a shot at the Guinness Book,"

"You'll either be here, or you'll find yourself lookin' fer another job. Decision's up ta you," Bob said with finality.

I stormed away, finished packaging five cases of chickens, and didn't talk to him the rest of the afternoon.

I walked out the door at the end of my shift, and Bob called out, "You comin' in t'morrow?"

I turned around, looked him right in the eyes. "No, I am not," and closed the door behind me.

The day after my birthday I went into the market and began boning shortloins, as usual. Bob was in the meat cooler when I came in.

Bob walked over to me and took the knife out of my hand. "What're ya doin? You don't work here no more."

I took off my apron, threw it in his face and stormed out. But I was actually mad at myself. I realized I had put pride ahead of intelligence and it cost me a well-paying job.

My next gig was at Rustler's, a popular college pickup bar. At my interview, the owner, Bill Howard, asked me, "Have you ever bartended before?"

"No, but I'm a quick learner," I plead with confidence.

I convinced Bill that I needed the job and that I'd work extra hard if given the chance. He hired me and showed me a mixology book—how to make drinks—in case I got confused. But who had time to read? Whenever a customer came up to me and ordered a mixed drink; say a Cosmopolitan. I'd go, "What's in that?"

They'd first look at me like I was nuts; then they'd tell me the ingredients.

I'd smile and say something like, "Just messin' with ya," though secretly thankful for the recipe.

Being a college bar, most of the young customers didn't have a lot of extra money. Consequently, most of the guys drank draw beer. Girls, on the other hand, tripped me up occasionally with some strange names for drinks. One evening around midnight, a good-looking girl sashayed up to bar and asked me, "Could I get a Slow Screw?"

I hesitated then said, "No problem, I get off at two o'clock."

She said, "No stupid, I mean the drink." Then she had to tell me what was in it.

A Budweiser man, myself, after a week at Rustler's I was introduced to rum and Coke. I'd kept trying different drinks until I found the one I liked best. My shift went until two in the morning. I had at least eight Bacardi & Cokes while working, adding just enough Coca Cola to give color to the rum. By the time I cleaned up the bar, and got back to my dorm room, it was 3:00 AM. Then I had to get up at seven for school. Between getting blitzed with the gas mask, and the hangovers, it is a wonder that I ever made it to class.

I started work at 7:00 PM. Bill grabbed at least a hundred dollars out of the till before he left. He went to a bar his mother owned to drink and play cards. Bill was a terrible card player. He lost most of the time.

One night around 11:00, Bill staggered into Rustler's and yelled, "Ever'body out! Bar's closed!"

I looked at him and said, "The bar is full of people, you can't close up. It's still early. Why don't you go home and sleep it off."

"I kin do whatever I wan'. I own this bar." Bill turned around and yelled again, "I says ever'body out!"

I immediately put my hands up for people to see and yelled, "Nobody leave. Bill will be leaving." Little did I know, Bill had gotten into a fight with his wife and she'd thrown him out of their house, so he had nowhere to go. Bill wanted to pass out on the pool table in the bar. It was his second bed.

I turned to him and said, "Bill, go home."

He started cussing at me and said, "You forgit who's boss?"

Behind the bar there was a button to push if we needed the police's help. When Bill wasn't looking, I pressed it. Two minutes later, two police officers burst in with their guns drawn.

"What's the problem?" one of them asked.

I quickly responded, "Bill is drunk, and causing all kind of problems. Will you please take him home?"

Bill slurred, "I ain't drunk. I jus' wanna go ta bed."

The cops came over to Bill, grabbed him by the arms, and escorted him out of his own bar.

As Bill went through the door, he turned back to me. "Rick, yer fired!"

Everybody in the bar was speechless. Nobody knew what to do.

I climbed up on the bar counter and yelled, "First drink is on Bill!"

Everybody started laughing. I gave the entire bar free drinks. There had to be at least fifty people in there. The good news is my gesture resulted in everybody staying until two in the morning, and Bill made lots of money the rest of that night.

The following night I drove to Rustler's expecting to collect my final paycheck and leave.

I walked in; Bill looked at me and said, "Hey, Rick, how ya doing? You ready for a busy night?"

"Uh…yes, Bill, I am."

Bill grabbed a fistful of cash, headed out, waved back at me and said, "See you tomorrow."

Bill didn't remember anything about the previous evening.

Rustler's had ten cent draws from three to five o'clock every Wednesday afternoon. Then the hungry students had to hurry back to the cafeteria before it closed at five-thirty. Frequently, a food fight broke out. Dinner buns were the weapon-of-choice, but several times I witnessed *Jello* squares flying back and forth.

The college complained to the bar owner, but he denied it was his fault. Bill said, "All I am doing is trying to draw students into my bar. Maybe if you had better quality food they'd eat it rather than throw it."

I usually ate dinner at 4:45 every day. I chose that time in order to beat the Trekies. They huddled around the TV in the lounge area watching *Star Trek*. The show aired from four to five every weekday. As soon as the show was over, they all piled into the cafeteria, creating a long line. On the way to eat, my friends and I laughed as we passed them, calling out, "Yo…Trekies!" and giving them the Vulcan hand sign. If you don't know what that is, ask someone who used to watch *Star Trek* and they'll be exceptionally happy to show you.

College life was so different from what I'd ever experienced because my parents weren't there to supervise me. Nobody came into my room and told me to get up for school. I wore whatever I wanted to class, if I even went. My new freedom made me feel like I was on top of the world. I attend Iowa Central for two years but ended up *thirty* hours short of graduating.

**\*\*\***

I met Gale Anderson, in John Benson's dorm room during a gas mask buzz. John knew Gale from classes they had together. Gale and I hit it off right away thanks to having several things in common: Both of us dabbled at tennis and basketball; but the sport we both excelled in was getting high, and soon became great teammates.

I've heard that we all have a look-a-like somewhere in the world; Gale was the spitting image of Tony Orlando. In later years, when we went to a restaurant, often the waitress came over to take our order and just stared at Gale. Of course, I never helped the situation out any.

I'd say, "Tony, go ahead and sing a couple bars of *Tie a Yellow Ribbon 'round the old Oak Tree* for her.

Sometimes the waitress got all excited and said, "Would you, please?"

Gale gave me a look that said, *Shut up, you're a dick.*

There were times where a waitress asked him for an autograph. He had to explain that he wasn't Tony Orlando —just Gale Anderson, mild mannered real estate broker.

Another good story about Gale: In 1989, he was flying to Hawaii for business. He drove to the Des Moines, Iowa airport, planning to park his car there for the week-long trip. Gale was running late as usual. He pulled up to the area where you check your luggage, handed over his bags, and ran for the gate. His layover was in San Antonio, Texas. When Gale arrived, he was summoned to the check-in counter to take a phone call.

He picked up and heard, "You left your car in the 'No Parking' area and we need you to move it immediately. It's blocking incoming traffic."

Gale chuckled sheepishly and said, "I'm in San Antonio, how can I move it? Can't you move it for me?"

The voice said, "It's locked up and still running."

Gale said, "I'll be right there," and hung up the phone.

I thought that answer was classic. In the end, Gale called a friend of his who went to his house to get a spare key, drove fifty miles to Des Moines, and put Gale's car in the long-term parking area. Luckily it hadn't idled out of gas yet.

I never would've heard about this from Gale. However, the event ended up as a syndicated news article. Mom read it in her local paper, cut it out, and sent it to me. She thought I'd get a good laugh. Trust me, whenever I have the chance, I still rib Gale about it.

After graduating from Iowa Central College, Gale went on to the University of Northern Iowa where he became the president of the ski club. Gale signed me up as a member. I never attended a meeting, but two years in a row I went on the club's ski trips to Colorado. Thanks to Gale, I got to ski Breckenridge, Copper Mountain, Arapahoe Basin, Keystone, Loveland, Beaver Creek, and Steamboat Springs. These are places I never could've skied in my lifetime if I wasn't a member of that club. Talk about having friends in high places. With sixty members, we were given a sweet group rate at the hotels and ski lifts.

Gale and I actually became pretty good skiers. At Breckenridge, as we were shooting down the slopes, we'd look for spots to get in some jumps. I was at least nine feet in the air and landed wrong, breaking one of the skis. The ricochet effect sent the broken ski into my butt bone, hurting like hell. As I lay there in the snow, someone going up on the chair lift saw me and told the Ski Patrol when they got to the top. I knew someone would come down with a snowmobile and rescue cart to pick me up. But I had too much pride; so I picked my sorry ass up and hobbled over to nearest lift going back down the mountain. On the way people coming up were shooting me looks like I was a chicken until I pointed to my L-shaped ski.

Once at the bottom of the mountain, I limped over to the shop where I'd rented the skis. They'd just been open a week and were new to the rental process. The kid at the counter said, "You didn't buy insurance. We're gonna have to charge you for a set of skis."

"And how much is that?" I said nervously.

"Two hundred and thirty dollars."

"I don't have that kind of money with me."

"You can use a credit card," he suggested.

"I don't have any."

Just then, Gale jumped in like he was my lawyer and began to rip them a new a-hole for not offering us insurance when we rented the skis. The manager came out of his office and they got into a shouting match. Gale wouldn't back down and the manger said he was going to call the police.

I put a calming hand on Gale's shoulder. "Go outside and let me handle this."

The manager and I went into his office. After I explained everything to him, he asked me, "How much can you afford?"

"All I have is sixty bucks."

He accepted it. I didn't rent another pair of skis since we were leaving two days later, and I could barely walk from the pain. Gale was a trouper in offering not to ski the next day himself. Instead, he rented a car and drove us to Vail to do some sightseeing. We couldn't believe all the security everywhere when we got there. We found out that President Ford was visiting **t**omorrow. Unfortunately, we had to fly out the next day, so we weren't able to stick around and see the president take a fall while skiing.

In 1976, Gale and I were hired by Boulder Valley VW and Saab of Boulder, Colorado to take pictures of a bicycle race. Gale's childhood friend, Ron Good, worked as the Leasing Manager at Boulder Valley VW; he was our connection. Gale was such a bull-shitter. He saw it as an opportunity for a free flight to Colorado and convinced Ron we could pass for professional photographers. Ron then told his boss that he was flying in some pros to take pictures of the race.

I had to borrow a 35mm Cannon camera from a friend. All I ever owned was those drugstore kind where you turn the entire cardboard camera in and a week later they give you the poor resolution shots back. I spent the flight out to Boulder reading the owner's manual to learn how to use it.

Once in Boulder, Ron set us up with a brand-new VW Rabbit to drive for the week. The race started in Keystone, then on to Estes Park, Boulder, and ended in Denver. Our job was to drive our car behind the pace car, in front of, and occasionally beside the pack of bicycle racers, and take pictures. We'd take turns driving while the other one snapped the shots.

Gale and I drove to Keystone for day one of the race. There was a big party to get things started. VW of America and Celestial Seasonings hosted the race. Mo Siegel, founder of Celestial Seasonings, was the MC. Also, several celebrities were there, like actress Susan St. James, Olympic downhill racer Billy Kidd, Olympic speed skater Anne Henning, and 7-time world bull rider Larry Mahan.

The first day we drove in between the racers along the mountains, and took some fantastic pictures. That afternoon, we turned our rolls of film into the media pool for developing. Then we had a seven-course meal in a restaurant (I forget the name) on the side of the mountain with an unbelievable view overlooking Boulder. We had to sneak out and smoke pot so we'd be hungry for the next course. After finishing the fantastic meal, we drove to Red Rocks to see the band America play. What a great sound resonated from the amphitheater! I'm not sure what was higher, the mountains, or us. The next day, Gale and I, excited as two kids in a candy store, went to the booth to check out our pictures. They were all pitch black. At first, we thought they didn't know how to develop them. They suggested we check out our camera settings and F-stops (whatever that is). It turned out, amateur and stoned photographers that we were, we'd forgotten to take the lens caps off our cameras.

While all the other photographers were critiquing and admiring their pictures, at least we had plenty of time to mingle with the celebrities. Gale had a crush on Susan St. James; he had me take pictures of them together. Most of the time, Susan didn't know that Gale was lurking beside or behind her when I was snapping away. She had to be wondering why I was always taking pictures of her, when in reality I was filling up Gale's photo album.

The following day, we did end up with some great pictures ourselves before the race was over. How could you not, when you have the beautiful Colorado Mountains as your backdrop. I took one picture of fifty bikes racing along the road with the red- and gold-colored mountains behind them. Several real photographers suggested that it was good enough to enter into a magazine photo contest. But I never got around to it. That's the thing that took me way too long to figure out… When you're doing drugs all the time, your priorities keep getting skewed. On the other hand, Gale & Rick's Big Rocky Mountain Adventure was one of those once-in-a-lifetime experiences you sometimes luck into growing up that makes you damn glad you went out of your element and took a chance.

***

In 1974, when I was nineteen. I dated Shari, a girl I met at Iowa Central Community College in Fort Dodge. She was five-two, long brown hair, brown eyes, and very attractive. Shari was from Osage, Iowa which is about seventy miles northeast of Fort Dodge. We got along handsomely. We laughed a lot. Maybe that was because she also liked to smoke pot. Of course, back then, who didn't?

In the end, there were two things that pissed me off about her. First, I had recently bought a brand-new white Ford Econoline van. We were going to visit her parents and siblings one weekend, who still lived in Osage. She absolutely *insisted* on driving. I kept saying no, since the van was new, and I hadn't let anybody else ever drive it. After *pleading* with me about how good of a driver she was, and how careful she'd be, I caved in and said yes. I'm sure you know where this is going. About forty miles into our trip, she was talking and not paying attention, ran a stop sign, hit a car. We were both okay and so was the other driver. Our vehicles on the other hand, didn't fare as well. My new ride was wrecked to a point it was undriveable, and had to be towed back to Fort Dodge to be repaired. The upside: My car insurance covered anyone who was driving my van. I only had to pay the deductible to get my vehicle, and the other guy's car fixed. The downside: My van never drove the same again. There was an intermittent rattle in the engine no mechanic could find or fix. The moment I drove into any repair shop, the noise *magically* disappeared. The question besieged me relentlessly: Why didn't I go with my gut instincts, and refuse to let her drive?"

The second incident took place on my twentieth birthday. Several of my friends were throwing a party for me in Snell Park, a couple blocks from my house. Shari had moved back to Osage, but we were still good friends. From time to time she'd visit Fort Dodge and spend the weekend with me. You know, "the friends with benefits" deal. Even with lots of presents, there is nothing better than sex on your birthday, which I was looking forward to in an after-party with Shari. My friends and I were all having a good time. There was plenty of good food, good pot, and various alcohol.

At one point, Shari had left the party to go back to my house—no reason given. I suddenly realized that she'd been gone for quite a while. I'd been busy with all my friends, so the time had gotten away from me.

My best friend, Gale, went back to the house to use the restroom since he had to take a dump and felt more comfortable doing it at my house rather than the bleak restroom in the park. When he returned, he found me and eerily said, "Rick, you need to go back to your house and see what's going on there."

I frowned. "Tell me what is going on?"

He shook his head. "You'll see."

I left the party and walked the two blocks back to my house. I went inside, looked around on the ground floor and didn't see anything unusual. Next, I went to check out the upstairs. As I passed the master bedroom, I could hear what sounded like moaning. I opened the bedroom door and there was Shari and another guy naked in my bed. It was Keith, the younger brother of a good friend of mine. I remembered seeing him at the party, eating food, drinking a beer...oh yeah, and he was talking to Shari. I went ballistic! Told them both to get the hell out of my house. I waited there while they both got dressed and took off. In my mind, our weekend "friends with benefits" deal was supposed to be with *me*, not some random pickup guy.

I went back to the party to be with my friends, but I really wasn't able to enjoy the rest of the day. Around dusk, the party ended, I went back to my house, still steaming. About an hour later, I heard a knock on my front door. It was Shari. Even for a woman, that took a lot of *balls* to show back up at my house. She tried to apologize, but I wanted no part of it. I told her we were done, for good. She asked to come in the house and talk, but I was too pissed off for that. Besides, I wasn't interested in being seconds.

She remained standing at the front door, looking left and right, then said, "I got a ride down here from Osage, and I don't have a place to stay."

"How's that my problem?" I said with a shrug. "You should have thought about that before you hopped into bed with Keith."

"I'm sorry." She gave me the sad eyes routine. "Can I just stay and sleep on the couch?"

I held up a finger. "Hold on, I'll be right back." I went in and a minute later returned to the front door. I led her back into the front porch, handed her a pillow and a blanket, then went back inside my house, locking the door behind me.

She knocked tentatively a couple times, but I just turned the TV up louder so I couldn't hear her.

In the morning, I was surprised she was still there, so I let her in long enough to call her sister to come get her. While I watched a baseball game, she waited back on the front porch for two hours until her ride arrived to drive her home.

To this day, I do not feel bad for making Shari stay on the front porch overnight. She made her choice to have sex with Keith while supposedly being with me on my birthday. Every thoughtless choice has consequences. The porch was hers.

# Chapter 13

# JUNIOR ENTREPRENEUR

During my second year of college, I applied for and got the RA (Resident Assistant) job. This meant I was head of the entire fourth floor of my dorm. One of the RA advantages was you didn't have to share a room with anyone. The dorm rooms were too small for even one person, but they really got claustrophobic when two people tried to occupy the space.

The first day on the job I was required to read the rules to everyone on my floor. I called everyone into the hallway and ticked them off of a 5 x 8 card:

"Rule # 1: No drinking in the dorms.

Rule # 2: No drugs in the dorms.

Rule # 3: No girls in the rooms after 10 PM.

Rule # 4: No parties in the dorms."

After I finished the fourth rule, I scratched my head and said to the guys, "There has to be some rule we can follow?"

Everybody laughed and, in that moment, they knew I was going to be a cool RA.

One evening I was awakened at two in the morning by a knock on my door.

"Come quick, I think you're needed in the bathroom," a fellow fourth-floor resident informed me.

When we got there, I saw an unbelievable sight. A guy had sat down on the toilet, then passed out, and fallen forward. His pants were around his ankles; there was a pile of vomit by his mouth and pile of shit by his ass. I wished I had a camera; it was one of those Kodak moments (Not to mention a sure moneymaker if the guy ever became famous). He had clearly passed out from too much drinking. I could see that he was still breathing. I made an executive decision and let him sleep it off. First of all, I wasn't going to clean the mess up, that was a job for the janitor. Second, I was hoping some of his friends would see him and have fun razzing on him tomorrow. Besides, this would make a great get even card if you ever needed one. Most of us have had those trump cards on our friends. He was just lucky cell phones weren't around then or his incriminating picture would've been all over the Internet.

I held the record in all the dorms for having the most people in a room. It started out as a private wingding, but soon the word got out. Next thing I knew there were thirty-five people in my room…and counting. A can of sardines had more elbow room. Just to let you know, we were breaking the first four rules, all at the same time. The room was so full of pot smoke you could barely see the person you were talking to.

There was a hard knock on my door. When I opened it, of course, some of the smoke went out into the hallway. It reminded me of the incident with the State Patrolman on the side of the gravel road.

The head honcho, RA Bill Matheson, was standing there. "Come out into the hallway, Rick," he said, both hands on his hips and a look of supreme annoyance on his face.

I followed his instructions and closed the door behind me.

"What's going on inside your room?"

"I'm just having a few friends over for a little uh…*study group*, got that big physics test tomorrow, you know," I said, not really thinking he'd buy my explanation.

"You need to keep the noise down, or break it up." Bill's eyes pleaded with me. "I've been getting complaints from people on other floors."

"Okay, I promise," flashing a thumbs-up.

I knew that I wouldn't get into trouble for the smell of pot coming out of my room. Bill had smoked weed with me on several occasions. He wasn't going to turn me in, or his little secret would be at risk. Besides he had more to lose than I did.

I went back inside my room and announced, "Party's over per Bill Matheson." Nobody complained. There was no way we could get much higher anyway. By the way, I wonder if I passed that test the next day…or even showed up to take it???

✳✳✳

Somehow, I acquired the nickname "Indian". I'd told the story of growing up around the Walthill, Macy, and Winnebago tribes, and all of a sudden my friends were getting a kick out of calling out to a blond-haired, blue-eyed, super-white-skinned guy, "Yo Indian!" I never knew that having an alias could come in handy, later on in life (more about that next chapter).

A few of my friends and I got together to purchase a small quantity of pot, then split it up evenly. As a junior entrepreneur, one day I realized I could buy it myself, charge a *little more* to my friends, and that made my portion either cheaper or free. I never knew then what it was going to turn into. I just liked the idea of being able to smoke for free. It had a real nice ring to it.

In the mid 1970s there was an excellent array of pot to smoke. I could get Columbian Gold, Columbian Red, Hawaiian, hash, hash laced with opium, Mexican, and Tai-sticks, to name a few.

After a while, I convinced my small-time dealer to introduce me to the big-time dealer he got his drugs from. I remembered that tactic from my earlier dealings with Nick Narc. Only in my case, I just wanted to move up the food chain, so I could buy from the supplier, and bypass the cut my go-to guy was taking. I could get larger quantities, and for a lower price. Why pay a middle man if you don't have to? Now, not only was I smoking for free, but I was making decent money on each transaction. I thought, *Could life get any better than this?*

All the time I was plying my new illicit trade, I still had to meet with my probation officer.

Lo and behold, a year short of my probation period, Dave Follet called me in and said, "I'm retiring. And I've decided that rather than turn you over to someone else, I'm going to send in the papers to end your sentence."

I could not "Thank" him enough. I was so happy that I rolled and smoked a cigar-sized joint on the way home. I was *free* and what a great feeling that was.

I moved out of the dorm and was renting a house with two other friends. Neither one of them knew how to boil water, pick up dirty clothes, or run a vacuum cleaner. "Cooking" to them meant a trip to the drive-thru at McDonald's. Once again, I was glad I had my earlier housekeeping training.

I'd long since figured out that radio broadcasting was not the direction I wanted to go with my life. For one thing, starting pay was only $7000 a year, and I knew I could make four or five times that in my new, budding, entrepreneurial career.

I approached my new friend, Sammy (last name withheld to protect the guilty), or Sammy Costello (if you believe that name is real, I know some New York bridges I can sell you real cheap). The big-time dealer, and told him, "I want you to teach me the ropes."

He introduced me to his connections in the drug business. They all come to trust me and we became good friends. We'd go to bars in town and listen to live bands. I was introduced to a couple of local bands, *Locust* and *Dakota*. After a couple of months, I found out two of the members owned a recording studio just outside of town. They invited me out to listen in on a recording session. That was really cool. I'd never seen how an album was recorded.

When I went inside the studio I was blown away. There in front of me was a large 32-track mixing board with all manner of knobs and buttons on it. A big plate-glass window separated the control room I was in from the "live room" where the bands played. There were two huge speakers on both sides of the window. I sat down and listened to the band FRB play a song. The music was so loud I thought the sound was going to pierce my ear drums. I could even feel the bass notes bounce right off my chest. It was incredible, like nothing I'd ever experienced. This was now the thing I wanted to do with my life.

After a few more visits to the studio, I convinced the guys to hire me as an assistant recording engineer. This was heaven to me; a job where I could get high, listen to music, and take home a paycheck for it. Bands played in the local bars Thursday through Saturday night, and during the day they spent their earnings on studio time making an album.

I was fortunate enough to be able to travel to Minneapolis with one of the owners to see an actual record being made. It was the same studio that was used by *Prince*, or *The Artist Formally Known as Prince*, or whatever iteration he was using at that time...*Hey, Remember Me; It's Prince, Again?* We took up a reel-to-reel tape and brought back a vinyl record. How amazing!

I helped record about ten bands and thanks to Keith, a fellow Husker and one of the owners who took me under his wings, I was lucky enough to get my name on an album as the recording assistant. I still have that record and I'm very proud to show it to anyone who wants to see it. To you non-believers, the band's name is Young Country, and the album is called *Barroom Blues*.

Most of the bands that came in to record liked to take the edge off by smoking pot during the long sessions, and/or doing lines of cocaine. Thanks particularly to the cocaine, we recorded for hours on end. A couple years later Disco became all the rage. Bar owners decided that instead of paying lots of money for a five-member band to play, they could just hire a DJ. Disco ended the live band scene in Fort Dodge. My work schedule was reduced to one or two days a week. Not enough to pay the bills. So guess what? It was back to dealin'.

***

I was buying pot and now cocaine from Sammy. To celebrate his 28th birthday, Costello threw himself a kick-ass party at his house, way out in the country. There had to be at least 150 people who came and went throughout the night. The only stipulation to get into the party was you had to eat a large spoonful of "silly mushrooms". They were the kind that took you on a trip without leaving the farm. Between the 'shrooms, the pot, and the bottle of rum I drank, I was flying higher than the Goodyear Blimp.

Sammy raised full-blooded wolves on his farm. One of the females, named Locust, was the meanest. She was tied up with the thickest chain I'd ever seen, but it was long enough to reach all the way to the back door. If she didn't know you, she'd go crazy and try to take a bite out of you; and you couldn't get near the door to get in. I was one of the lucky ones, Locust and I were friends. Sammy dug a hole right beneath her dog…er, wolf house, where he hid a large quantity of drugs. Nobody, and I stress *nobody*, was going to get them without Sammy's cooperation.

Costello gave me one of Locust's pups. The father was a Malamute, which is half wolf and half husky. That made my dog, Cochise, three-fourths wolf. For exercise, Cochise took me for a walk. He was so strong it felt like he was going to pull my arm right out of the socket. I lived on a steep hill and at the bottom was George's Pizza. When I ordered a pizza to go, I always took Cochise with. He'd pull me back up the hill.

The only problem with Cochise was, after dark, he howled at the moon, then the planets, then the stars, then the galaxies, then the black holes…you get my drift. All of my neighbors complained. I had to get up all hours of the night and open the window to tell him to shut up. People were afraid of Cochise once they found out he was mostly wolf, but he was a very friendly dog. He'd rather lick you than bite you. I even have pictures of my son Joe, when he was three years old, riding on Cochise's back.

When I moved, the new place didn't allow pets. I'd heard about a guy living in the country who had several part-wolf dogs, and asked him to take Cochise. A year later I ran into him at a grocery store.

"How is Cochise doing?" I inquired.

He shook his head sadly. "My neighbor thought Cochise was chasing his sheep, so he shot and killed him."

I was in utter disbelief. My mouth probably fell open. I now wished I would've found a place in the city that accepted pets. To this day, I've never gotten another pup. This was the third dog of mine that had died tragically thanks to me. I'd also gotten a puppy shortly after the one that got hung by his leash at Marsha's house. This one was run over by a car and killed right in front of our house. He'd run out into the street to chase a ball that I'd thrown. A person becomes so attached, almost like one of their children, and I cannot go through that pain again.

Sammy turned one of the bedrooms at his house into a game room. He installed a foosball table right in the middle, and he'd stage all-night tournaments. There'd be mushrooms, cocaine, and pot for refreshments during the games. Nobody wanted to —or could actually —go home. Like a line in one of Joe Walsh's songs: *It's hard to leave when you can't find the door!*

Costello and I became best friends. We did almost everything together. One of the best things I did for him was an "extreme makeover". He sported the hardcore-drug-dealer look with the long hair and beard, coveralls, and an over-big, about 8" long billfold in his back pocket with a freakin' log chain on it that was hooked to a belt loop in the front.

Back in the seventies, profiling wasn't the kind of police procedure it is today, but if it had been, Costello would've had "DRUG DEALER" emblazoned on his forehead. I convinced him to cut his hair, shave, wear casual business attire, and suggested a regulation billfold, or none at all.

Back then I never used a billfold. I figured that if I was ever stopped by the police, I could lie about who I was. Some habits are hard to shake; to this day I still don't carry a billfold.

Sammy was getting his drugs from Colorado. He decided it'd be easier for him to move out there. Sammy grew up in flat-as-a-pancake Iowa, and this was his chance to live in the mountains. When I was in high school, my friends and I talked about all of us moving to Colorado after graduation. I must've had the map upside down. In Nebraska, if you go *west* the next state is Colorado; if you go *east*, like I did, you end up in Iowa. Before he left, Costello let all of his local contacts know that I was taking over the Iowa territory.

Here was the bad news: I now had to drive to Colorado, in my 1973 Monte Carlo, in order to get my stock-in-trade. I made the trip once a month. My car both leaked and burnt oil badly. I had to stop once or twice along the way and check the oil level. I made sure I always had a couple of quarts of Quaker State in the back seat. I never put them in the trunk. Once the drugs were in there, I never wanted to open it until I got home. Heck, with my luck, I was worried the trunk wouldn't latch shut, and I'd have to tie it down with clothesline rope.

I'm not sure how my car made it. Looking back —knock on a giant redwood —I never had car problems on the interstate. It would've been awful embarrassing having a State Patrolman pull over to see if he could help me, and discover what I had in the trunk, especially with my track record with the law. I would've graduated from transporting over county lines to *state* lines.

This brings me full circle to where my story opened, and I had the flashback. God bless that Carlo that always got this Carle boy home safe, or I'd be handwriting this story on snatches of toilet paper from my prison cell.

## Chapter 14

# DEALIN' AND WHEELIN'

In 1978 after ten trips to Colorado, Sammy introduced me to the head honcho. We hit it off right away, and then I got to know most of his friends. They all drove brand-new shiny Corvettes, which was a far cry from my rusted-out '73 Monte Carlo. To me it was proof positive there was good money to be had dealing drugs. That is, as long as you didn't get caught.

The trip *out* to Colorado was always smooth and easy, but the one coming *back* was very nerve wracking. I usually made the round trip in less than twenty-four hours. On the return run, I always drove just under the posted speed limits, and obeyed all traffic signals and signs. I didn't want to give Johnny Law any reason to pull me over. If they had, the bust would've surely bumped them up to the next pay grade.

On a typical drug run, I'd bring back 150,000 hits of white cross or speed, at least a half pound of cocaine, and anywhere from twenty-five to thirty-five pounds of pot. I couldn't drive 24 hours straight without the possibility of falling asleep at the wheel, nor did I want to take any uppers and fog my thinking. And I wasn't going to stop at a Motel 6 for the night with a trunk full of drugs. I drove in the states of Iowa and Colorado, and Tony—I called him "Cruise Control"—drove both ways through Nebraska. Every time we'd meet a State Patrolman on the interstate, I had to turn my head around to make sure he kept on going. I was so nervous; I should have a severe case of ulcers today…wait a minute, I think I do.

Once C.C. and I got back home, the majority of the drugs were sold within one day. All Tony ever wanted for helping me out was a little sample of the cocaine, and a couple joints. I got off like the bandit I was since he did most of the driving.

I'd be the busy-bee in my basement, getting the contraband ready for dealin'. The white cross came in three bags with approximately 50,000 hits in each. I had a triple beam scale that I weighted everything on. I'd take the time to count out the first thousand hits and weigh them. Instead of counting out the rest, I went by weight only. I bought the white cross for six and one-half cents each, and sold them for eight, making $2,250 on each run just from the speed.

I sold the white cross to three guys, with each buying 50,000. It was easier to just give them a bag and let them split 'em up. But I got an extra one-half cent, or $750, for putting them in thousand lot quantities, plus the original bags usually had more in them, so I got what was left over, which I sold in one hundred lot bags for $15 each. I wasn't going to take the risk without being rewarded.

The same three amigos also bought the majority of the cocaine. Of the half pound I took out one ounce. Then I *stepped on* or cut the cocaine. I went to the local GNC store and bought large quantities of Inositol, better known as Vitamin B12. That should've set off a red flag but surprisingly it never did. I put an ounce of Inositol in with the rest of the cocaine and mixed it together… hey, at least I got them to take their vitamins. Then I sold the cut product in ounces. I bought the ounces for $1700, and sold them for $1900. With the remaining un-cut ounce, I split it in half. One of them I mixed with Vitamin B12 and sold them to people I called the "grammers" at $100 per gram, and the other half was mine for personal use. My stash, which I shared only with close friends, was pure as the driven Iowa snow.

Once again, the majority of the stuff was purchased by the same three fellows. They all lived in towns that were up to eighty miles from Ft. Dodge. In fact, in the three years of dealin' with them, I only saw their homes a couple times. We met close to halfway for both of us. We knew how long it took to get to the isolated gravel roads for the drop. Before we left our homes to make the drugs/$$$ exchange, we'd talk by phone. To be safe—wiretapping was just coming into vogue in Fort Dodge—we had a code system. I called and told them I just got back from a fishing trip.

They'd ask, "What'd ya catch?"

I said (for example), "perch (speed), crappie (pot), walleye (cocaine), and catfish (Quaaludes)." That way they knew I had all four. If I was only able to get three of the drugs that particular run, then I only "caught" those fish.

They answered, "Yeah, them fish is all good eatin'." And I knew that it was a done deal. Or, "I hate catfish, but I sure love them other three," told me they wanted everything but the Quaaludes. They always took the same amounts of drugs each month like clockwork. If the price was the same, I told them, "I caught 'em with nightcrawlers." If the price went up, I said, "I used minnows, and I was surprised when I had to pay eighty cents (dollars) more for them." Now they knew it was going to cost an additional $80. Then we'd just carry on a normal conversation for a couple of minutes.

Finally, I said, "Well, I gotta go, need to grab me some grub (meet me at the designated spot north of town)." Or, "Gotta go, I'm shakin' for a beer (meet me south of town)."

"Cool, Indian. Talk to ya soon."

We had it down to a science, so neither one of us had to wait more than two or three minutes for the other to arrive. We didn't want to create any kind of suspicion in the minds of random farmers on tractors who traveled the same back roads. Once we got to the selected location, we pulled up to each other's car. I handed them a bag full of drugs and they handed me a sack full of money.

There is some truth to the phrase *honor among thieves*. I couldn't afford to take the time to sit there and count the money, and they didn't wait to make sure the count was right on the drugs. The trust between us was what kept the system working. I met one of the guys late in the morning and another one that evening. The third transaction took place early the next day. The majority of the drugs, once again, were distributed within twenty-four hours.

I never sold the large quantities in the town where I lived. That was probably the main reason I didn't get caught. To the local police, if I was on their radar at all, I would've looked like small-time...a minnow. There was always bigger fish to fry when *la policia* made their busts.

I was scared many times for a couple reasons. First, I lived on what was called an "emergency road". It connected one side of town to the other. Ambulances and police cars always went by my house with sirens blaring and lights flashing. Many a time I headed for the toilet to start flushing whatever I had…even though it was always a false alarm.

Second reason, five houses down the street from me was another dealer, Kevin Robertson. We were never friends, but I knew about him. Kevin sold to anyone who came to his door. He was raided several times. Of course, the police had lights flashing, and couldn't do the raid with just one car, there was always a fleet. It looked like Christmas with all the red lights. But Kevin took the heat off of me. He was the big fish the police were trolling for. The last time Kevin was busted, he was sentenced to thirty years in prison. Sorry Kevin…and at the same time, thank you.

The pot came in large garbage bags weighing in at ten pounds each. I had to break it down into one-pound bags. The first thing, when I opened the garbage bag, I took out the large premium buds. Those were mine…all mine! Then I weighed out the rest of the pounds and sold them to my three guys. Depending on the quality of the pot, I usually paid between $300 to $500 per pound, making a $100 per pound profit. The ounces went for $50 to $100 each. It cost me around $60 for gas and $5 for oil round trip. On a good run I sold all the drugs for $25,000 (which in today's market would be $250,000) and I usually cleared around $4,000 —or today $40,000 pre-tax (yeah right!). Factoring in my limited skill-set, it was very difficult back then to find a legitimate job paying that kind of money each month —and all cash.

There was one thing a dealer never did: Deposited his drug money in a bank. When you're not working a legit job, it's hard to explain where all these huge wads of cash are coming from. Left to their own devices, some dealers hide it in their sock drawer, for quick and easy access. Others, who lack imagination, put it under their bed mattress (always the first place cops look). The clever ones stash their loot in a secret wall compartment, behind a hanging picture. But I wasn't that motivated. I just went to a sporting goods store and bought a tackle box; filled it with the cash and put it in the garage, all blended in with my mess of fishing gear. I called my little box the "Bank of Rick".

I was lucky that the local police were not trained by the DEA. As a rule, they set up surveillance for eight months to a year gathering evidence before they go to a judge to obtain a search warrant; and if I were in their minds at all, I wasn't worth investigating. There wasn't a Neighborhood Watch program to assist them. They had to do it all by themselves, and they only had a 24-hour window to nab me with the large quantities. Believe me, I've thanked God many times over that there was never a knock on my door with badges on the other side…or, more likely, a battering ram entry.

In the 70s it was no big deal to be at a bar and have someone put lines of cocaine on the table, or even the top of the bar counter, then roll up a dollar bill and snort away. Nobody even considered it the wrong thing to do, or think you might get busted. *Everyone* was doing it. Just like Bob Dylan sang, *Everybody must get stoned.*

Late one night I got a call from Sammy warning me about this big black guy, Willie Smith. His M.O. was to come to the house of someone selling drugs, sweet talk his way inside, then beat the shit out of you, steal your money and drugs. He'd pull out a gun if he thought you were still holding out on him. Mr. Smith knew you could not go to the police and report it…

"Officer, this dude came over to my house and stole my stash."

"Can you describe him?"

"Yes officer, he was black, about six foot tall, and carrying a Glock 9mm. Please help me, I need my drugs back, I got customers waiting!"

I'm sure that conversation would end up with handcuffs, and I'd be the one wearing them.

Sure enough, about two weeks later there was a knock at my back door. I opened it to a six-foot black man standing there.

He looked me up and down and said, "My name's Willie. You Indian?"

"No, my name is Rick," I answered quickly.

I knew what this guy's intentions were, and I was not going to let him in my house if I could help it.

"Sammy told me I could get some coke here."

I knew better…Sammy wouldn't set me up. Willie must've gotten this address from an unreliable source.

"I don't know anyone name Sammy. " I lied as straight-faced as possible; meanwhile my socks were filling up with sweat.

He rattled off three other names that I knew very well.

I pretended to give it some thought. I think I even scratched my head. Then I shrugged my shoulders and said with *sincere* regret, "Gosh…Sorry…Don't know those people either. I just moved into town a month ago."

It was perhaps the best acting job of my life; probably worthy of an Oscar. Otherwise, it could have been a completely different ending. He could've beaten me to a pulp, or even worse, filled me with lead. Instead, he stood there and stared at me for what felt like two lifetimes. In the end, I guess he either figured I was a fantastic liar, or that I wasn't worth the hassle. Without another word he spun around, and walked out my back porch. I never saw him again. A year later I heard Willie was killed in a shootout with the police. I was very relieved. One less thing to have to worry about.

I was living a charmed life with all the drugs I brought back from Colorado. They were fronted to me. My friends, the dealers, let me pay for them after they were sold. Most of the time, Sammy flew back to Des Moines and we met in a hotel room. We reminisced about old times and before I left, I ponied up for the drugs—normally between $25K—$30K. Sammy then flew back with money in his boots and taped to his body to pay his man so the process could continue the next month. Back then even the TSA wasn't smart enough, or didn't have the sophisticated equipment like they do today, to catch Sammy at the airport. This went on for almost three years without interruption or any problems.

On July 4, 1976 America celebrated its 200th birthday. Costello, all the other guys from Colorado, a few other friends, and I threw a big party at Lake Okoboji in northwest Iowa. One of the friends owned a bar there that ended up as the central party place for the weekend. The owner welcomed everybody by sitting at the door in nothing but a pair of Speedos with "Home of the Whopper" on the front of them.

Earlier on that Saturday, several of us decided to go water skiing. I knew a friend from college whose parents had a boat on the lake. We went to my friend's parent's house; each of us did a line of coke that was as thick as my little finger and more than a foot long. It took me ten attempts to get all of my line up my nose. When I finished, my heart was beating so fast I probably could've skied without the use of a boat. By the time Saturday night was over, we'd gone through two ounces of coke, and two cases of fifths of Bacardi rum. It is incredible how much rum you can drink when you're sharing the buzz with coke. This is how a bunch of drug dealers celebrated the bi-centennial. Happy Birthday America!

I was good friends with my next-door neighbor, Wilber, an elderly retired man. We shared the same driveway. When you drove up it, he turned right to his garage, and I turned left to mine. Wilber came over to me one day while I was raking leaves in my front yard.

He got right to the point: "Some of the other neighbors have asked me if you are selling drugs."

I about fell over. "What the hell gives them that idea?"

"They told me you seem to get a lot of visitors who stop over, but don't stay very long."

Here's the deal: When I sold cocaine to locals (aka grammers), they'd only pay for one gram at a time, rather than a larger quantity. Reason was, they'd take up a collection at a party and could only get the hundred dollars for a gram. The addiction of always wanting more had them buying one at six, another at eight, and last call was ten. Most of my neighbors went to bed around that time, and I didn't want them complaining to the cops about all the late-night traffic up and down our quaint little street. My then wife, Karla, and oldest son, Joe, were living with me at that time, and she didn't like us being disturbed during *Johnny Carson*, either. (More about my marriage later.) Hey, even drug dealers need rules!

"What did you tell them?" I asked Wilbur.

He gave a casual shrug. "I said you just have a lot of friends from college who stop by…and that you're too nice of a guy to be mixed up with drugs."

I wanted to give him a big hug. I could appreciate the neighbors' concern. No one wants a drug cartel operating in their little corner of suburban happiness—especially with toddlers needing to be raised knowing right from wrong.

After that, I began meeting my local contacts in remote areas of parks, or the far corners of shopping mall parking lots, where they'd get into my car to make the transaction. It is nearly impossible to see what is going on in the front seat of an automobile. Sometimes we just sat there; or else we went for a drive, if they needed to sample the product. For some reason, I never worried about being shadowed by the police…and I never was. Trust me, I never did anything stupid to give them a reason to. I always felt that I was smarter than they were, or at least one step ahead of them. You had to have that kind of confidence to keep dealin' month after month. But you could never let your guard down. I never got to the point where I was cocky. If you ever did, carelessness usually followed; and that was how you got yourself luxury (ha-ha!) accommodations at county jail.

My immediate profits were used to pay off Sammy. When I sold the remaining drugs, I first paid my monthly bills, then went out and bought *all* of the things I ever wanted.

I was on the go, doin' the deals. Even the day of my wedding was no exception. I'd made my connection with two of the players and I needed the third deal to go down in order to pay Costello, who was at my wedding., And the rest of the money was for my honeymoon. Everything was scheduled to take place a half hour before the ceremony; but every once in a while, a deal doesn't happen exactly as planned. Everyone but me was in the church waiting for Rick to walk down the isle.

Gale, my best man, came outside and said, "Rick, what's going on? People are starting to wonder if you got cold feet and are chickening out."

"I'm waiting for Anthony to get here," I said, glancing at my watch for about the twentieth time in fifteen minutes. "I can't pay Sammy his money, and I don't have anything for the honeymoon. Go in there and stall them for a few minutes. I'll be in as soon as I can."

If you remember, Gale was a dead-ringer for Tony Orlando; so I don't know if he went back inside and maybe sang a couple of songs to keep everyone entertained while I finalized the deal.

Twelve minutes and thirty-seven seconds later, Anthony drove up to the church; I tossed him a bag of drugs from my car and he passed me a bag of money. I could now go get married. None of the relatives ever knew why I was late for my own wedding... until now. Sorry folks...really!

One of my contacts was the Sergeant of Arms with a tough motorcycle gang in Iowa, the "Widows" (named after the spider— not husbandless women). Brian was six-feet tall, at least three hundred pounds, long greasy black hair and matching beard. He'd buy cocaine and speed then resell it to other bikers. We got to be pretty good friends. I told him the story of Nick Nark back in Nebraska and mentioned that he still lives on a farm outside of Lyons.

Brian asked me, "Does he have a large picture window fronting his house?"

"I'm not sure. Why?"

"I know a guy in Nebraska who'll drive by his house and shoot him through the front window for only $500."

"I don't like the guy, but...I...WANT...NO...PART...OF... MURDER." I spoke each word very slow, and enunciated them carefully, to make double sure he understood me.

"If you change your mind, let me know," he shrugged, like he couldn't believe I was passing up such a bargain.

"Trust me. I won't ever change my mind."

✳✳✳

Nick Nark wasn't the only snitch recruited in the area. The state patrol was able to persuade another kid, two counties over, to squeal on his friends. This guy's secret identity was easily uncovered, and he was found face down in a creek bed, with a fatal gunshot wound (execution style) to his head. To this day, no one has ever been arrested for the shooting.

The law wasn't going to take any chances and moved Nick Nark and his family to Idaho where they lived for five years. But Nick got homesick for the idyllic farm life of Nebraska and moved back.

One breezy autumn night at the Branding Iron bar in Lyons, as the saying goes, Nick was in the wrong place at the wrong time. He went to the restroom. A half-minute later, two guys got up from their corner table and headed in the same direction. The 350 lb. dude guarded the door while Joe Grudgeman, one of the twenty-six that Nick narked on, gave Nick one hell of a beating…18 months in jail's worth to be exact.

The interesting part was everybody in the bar heard Nick apologizing; then begging; then yelping in pain; and watched the other two slowly walk out of the restroom and exit the bar. But nobody dropped a dime to call the police. I guess sometimes justice has its own way of working itself out, no matter which side of the law you are on.

✳✳✳

The bikers lived by a different set of rules than I was raised with. Brian bought some speed one time and paid me with two one-hundred-dollar bills. He didn't like the quality and returned the merchandise, wanting his money back. When I handed him a fistful of twenties, he absolutely went ballistic.

"I paid you in C-notes and I want 'em back," Brian demanded.

"I don't have them anymore…just these twenties," I tried to reason with him. "It's still two hundred dollars."

"Then go to the damn bank and get 'em."

Lucky for me, my bank was still open, so I was able to appease him.

Brian was the reason I quit selling drugs. One time he never paid me for two ounces of cocaine. In the past, we'd always done the deal where I fronted him the cocaine for a week, then we met for the payment. This time Brian claimed he paid me when he received the coke. We'd never done it like that before, but he was a member of the *Widows,* so what could I do?

"The hell I didn't," he scowled. "It ain't my fault you can't remember."

So much for *honor among thieves.* A small guy like me wasn't about to argue with a biker his size—especially one who thought nothing of capping guys at a discount. He'd probably do me for free.

***

This biker group had an incident in Fort Dodge. One of the members was in a bar called Crinigans when he got into an argument with a trucker. The fight started inside the bar with fists flying and throwing beer bottles, glasses, or anything they could get their hands on at each other. The owner of the bar somehow moved it outdoors into the street. This was where the guns came out. They ducked behind cars and started firing at each other. It was the shootout at the *Crinigan's Corral.*

When the smoked cleared, the biker lay dead in the street with a bullet in his chest. I never thought the fight was fair since the biker was shooting with a .22-caliber snub-nose pistol, and the trucker (who hightailed it down the road before anyone could get his license plate) was using a .357 magnum...sort of like General Custer bringing a BB-gun to Little Big Horn.

Three days later, the funeral for the biker was held in Fort Dodge. Hundreds, and I mean hundreds of bikers showed up from five neighboring states, all wearing the colors of their bike gangs. The downtown businesses closed up shop for half a day until the ceremony was over. I remember staying at home that day. I didn't want any part of "guilt by association",

I was a good friend of Dave, the bar owner, where the fight started, and found out some of the gang members blamed him for the outcome. They went out to his farmhouse while he was at work, killed his two hunting dogs, and hung them from one of his trees. Dave told me it was a gruesome sight when he got home and saw blood everywhere. They'd slit the dogs' throats from ear to ear, and down their bellies with knives after hanging them up. If their intention was to send a message, it was well taken. Dave took a week off and left town. If it was me, I'd have moved to South America.

✳✳✳

After Brian stiffed me, I didn't have the money to pay Sammy. I'd already blown all of my profit on the most expensive TV, stereo, and other home entertainment equipment on the market. A bank loan to finance a drug deal gone south was out of the question. My only option was to call Dad and ask him for the money. That was one of the lowest moments in my life.

"Rick?" Dad said, acting as if he didn't recognize my voice. "It's been a while. To what do I owe the pleasure?"

"Dad, I need to borrow $3000," I said in my most humble voice.

"What for?" All kidding aside.

"I am in deep trouble. I got mixed up in drugs again, and if I don't pay this guy the $3000 I owe him, he is going to break some bones."

Sammy would never have hurt me, but I couldn't burn him after all the favors he'd done for me. I owed Sammy a lot more than money. So, I had to convince Dad.

Dad's voice turned to disgust. "I thought you learned your lesson the first time."

"I'm sorry."

"I will give you the money on one condition," he hung it out there.

"I'll do anything!"

"You are through with drugs as of right now." In no uncertain terms.

Hand on my heart: "I promise."

I got the money from Dad, paid Sammy, and I quit selling drugs. Ice cold turkey, man.

Once again, I want to take this moment to say, "THANK YOU, GOD!"

He watched over me more times than I probably deserved. I was never caught during those three years. If I had been, and was prosecuted to the full extent of the law, I might just now, twenty-five years later, be getting out…if I even survived prison. I can't imagine bein' nobody's bitch, so there probably woulda been a shiv with "R.C." on it.

Not selling was one thing…I still had my little circle of friends I smoked pot with all the time. It made fishing more enjoyable. When nothing was biting, we smoked. The golf course was another fun place to get high. It'd take away any frustrations you had from the game. Being stoned kept me from even thinking about throwing my clubs. Watching movies was also fantastic. The special effects were accentuated with the buzz. Driving was better stoned; the trip seemed shorter, and to the bleak Iowa countryside, it added a whole spectrum of color.

I never felt any harmful effects from smoking. Maybe my lungs were affected, but being stoned for thirty years made my life enjoyable and relaxing. Then again…

# Chapter 15

# DOCTORING ME UP

When I turned forty, I found out I had diverticulitis, an infection of the colon. I went to the emergency room at three in the morning bent over in terrible pain. I had to undergo a lower GI test where a tube with a scope is inserted into your rear end to probe your insides and check for cancerous polyps. The doctor gave me too much laughing gas. I remember counting backwards from one hundred, then waking up in a wheel chair in the recovery room with drool running down my chin. I was lucky enough not to feel a thing, and fortunate that I didn't have any cancer.

I was put on a diet where I couldn't eat peanuts, sweet corn, or anything with seeds in it. I guess they don't digest properly and that's how the infection occurs.

In the last five years I've had recurring stomach problems, and have gone through upper and lower GI tests to find out what's the deal. I think the doctor could shake his own hands while being inside me from the bottom and top, but he couldn't find anything wrong.

During one of my visits the doctor said, "The AMA did ten-year research on diverticulitis patients and found that you don't have to be on a special diet."

I looked at him with a deep frown. "So, all these years I could've been eating cashews, popcorn and sweet corn?"

The doctor shrugged. "Yes, you could have."

"You have no idea how hard it's been not to be able to eat those treats."

My doctor just laughed and said, "Well, now you can, but I'd suggest only in moderation."

I never forgot how good Iowa sweet corn tasted. I used to have to watch my family and friends eat it right in front of me. It almost killed me.

\*\*\*

Last year was good timing to be on Medicare. One of the reasons I got my upper and lower scopes was I had E coli and colitis at the same time. It was either from bad lettuce or uncooked meat. I'm going with the lettuce, since I know how to grill steaks. After that, I was told not to eat bagged lettuce, rather head lettuce only.

Let me tell you that was an experience. It started out with shitting blood for a week. After five days of losing blood, I decided it was time to go to Urgent Care. They ran a test on me and discovered my blood count was low. An average blood count is around thirteen, mine was seven point six. The nurse at Urgent Care recommended an ambulance to take me to the E.R. I told her, "No. I drove here from work. I can drive my car back to work and have my boss give me a ride there."

Urgent Care was only two blocks from Graham Tire and I knew I had the ability to make it that far. I staggered into Graham Tire and said to my boss, "I need a ride right now to the hospital."

He looked me up and down. "What's wrong, Rick?"

"My blood count is really f'ed up."

He quickly ended the phone call he was on and helped me into his pickup, then stepped on the gas.

More tests were run and the doctor determined I needed a blood transfusion. I was given a pint of blood, then more tests to see if I needed another pint.

Luckily, my blood count elevated with just the one serving. The transfusion had taken a couple of hours and I spent most of that time wondering whose blood I was getting. Will I be smarter afterwards? Or maybe a better athlete? What if I become a dumb klutz? Let me tell you it was none of the above. I'm still the same ol' me.

Within eighteen months I received two Covid shots, one booster shot, a pneumonia shot, two shingles shots, and one tetanus shot. I have so many vaccines running around in my body, I feel like I'm a human petri dish.

Here's how you know you're getting old. I used to have just a general practitioner who I went to for whatever ailed me. Now I see him plus a cardiologist, a dermatologist, a urologist, a gastrologist, a chiropractor, an orthopedic, and physical therapist. And no doubt there's more specialist to come.

After my youngest child was born, I decided it'd be easier for me to get a vasectomy than my wife getting her tubes tied, because I felt I'd fathered enough children. Before the surgery all of my pubic hair needed to be shaved off. I was informed a nurse would be right in to do the shaving. My first thought was, *I hope I don't get hard as she is touching me in that area.* A handsome young man walked into the room and said, "I am the nurse, here to shave you." Now I'm desperately thinking, *Please, please don't get hard.*

After that embarrassing moment was over and I was bald as a baby's butt, two "real" nurses came in to prep me for surgery.

When I was having this procedure done, it was shortly after Lorana Bobbitt was all over the news for lopping off her husband's penis. The surgeon came in, gloves on, ready to start. I looked at him in faux-panic and said, "Doc please don't give the scalpel to one of the nurses." He just stared at me in confusion. I had to explain to him about Ms. Bobbitt. He just shot me with nova cane and started cutting.

To this day I reference Lorana Bobbitt when it snows. If we get a measurable amount , I call it a "Bobbitt snow"—three inches on the ground.

In 2010 I had my first kidney stone. A nurse told me, "I've had three children and one kidney stone. If I had a choice to do it over, I'd rather have three more children before I had another kidney stone."

I asked the doctor, "Why it is so painful?"

He looked amused, "Do you remember when you were a little kid and you'd be playing in the weeds, and you'd get those sand burrs that attached to your socks?"

I nodded.

He went on, "They had sharp edges on all sides. Just imagine a sand burr going through your intestinal tract and coming out your penis. It's going to tear up your inside walls, cause bleeding, and hurt like holy hell."

I just shook my head in agreement.

Over the years I've had three kidneys stones. The last one was eight centimeters--too large for it to pass on its own.

The doctor described the procedure: "We are going to have to run a tube up your penis and blast the stone into pieces, so it will be able to pass."

After the shock of what I'd just heard passed, I said, "Is this going to hurt?"

"Not really," he assured me with a serious face. "It might feel a little uncomfortable is all."

"Let me ask you this," I retorted. "Has anybody ever come back and asked you to perform a second one?"

The nurses behind him were snickering as he stuttered, "W-Well n-no."

In 2023, my gastrologist recommended that I get both an upper and lower GI. The procedures are performed using scopes—tubes with a camera on it. The upper one goes down your throat, and the lower one goes up your butt.

The doctor highly recommended having both of them done the same day, one right after the other. This was so I could be sedated once for both procedures.

The day of the GIs, I got checked in and donned a gown that exposed my backside. A nurse came in and gave me a rundown on what was going to happen, then wheeled me to the surgery room.

The anesthesiologist explained that in a few minutes he'd give me the knockout juice and I wouldn't remember a thing until I woke up in my room.

I looked at him and said, "You can never use too much."

He just smiled.

The doctor came over to the operating table and introduced himself: "I'm Doctor Thompson, I will be performing the procedures today." He asked, "Do you have any questions before we start?"

I thought about it for a few seconds then said, "Yes, I do. If you are going to use the same scope, could you start with the upper first, then the lower."

Once again, all the nurses behind him were laughing.

"We use two different tubes!" he hurried to assure me.

I wondered if a requirement for med school is "no sense of humor." I was just trying to lighten up the moment a little.

Afterwards, I was thinking that might have been a bad idea. I was just glad that when I woke up, I didn't have a shitty taste in my mouth.

✳✳✳

I once thought that because of all the drugs I did early in life, I wouldn't live to see fifty. Now that I'm over that hurdle, I do watch what I eat, and I exercise regularly. I want to be able to enjoy the remaining years that I have left with my kids and grandkids.

I have to admit, life still feels pretty good without drugs or alcohol. I confess there are times I miss smoking pot, but I am over the urge to ever start up again, and I've had plenty of temptations since I quit. I figure, life is short enough, and it is constantly changing, and I'd be a fool to stay stuck in the past smoking pot each and every day. God bless my friends who still do; and I'm not being critical, or judgmental of *their* decisions. But sometimes you have to make yourself walk through the door to the future, just to see what it has to offer.

*Me and my first son Joey, 1978*

## Chapter 16

# EX – CUSE ME!

In 1975, I was running low on pot and went over to Arley's apartment to see if I could score some from him. He was my friend who had introduced me to Sammy. Arley was living with a hot-looking babe named Kathy.

I nudged him, "Arley, your girlfriend wouldn't happen to have a sister?"

"Why yes, she does," he let loose with a big grin. "And she's coming over tomorrow afternoon."

I planned on stopping by, but I wanted to bring something to impress her. Of all the things there are in the world, I came up with tomatoes. Little did I know the bag of tomatoes that I brought her had a rotten one in it. You'd think that with my teenage produce training, I should've picked out the bad one, but I didn't.

It was kind of ironic that I gave her a rotten tomato; when in the end, things turned out rotten for us. "Karla" and I laughed about my first gift to her many times. (It wasn't so funny when the tomato became a metaphor…but more about that later.) Evidently my charm and charisma must've been overwhelming. She still went out with me.

Karla became the second love of my life. When I first saw her, I was pleasantly surprised. She had a pretty face and a smokin' hot body. Karla had a twinkle in her eye that could make the stars jealous. When Karla smiled at me, I was transfixed, and I'd do anything to keep her smiling.

When we stated dating, I was still smoking pot and selling drugs. She didn't partake at this time, but I found out later that while in high school her best friend was Sammy's younger sister, Sandy.

Sandy told me, "Karla and I used to steal pot out of Sammy's stash and smoke it up. Sammy was so high all the time he could never figure out how it was disappearing."

Our dating years were quite romantic. We did all the fun things young couples in love do; we went to the movies, to the clubs to watch the up-and-coming local bands, and even attended big-name-band concerts. The sex was good—probably too good—and during the first year of dating Karla got pregnant and gave birth to our first son, Joe. Karla wanted to get married so Joe didn't have the stigma attached of "a bastard child born out of wedlock."

I had ongoing peer pressure from Sammy, and other close friends, telling me that my life as I know it would be over if I got married. Karla and I fought over the subject of marriage a lot, but I held out for two and a half more years.

Against my better judgment, in 1978 I still asked her to marry me. I hoped that tying the knot would magically make Karla happy and reignite the love we once felt for each other. It was too late by the time a friend who was a therapist explained it to me: "Marriage," he said, "doesn't change you, it reveals you."

After our wedding at the church in Badger, Iowa, we decided to spend our honeymoon in Kansas City. I booked the honeymoon suite at a hotel near the Worlds of Fun Amusement Park. Being the romantic that I am, I wanted to set the proper mood. I arranged for roses, chocolate covered strawberries, and champagne to be waiting in the room.

I was about ready to make my signature move in bed and get things heated up. But Karla had a different idea about foreplay. She said, "Hurry up and get it over with." My friends had warned me that women lose interest in sex after marriage. But on the first night? Just to get even with her, I took my sweet time.

As I mentioned earlier, Karla didn't like the idea of me selling drugs out of the house. She said in a panic, "If you get caught, the State will take Joe away from us. How will you be able to live with that?"

"I won't get caught," I assured her, "I'm too careful. Besides that, I'm smarter than the police."

Karla did like the money though. We had all of the state-of-the-art stuff during those years: A new 1980 Ford Escort, a waterbed mattress for Joe's crib, 50" console Curtis Mathis TV, and a Yamaha stereo system—I even became my dad and filled up my garage with tools I never used. I didn't have a checking account. Everything was paid for with cash.

In 1980, our second child, Katie, was born…a blue-eyed, blonde, angel. As a joke between Katie and me, I've always called her "my favorite daughter". She was the first girl born to Karla's and the Carle's family. Karla's older sister, Kathy, and her aunts, all had boys. When Karla's family came over to our house, they made such a big fuss over Katie...and ignored Joe.

With Joe no longer getting the attention that a firstborn is used to, he became jealous, and vengefully angry. There were times when I'd hear Katie crying from her bedroom. One time, when I went in to see what the problem was, I found Joe with a clump of her hair in his hand. This was also at the same time that I quit selling drugs and had to get a regular job, so the money was tight. Joe wasn't getting the toys he was used to, and I think he blamed that on Katie.

I got hired on at Iowa Beef Processors. I switched between two jobs there: Cutting off the lower leg including the hoof with a hydraulic machine that zapped right through the bone. You wanted to make damn sure your other hand, or fingers, were nowhere near when you pulled the trigger, or they'd be lying on the cement floor in a split second.

The other job, and I am not making this up, was cutting out the cow's asshole. You heard it here, folks. That was step one. Step two was ripping the hide down as far as you could reach. Down the line, another person continued where I left off all the way to the throat, so the hide could be removed. Knowing what I know, and seeing what I saw about what goes into making one, I'm thoroughly surprised I'm still able to enjoy a hamburger.

As you could imagine, I didn't talk about the asshole job amongst friends and family over the supper table, or next to the cheese dip bowl at parties. I'm not sure why I'm mentioning it now.

I was on an assembly line where a cow, hanging upside down, came by you every thirty seconds. You had to do the job quickly, in order to get any kind of rest, before the next one came along. The hide was very tough, so you spent your free seconds sharpening your knife as fast as you could.

Thank God, within two months of working there, the employees went on strike, and the plant closed down. I wasn't sure how much longer I would've lasted. I hated the job, but pride, and the necessity to put food on the table, kept me going.

With a growing family to provide for, I had to find work quickly, and I took the first job I was offered: A door-to-door salesman hawking Electrolux vacuum cleaners. Now there's a job where you learn humility, and how to quickly get your nose out of the way when the door slams shut. I did get good at the job, the company-wide national average was a salesman sold a machine in every three that they showed. I sold one in every two—but only if I got inside their house.

The job was mostly cold calls with *very few* leads provided by the Electrolux phone force. This was my system: I'd go in to the office in the morning, walk over to the wall map of Iowa with my eyes closed; wherever I pointed to was the town I canvassed that day. I parked my car on one end of the block and walked down one side and up the other, knocking on doors, hoping throughout the day that at least two people would let me in so I could do a demo. There were times I felt that when I got to the last house on the right side of the block, the left side would see me coming and shut off the lights and the TV.

I enjoyed selling, the only problem…it was a commission-only job. If you didn't sell, you didn't eat.

Plus, it didn't help that every night when I got home, as soon as I walked in the door, Karla repeated her mantra, "Did you sell anything today?"

When I answered, "No," the next thing I heard, in the most belittling voice she could muster, was, "Well, how the hell are we going to pay the bills then, Ricky?" *Ricky* for emphasis, not Rick.

That alone put extra stress on me. It was hard enough selling vacuum cleaners without the added pressure, but she didn't understand that.

It seems a good wife should support her husband with encouragement like, "Don't worry, you'll get 'em tomorrow. I have faith in you." But all I heard was bitching and complaining. Believe me; I got tired of it real quick.

My boss could see my mood swings and asked, "What's going on? You don't look happy anymore."

"Yeah, Dan," I frowned, "Karla keeps ragging on me when I come home with no sales. She's constantly ripping my ass about finding another job that pays better. I like this job, but all the arguing at home isn't helping me."

"I see," Dan said. "I'm going to say something to Karla."

"Whatever you do don't piss her off," I cautioned him, "I do enough of that myself."

The next day while I was out hustling vacuums, Dan went over to the house and said to Karla, "You have to give Rick support when he gets home at night. He can't sell during the day with all the pressure you're putting on him."

After the talk, Karla was understanding, and even encouraging for *one whole week* before she went back to her old self. Between the fighting, and *once-a-month* make-up sex, the baby of the family, Josh, was born. That was my quota. Even then, there were times I had to point to the calendar and go, "Uh, Karla, it's the thirty-first, time for you-know-what." Josh was not planned, but happily welcomed, and completely loved.

I showered Josh with extra attention knowing how it felt to be the youngest. I made it my responsibility to see that he wasn't going to get the same treatment from his older siblings that I got from mine. I wasn't letting him grow up saying, "I Love Aunt Ethel!"

With three kids, I realized I had to find a job with a dependable paycheck. I landed a retail sales position with Goodyear. I was no longer selling vacuums, now it was round, black things, called radial all-season tires.

Fortunately, I didn't have to be at Goodyear until 9:00 in the morning. That gave me time before I left for work to get the kids up, dress them, and made sure they had a decent breakfast. When I got home there was rarely food waiting on the table. I usually made supper because I was a better cook than Karla. I used to joke with my buddies at work, "Karla is the only woman I know who can burn water." After supper, I did the dishes, gave the kids a bath, and got them ready for bed.

Karla's P.O.V. was: "I watch them during the day, and then my job is done." When I got home from work it was my turn so she could sit in her Barcalounger and watch TV. I admit, I didn't mind because I love my kids, and I only saw them for a few hours in the mornings and at night.

I also did the vacuuming, which I was good at from all the practice I had from doing in-home demonstrations. The training I got as a youngster helped a lot too.

By the time Josh was two, Karla and I were fighting about everything under the sun.

"We don't ever have any extra money anymore," was Karla's #1 complaint.

"I'm trying to make money without selling drugs. It doesn't help that you keep buying Avon and Home Interior products with our 'necessities' money."

Karla was also upset that I was still smoking pot. But how else was I going to keep my sanity around her? We constantly yelled and cussed at each other; and sadly, in front of the kids. I seriously regret that. I could see in their faces how it was upsetting and hurting them, and yet we couldn't stop ourselves. Why do parents do that?

Karla never worked the entire seven years we were married, unless you call it a job to watch soap operas from eleven in the morning straight through to three in the afternoon.

I told my work buddies, "If there was a way to get paid for watching TV, Karla would be a millionaire."

A lot of people, including her family, asked me, "Since Karla isn't working, why doesn't she do the housework and cooking?"

My stock answer: "Good question. Why don't you ask her?"

Five years into our marriage, to reduce the rent, we moved to a farmhouse a couple miles outside of *Hicksville*, aka Badger, Iowa. It's where Karla grew up, and most of her relatives still live. It had a population of just under 500 people—one of those places that if you left your shades open the entire town knew what time you went to the bathroom each day.

The farmer we rented from had let the place go to seed and I had to be the handyman around the house. But I couldn't fix a thing. One of my "repairs" is a legend around Badger. Our kitchen tables' legs were always wobbly. After a Thanksgiving turkey slid onto the floor, I decided I'd had enough. I was going to solve the problem once and for all. I thought the solution was I just needed longer screws. I turned the table over, removed the 1 ½ inch screws, and put in three-inch ones. I tried the legs, and they were as steady as a captain on his ship. I went to turn the table back upright, but it wouldn't budge. I had screwed the legs into the kitchen floor. I have never heard the end of it, nor have I been asked to help on any local construction crews.

My boss, Dave, at Goodyear, sent me to a nine-week Truck Tire Sales Course in Cuyahoga Falls, Ohio. In my fifth week of training, I got a call one evening, at my hotel room from Karla.

I could hear anger in her voice as she informed me, "Things aren't working out, and I'm tired of fighting. I want a divorce."

How in the hell do you answer that when you are hundreds of miles away from home? I was silent on the phone. I didn't know what to say except, "Can we talk about this when I get home?"

"We can talk, but it won't solve anything." Karla's voice was getting louder. I remember thinking. *What kind of a person asks for a divorce over the phone?* The answer: the Karla kind. It put a new twist on the company phrase: Reach out and clobber someone.

The rest of the course, while I was supposed to be learning, tortuous thoughts were going through my head... *When will I see my kids? Where am I going to live? What am I going to drive?* We only had one car. *How can I pay rent, the bills, and child support, and keep my head above water?* In short, I was a wreck.

A few months after I got home, my boss had been fired—for reasons I am not at liberty to discuss. A good friend of mine told me that while I was in Ohio, he had seen Dave and Karla together in a bar, and they looked awful intimate, with her head on his shoulder.

I confronted Karla, "I heard you and Dave were cozying it up at The Golden Eagle. Is that true?" She did not admit nor deny it. I thought to myself, *That's great...treat my heart like a piece of garbage. When you're done with it just kick it to the curb.*

Karla hated the country life. "I will help you and the kids move into Badger," I offered, "before I move out." I kept my word. For a long time, Karla and I put on an act in front of the kids, and the public, with fake smiles, and we even made it look like we enjoyed each other's company.

Meanwhile, I was also looking for a place of my own. I decided to move in with Danny, a guy who used to date one of Karla's younger sisters. I packed up and left on a Sunday morning while the gossipers of Badger were in church. In less than two months of my moving out, Dave moved in. I guess cozy turned into much more. In fact, they ended up getting married, and still are today.

I caught a lot of flack from people at Goodyear about Dave and I trading places.

I'd tell them, "I got the better end of the deal. I'm making more money, and now he's the one who has to put up with her bitching."

Karla and I stayed together a lot longer than we should have. The love part of the relationship was over a long time ago. The only reason I was hurting was I could only see my kids every other weekend.

I was back living on a farm near a town called Kneriem, seven miles west of Fort Dodge. It was refreshing to be out in the country again. You could go out the front door and take a piss off your porch without the fear of being seen. I lived there for almost a year until I woke up one morning, went down stairs only to find Danny passed out on the couch with a Colt 45 beer can in one hand, and in the other a cigarette that had burned all the way down to the filter. The burn on his hand from the cigarette didn't even wake him up. That scared the shit out of me. I found a place in Fort Dodge and moved out in a week. I wasn't going to have myself, and especially my kids, die in a fire that was started by a careless drunk.

My new tiny five-room house had no insulation in the walls. During the cold winter days you could see the curtains rustling even with the windows closed. I put plastic on the windows in an attempt to help; and bought a kerosene heater for extra warmth. Without it you woke up with frozen snot in your nose.

I didn't find out until a few years ago that Katie got headaches from the fumes, when they came over on every other weekend. Katie never told me because she didn't want to hurt my feelings.

I paid child support for sixteen years. In Iowa, the law reads that you pay even though the ex remarries—unless you give up your rights to your kids, and I'd never do that. In fact, one day Dave asked me if I'd ever consider it. I told him, "Not in my lifetime."

My divorce decree stated that I had to pay until all of my kids graduated from high school, or college, if they attended one.

At first, I didn't mind. I thought the money was going to help my kids. But then I'd become furious when they came over for the weekend and told me about the new chair or couch the ex had just bought. She wasn't working, and Dave was between jobs, so the money to purchase the luxuries had obviously come from me. It also rankled me when I got calls at work from Karla to see if I had mailed my check yet, which led to another line I said to my coworkers: "If women had balls, my ex could use hers for bowling on the weekends."

I was promoted to Commercial Truck Tire salesman at Goodyear, and paid $650 a month plus commission. I had to pay almost $400 a month for child support, which didn't leave me with much. I was paid on the 15th and the 30th. Goodyear automatically sent my child support into the State at the end of each month. The check for January won't arrive until February.

I went round and round with the people who work for the Child Recovery Department. I told them the check they received in February was for January.

One of the women there said, "We can only process the checks for the month they're received in."

I got pissed. "My checks come from Ohio, and they take a few days to get to your office."

"It doesn't matter where they come from—they have to be here before the end of the month to count for the same month."

It didn't take me long to figure out that you don't need compassion to work for the Child Recovery Department, just an attitude.

At the end of the year, according to the state, I was one month behind in my payments. According to my divorce decree, in this instance, the ex could take away my right to claim the kids on my taxes. Of course, she took two of them away from me, leaving me with just Katie. Little did I know this would bite me in the ass later. I decided the smart thing to do was to pay an extra month of child support to make sure I wasn't behind the following year. Otherwise, I knew that Karla would make it so I couldn't claim Katie.

There were times when Karla called me out of the blue, just to bitch at me, as if for sport. After a few seconds I'd cut her off: "Hold on, just hold on. Did you get your child support check?"

If she answered yes, I'd hang up. The divorce decree didn't state that I had to listen to her shit.

When Katie graduated from high school, she went on to nursing school for two more years, meaning I had to keep on paying child support even though Joe was out of school, Katie wasn't living with her mother, and Josh was living with me. I asked Katie if she'd delay college for six months so I could get the papers submitted to the State and end my payments. But she wanted to start college in the fall, and I respected her wishes, even though it was going to cost me. The only way I could get it changed was to hire a lawyer and go back to court. I didn't have the money to do that, and I had to continue to pay the ex until Katie graduated from college.

Of the three kids, Joe took the divorce hardest; he thought he was the reason, and turned mean. He refused to do as he was told, and called Karla every dirty name in the book. I have to say it wasn't fair to her. By the age of fourteen, he got to the point where the ex could not handle him. With my job, I wasn't able to be at home when he got out of school, and a babysitter wasn't in my budget.

The ex decided to put Joe in a boys' home. I wasn't thrilled with the decision, but Karla, the primary parent in the divorce, had the final say.

All Fort Dodge had was a temporary facility. Joe was transferred to Orchard Place in Des Moines, a behavior unit for children under eighteen. It was a hundred miles away.

One of the first things the facilitators want to do is take away a child's control, and temper their bad attitude. To accomplish this, when a kid arrives, they are put in an 8 x 6 padded room with just a mattress in it. The only time the kid can come out is to go to the bathroom; and he, or she, stays in there until they're willing to say, "I love Aunt Ethel!" Or something to that effect. This means that you are now going to listen and do as you are told.

During this period, neither parent was allowed to visit, but you could call on the phone after the first week. They figured in a week's time your child will be broke like a wild stallion. They underestimated my Joe. I called down there on the eighth day, and was informed Joe was still in the detention room. They said I'd get a call when Joe toed the line. A few more days went by, and I was getting furious. I still hadn't heard from them.

I couldn't wait any longer. I picked up the phone: "This is Rick Carle. Can I please talk to Joe?"

Business-like voice: "Joe is still in the holding room."

I yelled into the receiver, "How can you leave a boy in a room by himself for that long? This is inhumane! What kind of a place are you running, a prison?"

Without raising his voice, the administrator said, "Please settle down, Mr. Carle."

"Settle down my ass," I barked. "Would you settle down if it was your child locked up in a closet-size room?"

"Every morning when we go in there, the first question we ask Joe is, 'Are you ready to start doing as you're told, so you can get out?' And every day his answer is 'No'. All he has to do is say 'Yes', and he will be let out immediately."

"Why won't he answer yes?" I demanded. "I know I would've by now, even if I didn't mean it."

"Most kids by now would've answered yes. But Joe is not ready to give up his need to be in control. We can't move on with the program unless we have total control of every child here. When Joe makes up his mind that he's not going to win, then we can move forward. I hope that makes sense to you, Mr. Carle. We're not mean people here, but we have to be the ones in charge."

I think a type of genetic claustrophobia finally won out, because Joe gave in the next day, and was able to join the rest of the kids at Orchard Place.

Goodyear had a retread plant in Des Moines. Just about every Friday I made up an excuse that one of my tire accounts needed new rubber, and I had to go to Des Moines to get them. En route I always made a stop at Orchard Place to visit Joe for a couple hours.

I also went down there on the weekends when I didn't have Katie and Josh. I did not want them to see their brother in a facility like O. P. You had to walk through security locked doors to get in and out. That alone made me feel like it was a psych ward. I know it really was a behavioral unit, but I hated it every time I left and I heard the *CLANK!* as the door locked behind me on my way out.

Joe was stubborn, and remained at O.P. until he was eighteen and they could no longer keep him. I felt bad that he lost out on those normal memories and experiences that kids have growing up, like playing sports with buddies, going fishin' with his dad, or just the freedom of coming and going. Plus, every summer for one week, I'd take my kids on a family vacation. The ex and Dave never took them on trips. In fact, Karla called me at work every January to find out when I was taking my vacation, so they could plan theirs at the same time—without the kids. For fifteen years, all the summer vacations the kids went on were with me.

I did get some gratification with the ex one weekend when we met at O. P. to visit Joe. I was trying to buy a house in Fort Dodge and I needed her signature on a paper stating that I was current on my child support. She always wanted her own house, and I was about to buy one without her. Karla was pissed that I had the gall to bring the papers out in the parking lot to get signed. I had a smile as wide as the Nile River as I walked back to my car with her signature in hand.

\*\*\*

During the summer I took my kids fishing in Minnesota and South Dakota; trips to the Wisconsin Dells, to the mountains in Colorado, to San Antonio, Texas to visit their grandparents, and to Lincoln, Nebraska where my brother Jeff, and his wife "TC", as we called her, resided.

We went to Lincoln many times. It was only four hours away, which made the trip easier on the kids. Besides, I didn't want to become my dad while traveling in the car with my kids. Another reason was, I'm a huge Husker fan, and Jeff worked for the University of Nebraska; so we were able to get onto the football field during the summer off season.

One time, Jeff and I took Josh to the store across from the stadium that sold Husker items. I bought Josh a new hat and a Husker pen. We decided to go inside the stadium to the 50-yard line for some pictures. This tall man was jogging around the track; as he got closer to us Jeff and I recognized him: Tom Osborne, the head coach of the Huskers.

As he went by us, Jeff and I said, "Hi coach."

He nodded and kept on running.

Josh looked at me and said, "Do you think I can get an autograph from him on my new hat?"

I figured it for a long shot. "I don't know…you'll have to ask him when he comes back around."

Coach Osborne was passing us a second time, and Josh yelled, "Hey, Tom, Can I get an autograph?"

Jeff and I couldn't believe our ears—Josh calling him "Tom" instead of Coach.

But Coach Osborne stopped and said, "Most certainly, my young boy, where do you want it?"

"Anywhere on my new hat will be fine."

Tom…I mean, Mr. Osborne, signed Josh's hat, and off he continued to jog. What a class act!

On another trip to Lincoln, we were at Jeff's house, and Josh who was four at the time, reached into a candy bowl, took what he thought was a gum ball, and stuck it in his mouth. When it turned out to be a jaw breaker, he decided just to swallow it rather than spit it out. The jaw breaker got stuck in his throat. He came running over to me for help pantomiming "I can't breathe!" I grabbed him, and hit him gently on the back to dislodge it. Didn't work. The other kids were screaming and crying. I must admit I was getting scared shitless myself.

I yelled at my brother, "Call 911, I can't get it out!"

Thank God, I had some medical training. I tried the Heimlich maneuver, but to no avail. Josh was starting to turn blue. I couldn't let him die, especially on my watch. I thought to myself that if I had to break a rib it was better than Josh dying. I reached around his abdomen a second time, and with all my might gave a hard quick thrust. The jaw breaker flew across the room, and ricocheted off the wall. We all breathed a collective sigh of relief. It was all over by the time the ambulance got there. They looked Josh over, and concluded he was okay.

Josh has kids of his own now. I've been over to his house numerous times, and although I've never commented on it, I've noticed there's never been any jaw breakers in the candy bowl.

When Josh turned eighteen, he got a job with a construction company in Ft. Dodge. He liked the work a lot, but a big problem ensued. Josh was introduced to methamphetamine on the job site by a fellow worker, and got hooked on the stuff. Then he got mixed up with the wrong guy, Tommy "the thief" Baker, who taught him how to break into cars and steal the stereos to sell for meth money.

One day when Josh was pulled over by the police, he had special tools in the back seat that are used to break out the windows of cars without making noise. Add to that, without his knowledge, he'd been followed by a "spy in the sky" helicopter after leaving the scene of a meth lab out in the country. The police had enough evidence to convict Josh and his accomplice in three counties. The police had been building a case and Josh was finally arrested.

He spent time in each of the county jails until I could raise the bail money. (Kind of has a familiar ring to it, doesn't it?) Maybe this was God's way of paying me back…for all those drug dealing years when I never got caught. I was fortunate that I never spent any time behind bars. But as a parent, I swear I would've happily done the time in exchange for Josh's.

To ease the tension, the third time I bailed him out, I asked Josh, "Of the three jail cells, which one was your favorite?" I thought joking about it would lessen some of the pain he was going through. But he didn't find it as humorous as I did.

Josh was living with me during his crime spree. I got a call from the Fort Dodge Police Department wanting to ask Josh some questions about an unrelated investigation they were doing. They wanted to know if I'd be willing to bring him down to the station. I talked to Josh about it, assuring him that I'd be with him, and he agreed. When we got there, Josh was arrested on the spot, handcuffed, and led away to a jail cell. I was told there was a warrant for his arrest in another county, and they were going to drive him up there in a transport vehicle.

I felt like shit. I thought I had betrayed Josh by convincing him that going down to the station was the right thing to do.

I was also infuriated at the police for using me to do their dirty work. "This is bullshit," I screamed at the sergeant, "having me bring Josh in like this just to arrest him! Why didn't you tell me upfront what your intentions were?"

"If we had, Mr. Carle, would you have brought him down here?"

"Hell no, but goddammit you tricked me."

"Would you have preferred we came to your house, sirens blaring, and hauled him out of there in handcuffs, with all your neighbors looking on?"

"No, but it's still bullshit, and you know it," I said storming out of the station. I slammed the door on the way out. My first thought as I was going to my car: *Is a cop gonna come after me to make me go back and close the door the way you're supposed to?* I just knew I had to get out of there before my mouth ended up putting me in the cell next to Josh.

Meth is a much more serious crime today than pot and speed was thirty years ago. I had obtained the services of three different lawyers, one for each county. I attended all of his court proceedings. It took over a year to complete them all. Josh was sentenced to thirty months in prison for his crimes. One of the hardest things for a parent to bear is to be sitting in the courtroom as the verdict and then the sentence is read. You feel absolutely helpless as your child is handcuffed, and led away to prison right before your eyes, and there isn't a damn thing you can do about it. The pain that goes through your heart is almost as close as it'd be if your child died. I sat there for at least five minutes before I could get the strength in my legs to stand up and leave. All of Josh's life I had tried so hard to protect him, and at that particular moment I couldn't do a thing to help him.

The prison was in Ft. Dodge. I visited him every Monday night. To prevent smuggling drugs into prisoners, you had to be searched and X-rayed before they let you in. I began to worry about getting radiation poisoning.

We'd sit and talk about what was going on with him, or the family. Some of the time we played cards. The visiting area had fifteen tables in it. I found myself looking around the room at the other visitors, or prisoners. I was surprised that I recognized some of the other parents there. Many of them had bought tires from me. Guards sat at the front of the room making sure that the girlfriends, or wives, didn't get too close. It was a crime if a prisoner was caught copping a feel.

I always reassured Josh before I left that I'd be back the following Monday, and I rarely missed one. That gave him something to look forward to. I'm sure he counted the days. It tore my heart apart to see him go back through the locked door from the visiting room knowing he was going to be strip searched before he was led back to his cell. That procedure was done every time both coming and going.

When Mom came up from Texas for a visit, Josh wanted to see her. He had to write a letter to get special permission since she wasn't on the visitor list that he had to turn in. Since the list was already full, without the letter it would've meant somebody had to be dropped off. Mom was approved and I took her out to the prison. I saw the tears in her eyes, and imagined how much she was hurting in her heart when we had to give our hugs before we left. It had to be as bad, or even worse, than the days Mom had to be with me during my drug trials. Now her grandchild was in prison. I wondered, *How much pain can this woman be subjected to in her lifetime?*

I want to make it perfectly clear that I never considered Josh a disappointment in my life. I'd been down the same road. I was just lucky I never got caught. I love Josh the same as my other two children, and always will.

**\*\*\***

When each of my kids turned 16, I bought them their first car. It was always a used car—that was all I could afford. I managed a tire and automotive store, so I had the technicians go over the car from bumper to bumper to make sure it was safe before giving my kids the keys. The car had to have good brakes and I always put on new tires. Joe's car was a 1970 Rambler, almost like my first car. One late afternoon Joe came by Goodyear to tell me he had a flat tire.

I said, "Bring it inside and we'll fix it."

"You can fix them?" He blinked.

"Why yes, what did you think?"

His face turned red. "I didn't know that, so after I put the spare on, I just threw it in the ditch."

"You threw a good tire and the rim in the ditch? What in the hell were you *thinking?*"

"I guess I wasn't."

"That's obvious," I fired back. "Go find it and bring it back."

By then it was dark, and Joe had to use a flashlight. He returned about four hours later with the tire. Since then, Joe has had to take a lot of shit from the technicians at work: "We never knew we were selling disposable tires." You would've thought that since I was in the business a little common sense about cars would've rubbed off on Joe; but in this case, it must've gone in the ditch.

Katie finished nursing school and started working at Trinity Regional Hospital in Fort Dodge. Within a couple of years, the hospital closed one of the wings…of course, the one where Katie worked. She bounced right back and got hired on as a traveling nurse for a three-month stint out in Southern California. At her assigned hospital most of the patients were Hispanic. Katie went into a room where a woman was having an emotional problem. Katie spent some extra time with the distraught lady, comforting her.

When she left the room, the head nurse took Katie aside and said, "Don't spend so much time with the patients, they're only Mexicans."

That turned Katie sour on the hospital. She didn't give a damn about the nationality, Katie just wanted to give her patients good care. She left California shortly thereafter.

Katie returned home and got a job at the Wolfe Eye Clinic in Ames. She travels to several towns in the immediate area with the doctor performing eye surgeries. She absolutely loves her job. I've had many people come up and confide in me that Katie is one of the most thoughtful persons they've ever met. She will go out of her way to help someone, even if it is a stranger.

The best thing that came out of my marriage was my kids! They in turn have kids of their own. It was hard at first hearing the word *grandpa*. It makes a person at once feel thirty years older. I'm fortunate that they all live within six miles of Fort Dodge. I can see, and spoil them, whenever I want to. The best thing about grandkids is they see grandpa for the kind loving, cool dude he is today, not the drug dealing guy he once was.

## Chapter 17

# AFTER DIVORCE: THE FUN FRONTIER

I've been divorced over thirty wonderful and happy years. I celebrated August 15th every year at work by making a huge spread that includes several crockpots of food, and baking batches of cookies, or a layer cake. My fellow employees loved *Divorce Day* as I called it. My daughter, Katie, even told me that the ex knew I did this, and she thought it was silly. Of course, she would!

I always get a laugh when I go to the doctor's office, and the nurse asks me, "Are you allergic to anything?"

My answer is, "Marriage." The look on their faces is priceless.

Most people who find out that it has been so long ask me, "Why haven't you remarried?"

I used to tell them that I live by a motto, from a song by the band White Snake, called *Once Bit Twice Shy.* Now, I can tell them to just read Chapter 16 on the Ex, and it will answer all their questions.

I met with my lawyer to discuss the divorce and he told me, "Since all of the loans for the household items are in your name, you're responsible for them."

"What?" I threw my hands in the air. "That isn't fair—she's keeping all of them."

"You can file for bankruptcy, and that will relieve you of the bills," he counseled.

I didn't want to, but there was no way I could afford child support each month on top of the home furnishings bills. So, I paid my lawyer for a divorce and bankruptcy at the same time. I've always said that there are three things in life that make a person go crazy and do something stupid: divorce, bankruptcy, and unemployment. I've done all three, and survived.

There are more fish in the sea, different jobs, and starting over financially is hard, but as long as a person keeps a positive mentality they can get through anything that they set their mind to. Most of the time, *losing it* only gets you jail time, or worse, having six feet of dirt heaped on top of you. In life, most of us get handed a shit sandwich, the people who are successful are the ones who figure out how to make it taste like peanut butter and jelly.

&#42;&#42;&#42;

I have dated many girls since my divorce. The first one was Dawn, a wild, big-breasted, kinky girl. Dawn was the secretary at one of the trucking accounts I called on. She was one of those women a man deserves after being married and *cut off* as the saying goes. We clicked right away, started dating, and of course having sex everywhere and anytime. When her work day was over, all she thought about was attacking me.

One morning, we woke up in my bed and Dawn said, "How do you like your eggs?"

I answered, "Scrambled." I thought to myself, *Great! This is a woman who can cook, too.*

Dawn went to the kitchen and came right back into the bedroom with two eggs in her hand. She proceeded to crack the eggs over my private parts, and said, "Now I'm going to scramble them."

Dawn was just what I needed at the time, but we both knew it was not a permanent thing. Thank you, Dawn, for making a man out of me again!

***

Sandy was twelve years younger than me, and kept herself in great shape. She came into Goodyear badly in need of some tires. Money was an issue, and I gave her a real good deal on some used tires. We installed them, and Sandy left with a smile on her face.

Three hours later, I'm in a tire bay, shootin' the breeze with one of the mechanics, and I get paged over the intercom: "Rick, you have a call... from Sandy."

"Hi, Rick," cooed a sweet, sexy voice. "I wanted to thank you in person for today. So I was wondering if you'd like to come over to my house tonight for supper?"

Now, how could I resist an invite like that? "Sure," I said, "what time?"

I arrived to find she had grilled steaks, and man they smelled good. As soon as I finished the last bite, Sandy took my plate, set it in the sink, and proceeded to undress me at the dinner table. I'll have to admit she served a great steak, but desert was even better.

After a few months of practically nonstop sex, Sandy and I moved on. She desperately wanted a husband…and kids, and I didn't —actually couldn't , because of my vasectomy. Sandy and I did get together, just for sex, on a few occasions when we were both in between relationships. We became "friends with unlimited benefits." I like the kind of a woman for whom foreplay means, "Let's see who can get their clothes off first."

*** 

Sara was a wild child and that's putting it mildly. Blonde, good looking, and exceptionally thin. I think she weighed less than ninety pounds. Sara lived a block away from my little five-room house. She had two children, a boy and a girl. They were about the same ages as Katie and Josh. My kids and hers got along great, which made things easier when they came over on weekends. And living so close to Sara was advantageous for nightly rendezvous.

I knew Sara from my college days at Iowa Central. As she did back then, Sara still enjoyed her cocaine. I smoked pot, but nothing more. I knew of connections where I could score cocaine for her, and I did…but I wasn't happy about putting myself at risk again with hard drugs in my possession. On the other hand, I credit Sara for teaching me the proper method of giving oral sex to a woman. Many women since have benefited from Sara. But after a year of trying everything I could think of to help her kick the coke habit, I could see it was futile. With my past record, the cost of sex (becoming a third time offender) was out of my price range.

*** 

Carol, a gorgeous, long-legged blonde, was a recent divorcee. She'd been married to the son of the owner of a large trucking company in a nearby town. If you haven't noticed, I have a thing about blondes…no idea why.

Carol came in to Goodyear to get an oil change. After recognizing the family name on the work order ticket, I went over to the customer waiting area and started up a conversation with her. Carol was not very easy to get to know. Thanks to her cheating ex-husband, I think she had a distrust of men, but I was smooth (i.e., funny), caring, and very persistent. I learned from my days with Electrolux that "no" means they just haven't said yes yet. It didn't take very long before we began dating.

Although I was still smoking pot, I was able to keep her from finding out. She was absolutely against it and would've dropped me like a lead potato. I should've sent a "Thank You" card to Old Spice cologne and Wrigley's Spearmint gum. Carol was raising her three children and didn't have a lot of extra money. She needed a washer and dryer to keep from having to go to the laundromat. At Goodyear we also sold new appliances, and occasionally we'd get decent used ones as a trade-in. I thought I was doing a good deed when I brought a used dryer over to Carol's house. But Carol took one look at the dryer and screamed, "Get out, I never want to see you again!" I had no idea what was going on in her mind. I'd been forewarned by a couple employees from the trucking company who knew her to be careful: "Carol has a tendency to just go ballistic." Until that moment, I had never seen any indication of that side of her.

"Carol? What is going on?" I said, trying to calm her down, "I just brought you a dryer."

"I said get out, and take that goddamn dryer with you!" She actually pushed me out the door.

Ten minutes later, I got back to Goodyear. My boss called me into his office.

"Rick, what the hell just happened?" He had a look of puzzlement on his face.

"Nothing. Why?"

"Some gal just called here screaming at ME, and said that she never wanted to see you again. Then she hung up."

"That would be Carol, the girl I'm seeing."

"Make sure it doesn't happen again," my boss said, then dismissed me.

I went to my desk to play back the events at Carol's house in my head.

I tried calling her that night, but she screamed, "It's over!" and slammed down the receiver. I left it at that. Our passion for each other had lasted about three months then *Carrie*, the real Carol came out.

\*\*\*

Mary was a tall brunette (okay —a couple of blonde streaks) who worked at a local dry cleaner. When I dropped off some shirts, she looked past me to my car, a Cadillac Seville, and said, "Is that yours?"

I nodded.

"I've never ridden in a Cadillac."

"So, you want to go for a ride?" I winked. Smooth huh?

Mary had two kids, a boy and a girl. I thought she was overly strict with them, but I'm sure it was difficult raising kids without any support from her ex. He had chosen not to see them on weekends, and not even on holidays, either. He was such a dick that at Christmas he'd drop their presents off at his dad's house to give to them. He was remarried. He and his new wife had a child of their own, who they doted on, and he just gave up his first set.

To make matters worse, he lived only eight blocks away from them. His prize for refusing to visit them was he didn't have to pay any child support. What kind of legal system *rewards* desertion? I'd heard about deadbeat dads before, but he was the president of the club.

Mary was strong in her Catholic beliefs, except for the part of sleeping with someone outside of marriage. She enjoyed that very much, and as often as possible. She didn't like my marijuana habit, but was willing to put up with it if she could land me as a husband. Probably figured she could put her foot down then.

Mary and I went to a hotel in Des Moines for a weekend of romance, movies, and dancing. When we checked in, I paid for the room in advance. This was the first, and last time, I've ever done that, as you will soon see why.

Mary and I were getting ready to go out for supper, and I decided to work up an appetite by smoking a joint. I put towels at the bottom of the door, and opened the window. I'd gotten stupid in my older years, and didn't realize that I had created a backdraft. After two minutes of smoking, there was a hard knock on the door. I looked through the peephole, and saw two security officers standing there. Fear washed over me.

I cracked the door, and one of them said, "We know what you're doing in there, and you'd better stop it."

"No problem," I apologized profusely, "it won't happen again."

They left, and I thought, *Whew I got lucky!* I started to change my clothes to go out to eat, when there was another knock, even harder this time. I thought, *Who could it be now?* Once again, I looked through the peephole and all I could see in the hallway were three sheriffs' uniforms. I knew I was in big trouble. My heart started racing as I opened the door.

They barged right in and the biggest one said, "We know you're smoking pot. We want all of it right now."

"I smoked all I had with me," I lied.

"We don't believe you. If you don't want to go to jail you'd better show it to us."

I thought, *How in the hell do they know I have more?*

I gave them the container with the pot and the rolling papers, pleading with them, "Please let us go. I can't afford to be arrested. I'll lose my job."

He sized me up, then asked, "What do you do?"

"I'm a salesman up in Fort Dodge."

"You should've thought about that before you decided to smoke pot in this hotel."

"It will never happen again," I promised. "Besides, as you can see there, I didn't have very much on me. Please let us go."

I kept pleading with them, like a kid in a candy store caught stealin'.

After ten minutes of lecturing me, in between my begging, they took down both of our names and addresses, then escorted us out of the hotel. I'd paid for two nights, and thanks to my stupidity, we never even got to stay one.

In hindsight, I should've gone out to my car and smoked. Since they never booked me for possession, I've always wondered what they did with the rest of my pot and papers. Perhaps what they had in mind all along: *Party on!*

I felt sorry I'd put Mary through that hell. The whole time the cops were putting me through the paces, she just sat on the bed and cried. Mary was scared that if arrested she might lose her kids, and they meant more to her than I ever did. I knew I'd been a JERK. It wasn't her fault I dragged her into my situation; I did apologize, big time, for that.

I told the officers at the time, "The pot is mine. She has never smoked in her entire life. Please don't take down her name. It's all my fault." But they couldn't have cared less. She was in the room—she was an accessory.

Mary thought she could change me. But you can't convert someone who is not willing to try. Without my knowing, Mary had scheduled us a meeting with her priest to talk about me renouncing my religion, so we could get married in the Catholic Church.

Twenty minutes in, and probably because of my nonparticipation (arms folded as if to say, "What the hell's going on here?"), the priest looked at Mary and said, "I think Rick does not want to do this. Maybe you two should talk about it some more, and then get back to me."

It took Mary seven years of putting up with my noncommitment, which included my invisible shield, (my defense mechanism to prevent getting hurt), before she realized that I am who I am, and we parted company.

&#42;&#42;&#42;

I took a two-year hiatus from women. Like John Lennon's *Lost Weekend*, I called this period of my life "Rick's Time". It was a point that I did whatever I wanted, when I wanted, and without any woman to have to ask permission from, or explain myself to.

I played my best golf during these two years. I was playing five to six times a week, and sometimes even up to forty-five holes a day on the weekends.

I'd finish eighteen holes, and ask myself, *Do you want to go home, or keep playing?* I'm sure you can guess on one try what I ended up doing.

My friends had to call their wives to see if they could play longer, I just had to ask *myself*, and I got along real well with me.

Life was great, but after a while I began to miss the company of women. In addition to lonely, I must have been getting sensitive.

I got on the Internet and began to do some window shopping for a date. I found one in Cedar Rapids; she was eventually going to be moving to Fort Dodge. We hit it off real well and wrote back to each other daily. I looked forward to coming home from work and jumping on the computer to see if I had an email from her. We then sent pictures to each other. You wonder sometimes if the photo is really them today, or when they were just out of high school, but I decided to roll the dice. It was time to meet one another. She drove to Fort Dodge since she had family here, and a place to stay for the weekend.

Open the door for the third love of my life: Her name was Deb. Five-feet one-inch tall, dark hair (go figure!) and with her killer smile and effervescent laugh, my heart once again melted. She had something about her, that when I saw her, I wanted to give her a big hug even though she wasn't a blonde. My work buddies always said that whenever Deb walked into Goodyear my personality instantly changed—I lit up like a Christmas tree.

Deb was just getting out of a nasty marriage. Her soon-to-be second ex-husband liked to tee off on her with a closed fist. She rented a moving truck, and I, with a couple of friends, went to Cedar Rapids and cleaned out the house. The only thing she left him was one chair. A small part of me felt sorry for him. I was on the side of being screwed by an ex; but I have never hit, nor would I ever, hit a woman in my life. So, the larger part of me thought, *He had it coming.* Besides it felt good to see a deserving asshole taken to the cleaners.

Deb took some of the items to a storage unit; the rest went to my house. That's right—she was moving in with me. She even brought her cat, Socks, with her. We instantly went from emailing and talking on the phone to living together. My friends thought I was making a huge mistake, going so fast. They thought I should have moved her into an apartment and continued dating for a while. What do friends know, right?

I didn't want to let my invisible guard down that kept women from getting too close to me, but Deb and I fell madly in love with each other. For the first time in thirteen years since my ex-wife, I was vulnerable to the pain that was about to hit me alongside of my head, like a runaway locomotive.

I'd never been with a woman who had been battered by a man. I wasn't sure how to treat her, so I went overboard, and put her up on a pedestal. I did everything for her from never letting her wash a dish, to rubbing her feet almost every night. I cooked supper for her unless we went out to eat. There was nothing that I wouldn't do for Deb. Get this ladies: I even let her run the remote. I loved her that much. I didn't know I had it in my heart to love a woman like that again. It felt absolutely wonderful! I was on cloud nineteen. I wasn't afraid to show my affection for her no matter where we were. I even enjoyed holding hands when we went for moonlit walks at night.

To do my best to make up for the brutal ex-husband, I tried to smother her with kindness. In a million years I never would've guessed that it'd backfire on me. Deb was not used to being treated that way. Even her first ex-husband had smacked her around. And she was waiting for me to one day come unglued and do something mean to her.

After about a year, out of the clear blue, while relaxing on the couch, Deb asked me, "When are you going to hit me?"

"Never," I said in shock, "it is not in my character. Besides, my dad always said if he ever heard of one of his boys ever hitting a woman, he'd clobber us."

I knew that Dad meant it. I still had that fear of him no matter that we lived in different states.

I've never understood why a man has to beat up on a woman. What satisfaction could he ever gain by it? It sure the hell doesn't make him a tougher man. Even more, why would a woman stay with a man who has battered her? I've been told that it is all about a man's need to control. There has to be a better life than living with abuse, whether it is mental or physical. I'm sure it is hard just taking the first step to get away. It's good that there now are shelters available for abused woman and their kids.

For two years I got along really well with Deb, her mom, brothers, and sister, and her two children. We did everything together, and laughed constantly. We really enjoyed each others' company. I thought for sure this was the woman for me. I was even seriously considering taking the next step—asking Deb to marry me.

Then one night she said, "We need to talk."

Whenever us men hear those four words from a woman, we know what is about to come next can't be good.

And true to form, Deb said, "I'm going to move out and get a place of my own."

"Why?" I asked as my jaw was bouncing off the living room floor.

"Because I need to see if I can make it on my own. I married my first husband right out of high school, and started seeing my second one while I was leaving the first ex. I haven't been on my own since I was eighteen, and now I'm forty-nine."

"Are you sure that is what you want? I love you, and I want you to stay here," I pleaded; tears were rolling down my face.

"Rick, I can't breathe here. You are suffocating me with all of your kindness. I've never had that before, and it scares the shit out of me."

"I can change. Please don't go. You can trust me."

"You are the only man I've ever completely trusted, but I have to go. Please don't make it any harder than it is."

And with that, Deb moved out. Along with her possessions she ripped my heart right out of my chest, and took it with her. I was in humongous pain for a very long time. I had opened my heart for the first time in years, and I couldn't believe what I got in return. What's a guy gotta do to make a woman happy? And find happiness for himself?

Deb left her cat behind—she thought he'd be good company for me. I knew she loved Socks with all of her heart. I figured as long as Socks was here, Deb might see that she'd made a big mistake and come back. It has been five years since Deb left, and Socks is still here. I guess that strategy didn't pan out.

I went for two years with the thought in the back of my head that Deb would call someday and want me back. I never received that phone call. Part of me says move on, and the other part has saved a special area in my heart for Deb.

Many of my friends have asked, "If Deb ever knocked on your door, would you really let her back into your life?"

I tell them, "In a heartbeat."

***

With the first love of my life, we split because of the situation with her parents, the child, and me going to college in Iowa. The love was gone a long time before the ex-wife and I split up. But with Deb, I was still madly in love when she moved out. I had no control over our parting, so it hurt the worst.

I started having worsening back problems while working at Goodyear as the Commercial Salesman. I was picking up truck tires, still on rims, which weighed over 150 pounds. My pickup didn't have one of those Tommy Lifts, where the tailgate is operated up and down with a hydraulic motor. My truck only had a Rick Lift, and as I was loading one of the tire assemblies, I felt something give in my lower back —it hurt way more than the first time I jacked up my back, in my teens. I fell immediately to my knees in excruciating pain.

I made appointments to see a chiropractor and a massage therapist. One evening I got a call from Patti, the therapist, a tall, attractive woman. She had worked up the nerve to ask me out. After Deb, I had welded the invisible shield back up around my heart, and wasn't sure if I wanted to.

Patti said, "It'd be good for you to get out of your house and laugh again."

"I don't know if I can," I protested. "I've been hurt very badly, and I'm not ready to have it happen again."

"I'm not asking you to marry me," she teased, "I just want to go out for supper."

I agreed, and we dated for three years. Unfortunately for Patti, I never let my guard down. I was afraid to. Even when I tried my best, I couldn't. I took Patti to Nebraska to visit my brother Jeff, and his wife TC. We saw Nebraska Cornhusker football and girls' volleyball games while we were there. Patti even became a Big Red fan. We flew to San Antonio, Texas where my parents lived. Patti and I saw all of the sights of San Antonio, Corpus Christi, and Padre Island.

Patti treated me better than I deserved. She had fallen in love with me, but I couldn't requite the feelings. It wasn't fair to her, and I was a butthole for not ending it sooner than I did. But I was always honest with Patti that I didn't think the way I felt was going to change. My heart wouldn't let me.

All of my family thought the world of Patti. She was always doing nice things for them without asking for anything in return. They all thought she was *the* one for me. But I felt differently. I was hurting inside knowing I was leading Patti on, and I never wanted to do that. With my broken heart, I pretty much knew that whoever came after Deb, I probably wasn't going to be able to give her what I could and should have.

We broke things off while I was writing this book, and I want to express my deepest apology to Patti for not being able to show her the feelings that she absolutely deserves. I wish her the best that life can give a person who is so sincere and loving. I also hope Patti can find what she is looking for in a man, and that he treats her like the "queen" she is.

**\*\*\***

In all the years, after breaking it off with each of the women you've read about in these pages, I have not burned a bridge with them—we are still on speaking terms (whoops, minus Carol). This includes the ex. Usually, when the grandkids have birthdays, the party is held at Karla's house. It took us long enough, but we have finally learned that *the kids come first*, and we actually get along quite well these days.

As far as the other ex-girlfriends, I run into most of the ones who live in the Fort Dodge area and we instantly start talking about our kids and grandkids. I've always done my best to remain friends. Life is too short to hold grudges.

I want to take this moment to thank all of you women who have come into my life for shaping me into the man that I am today. I'm truly blessed for knowing each and every one of you.

For myself, I'm still not really looking for a woman. I know there is one out there for me. I will be picky in my search. I'm in no hurry to find her. She is going to have to be extra special for me to fall in love again. I'm hopeful that I will find her before my time is up on this earth. I can't imagine that marriage is in my future, but one never knows. I don't have a crystal ball. Yesterday, I was driving in my car, listening to the radio, and on comes the Eagles' song *Desperado*. A chill went through me when I heard the line, *You better let somebody love you, before it's too late.*

*My son Joe and me, 1985*

## Chapter 18

# WORKING OVER TIME

After my parents' store, Lou's Market, burned down, I hired on with Benson Sodding Company. George Benson, the owner, was the father of the two kids who were killed in the pickup accident I mentioned earlier, where I was invited but couldn't go throw snowballs that cold Saturday.

We started each summer day at seven in the morning. The sod field was acres and acres of land where as far as you could see was green grass. The sod cutting machines looked like a garden plow with a sharp blade eighteen inches wide that went three inches under the earth to cut a swath nine feet in length. We rolled the sod up, dirt side out, and stacked them on pallets. Each sod roll weighed approximately fifty pounds and we put seventy-two on each pallet.

Mr. Benson paid us two dollars per pallet to stack them and we could do four per hour. Our crew only cut and stacked what was sold for each day. That would keep the grass fresh. The pallets were loaded on a semi flatbed and transported to Omaha, Nebraska. Some of us rode along to unstack the sod then lay them on the ground at new houses that were just built. Instant green grass yards by evening.

We were paid four dollars a pallet to lay them. In a day's time we could make up to fifty dollars, which was a lot of money for a sixteen-year-old. Some of the yards were easy to work on, and others had steep embankments where we had to put stakes in the sod to keep them from sliding down. The job was not easy; it was hot and strenuous. There were not many other opportunities for employment in Lyons, and detasseling corn was out of the question.

One day, as I was lifting a roll of sod onto the pallet, I felt a sharp pain in my lower back, and I dropped immediately to my knees. I was off work for an entire week recuperating. It was the beginning of the forty years of daily back pain that I've had to live with.

✳✳✳

With the lingering pain, I abandoned the lucrative sod business and applied for a job driving a truck with the Bancroft alfalfa mill. You worked twelve-hour days, either six in the morning to six at night, or vise versa. I had more overtime hours than regular ones. It made for a good paycheck, and it was hard to spend the money when you were either working or sleeping all the time.

I had to drive out into the field, wait for the chopper to finish cutting the alfalfa, then it loaded the cut product onto my truck. I'd return to the mill where I backed into an unloading area and dumped my load. The alfalfa went through a huge incinerator that turned it into pellets that was used to feed cattle.

The job became very difficult the nights I took my girlfriend, Marsha, out on the town. We stayed up till all hours, then I had to show up for work at six in the morning, with maybe two or three hours of sleep.

One night, my coworker, Jimmy, and I stayed out drinking all night. We had just enough time to change clothes before going to work. I took a couple hits of speed to make it through the day, and held out two more for my buddy. But Jimmy wanted no part of any drug.

He should've taken my offer. Jimmy fell asleep while driving the large dump truck. He awoke right after he ran a stop sign, and hit a car. Thank God nobody was hurt, but Jimmy was fired before he could climb out of the truck.

Two weeks later, I was working the night shift. As I was coming out of the field, I turned too sharp. The next thing I knew, the truck, loaded with three tons of alfalfa, rolled over onto the left side. My head banged into the window. I had to crawl up and out the passenger side of the truck. It was all I could do to open the door by putting my feet on the steering wheel for leverage. Once on tera firma, I made sure I was okay and not bleeding anywhere. A coworker, driving the chopper, saw the accident and radioed back to the mill. My boss called the local wrecker company to set the truck back up on its tires. He met the wrecker out at the scene of the accident.

"How did this happen?" he yelled at me.

"I must've turned too sharp," I offered, "and the next thing I know the truck flipped over."

"You were coming out of the field too fast, weren't you?"

"No, sir. I was still in granny gear," I tried to explain to him.

"I bet when this truck gets turned over, I will find it in at least third gear. If it is you're fired," he yelled, shaking his finger at me.

Once the truck was back on the tires, my boss ran over and yanked open the driver's side door. He looked in, then turned back to me and said, "You're lucky, Carle. It's in first. I'm not going to fire you..." he walked over to his truck and reached into the bed, "but you're going to take this pitch fork and put the alfalfa back in the truck. By the way, you'll do it off the clock."

I should've told him where he could stick the pitch fork, but it was the summer before I went off to college, and I needed the money. The alfalfa was in the ditch, and I had to walk down to get a forkful, walk back up to the road, and throw it in the back of my truck. I can't tell you how many trips it takes to carry three tons of alfalfa from a ditch twenty feet to your truck, because I did not count them. I do remember it took me until noon to finish. This did not help my back pain at all. It was a Catch 22. If I took smaller loads, it meant more trips...a lose-lose situation either way.

**\*\*\***

I had two jobs that lasted one day. The first, was baling hay for Farmer Anderson. My job was to walk alongside a trailer pulled behind a tractor. The hay bales in the field were fifteen yards apart. I picked up the bales and tossed them onto the trailer where someone else stacked them. I had no idea Farmer Anderson was going to drive in third gear. This meant I had to run ahead like a maniac to grab and toss each bale, so I could get a five-second breather before the tractor came alongside me.

At lunchtime, Mrs. Anderson had a spread of food that filled the entire table. We ate like pigs; we were so hungry. Afterwards, I'm thinkin' it's naptime.

Farmer Anderson had other ideas, "Let's go boys, back to the field."

I thought, *What, no siesta?* I can't even *walk* let alone go run beside a tractor.

Farmer Anderson let out a chuckle, "I thought you boys were sure eatin' a lot of food for havin' to work, rest of the afternoon."

"We thought we were done and lunch was part of what you were paying us," I said in a panic.

"Nope" he shook his head, "I told you boys I'd pay you five dollars an hour for a day's work, and you agreed. So, let's go."

It was the hardest afternoon of my life. Several times I thought lunch was going to revisit me. At the end of the day, Farmer Anderson paid us in cash and said, "See you tomorrow."

I thought, *Yeah right—if you come look in my bedroom window, you might.*

✱✱✱

The second one-day job: A year after my best friend Tom died; his parents bought a chicken farm and moved out to the country. Besides the beautiful ranch house, four Quonset buildings were home to a total of 30,000 birds. Six hens were kept in each cage for the purpose of laying eggs. Once the hens had outgrown their cages and/or their egg production diminished, their next stop was chicken soup. At this point, they were taken out and loaded into a waiting semi to make room for younger chicks (kind of like the Hollywood starlet system, eh?). Tom's parents hired a few of his old buddies to do the removal process and I was one of the select few who got the nod.

Before that moment I had never been up close to a live chicken. We were told to take two out at a time. I reached in to grab one in each hand and discovered they were not at all happy about being pulled out of their home for a trip to the slaughter house. I got scratched by their claws and pecked by their beaks. It hurt so bad I often dropped the chickens into the manure traps below the cages. Now I had to reach into their crap to get them. They'd flap their wings like crazy, throwing chicken shit all over my face, in my hair, and on my clothes. Sometimes they'd take off running and had to be chased down.

When the day was done, I had cuts from my fingertips to my shoulders. It would've been nice to be forewarned that gloves and a long sleeve shirt were recommended. When I got home, I couldn't take my clothes off fast enough. The stink was so bad I couldn't even ask mom to wash them. Instead, I threw the funky pile into the burn barrel.

A week later I got a call inviting me to come back out and do the next barn. I was still having nightmares of being chased down and pecked to death by a ten-foot rooster. I had to decline and tell them that my chicken eviction days were over.

*** 

Once I got to college, in Fort Dodge, Iowa, my first job was at Gillman Drug Store. I stocked the shelves and waited on customers. I always thought it was strange that Mr. Gillman rented the building his business was in. He retired after sixty years, and paid rent the entire time. I guess when Gillman got started, he thought he'd never stay that long in the drug store business.

Mr. Gillman instructed me: "The first thing you need to know is where the condoms are behind the counter. We sell lots of 'em."

I had never used one before. (Remember, my first sexual encounter ended up with a pregnant girlfriend.) I tried to learn the different brands.

My second day there, a well-dressed man in a suit walked in, came over to me at the counter and said, "Give me a dozen wets."

I looked behind the counter, on the shelves for what seemed like five minutes trying to figure out what the hell *wets* were. I didn't want to look stupid by asking him.

Luckily for me, Mr. Gillman came out from the back room and said, "Hi Doc. How you doing? Do you want the usual?"

The doctor nodded his head. Mr. Gillman reached behind the counter and handed him a dozen *lubricated* rubbers. How would I have ever known that?

Randy, a sixty-year-old, part-time worker, and I, were running the store one Saturday afternoon. In walked what looked like a sixteen-year-old kid and he headed right for the counter where the rubbers were.

Randy winked at me and said, "Come with me to wait on him."

We walked to the counter, and Randy said, "Young man, how can I help you?"

The boy answered, "I'm looking to buy a rubber."

"You can't purchase just one, they come in packs of three," Randy informed him.

"How much are three of 'em?" he asked.

"Two dollars and seventy-five cents," Randy said with a huge grin on his face.

The boy took all of the change out of his pocket, and realized he didn't have enough money.

He left every penny he had on the counter and said, "I'll be right back."

We watched him go outside to a car in front of the building. There was a girl in the front seat. We saw her get into her purse and give the boy some more money. He strutted back in and put all total three dollars on the counter.

Randy smiled and said, "What size do you want?"

"What? They come in different sizes?"

Randy was doing all he could to refrain from laughing. "Yes, they do, small, medium, and large."

The boy looked down at his crotch area, then raised his head and said, "You better give me the large."

Once he left, Randy and I laughed about it for hours. After that incident, I always enjoyed working with Randy. He found many ways to make the job entertaining.

Gillman only paid minimum wage. After six months, I found work in the meat store across from the jail. (The job where I worked until I didn't get my birthday off and stormed out.) Not much exciting happened there.

\*\*\*

My next gig was at Rustler's, the college bar. Bill Howard, the owner, was a drunk and a gambler. Not a wise combination when you own a bar.

Bill had a way of tracking beer and mixed drink sales that I never figured out. I got chewed out about the sales not matching up with the number of shots you are supposed to get out of a fifth. Reason why: I was drinking my rum and Cokes without paying for them. I tried to outsmart him--I started selling beer and ringing it up as mixed drinks. Bill had a couple of college football players working part-time during the day. He yelled at them for drinking beer for free. They were never smart enough to figure out what I was doing to mess with them.

Rustlers also served homemade pizzas and sausage sandwiches. They were cooked in a big drop-down-door oven like you'd see at a pizza joint. Bill figured if people were going to drink, he could make money feeding them as well.

Everything was made from scratch. He had a couple college guys who took turns working in the kitchen. I always had a good laugh. Most of the time they were high on acid, blitzed on cannabinol, or stoned out their minds. Whenever I got hungry, I made my own food. I didn't trust them. I figured either they'd screw up my order, or slip in something I wasn't expecting. There weren't too many complaints from the customers, though—maybe an occasional overcooked pizza. Most of the cliental were drunk when they ordered, and their taste buds were as wasted as they were.

Rustlers had both a pool and foosball table. One evening around midnight a fight broke out around the pool table. Fights were pretty common at Rustlers. That was why the button to summon the police was installed.

I heard a loud crack. I looked toward the pool table and saw a kid drop to the floor. A pool cue had been broken over his head. Blood was spurting out and pouring all down his face. I couldn't believe the fool stood back up to try and retaliate. Before he could even get his fists up to take a swing, he was hit again. *Down goes Frazier for the second time*, I could hear Howard Cosell saying. To my surprise he got back up. I know I would've stayed on the floor, or crawled out the door, after the first shot. Of course, it is the bartender's job to break up fights, but I was staying out of this one. Luckily, two other guys jumped in and grabbed the guy with the broken pool stick in his hand.

I suggested to the guy who was bleeding, "You need to go to the hospital and get stitched up. You are cut up pretty bad."

He looked back at me and said, "Hell no, I going to beat the shit out of this guy."

A couple of his friends came over and convinced him to leave. A half hour later, on my break, I went out the front door to go to my car and smoke some pot. There he was sitting on the hood of a car, just outside the bar, waiting for the other guy to come out. He hadn't gone to the hospital, but his blood had coagulated on his face. Even though he looked like a mangy Chihuahua in a pit bull fight, he was determined to finish it, or to get at least one punch in, even if it was a surprise one. The guy who cracked him over the head played pool for another hour or so. When he left the other kid was sprawled on the hood, passed out. I told his friends and I think they finally took him to the hospital.

Rustlers had a storage room in the back of the bar. The door wasn't locked and people went in there to snort coke, or once in a while smoke a joint. Rustlers was so full of cigarette smoke that the two smells blended together. Girls went into the room to *trade favors* for getting high. I was always amazed at what a girl would do for a line of coke.

One Friday night, a guy I knew came into the bar and sat at the front counter. I made him a drink, and was waiting on another customer when I heard,

"Indian, your turn."

I went back to where he was sitting and I saw four lines of coke on counter. I was shocked. I looked around and saw two men in business suits sitting only a few chairs away. I turned around like I didn't hear anything, and headed to the back of the bar.

The next night when I came to work, Bill said, "Rick, did you see anybody put some kind of drug on the counter last night?"

"No, I didn't," I quickly answered. (Yes, I saw the four lines of coke, but technically I didn't see anybody *put* them there...same tactic I used as a kid with my Dad.)

He eyed me warily. "A couple of my friends were in the bar, and told me they thought it was cocaine, or some other illegal substance."

"I must've been in the back of the bar, or cleaning bottles off of tables."

"Okay…" Bill raised an eyebrow, but he never asked me again about the incident.

I'd been working at Rustlers for two years when one evening Fort Dodge was hit by two tornados—what are the odds?— on opposite sides of town. One of them came right down Rustlers' road and leveled the bar. I was lucky it was my night off. I was at home. I lived up on a hill, and from my vantage point I could see trees and wood (and I figured my job) flying up in the air. The second tornado actually passed over my house before it landed in a new residential area. I was standing in my front yard watching the destruction of the first one out by Rustlers; when I looked up in the air and saw *dos* tornado directly overhead. I could've beat Jessie Owens to my basement.

The next morning, I drove out to where the second one came down. I saw firsthand the destruction a tornado can do. It was amazing that some houses were completely demolished, and others right next to them had only a few shingles blown off. Mother Nature does work in mysterious ways, and a tornado will definitely prove it. It took Fort Dodge the rest of the summer to clean up the damage and start rebuilding.

❋❋❋

With Rustlers gone, I worked at the recording studio. It was a great job with (high) benefits. I loved the music industry and even tried to sell businesses commercials that we made at the studio. In a small town like Fort Dodge, it was cheaper to have a poorly made commercial done by the radio station that they advertised on, than to pay for a quality ad by us, and then pay the station to run it.

With bars closing where the recording bands once played, I was only working a couple of days a week, and that didn't pay the bills.

*** 

I decided to go back to my roots in the meat cutting business at Myers Provisions. Two brothers, Roy and Bill, who were in their late sixties, owned the business. They had been meatcutters for over forty years. We were the middle man between Iowa Beef Processors and the local grocery stores.

Myers also made and stuffed several kinds of sausages. I helped Adolf, who was an old German sausage maker. He had all of his recipes scribbled down on index cards. He'd never let me see them. Apparently, Adolf thought I'd steal his secrets and sell them to the Americans.

I always thought it was funny how the sausages changed depending on whether or not the inspector was showing up that day. All companies were required to list their ingredients on the packages. When the meat inspector wasn't there, we used cow hearts and brains in the sausages.

Adolf confided to me one day: "It make for better flavor in sausage."

"Why don't you list them on the packages then?" I pressed.

"America people don't buy if offal is ingredient."

"But if it makes them taste better, why not include them?"

"You eat someting if it taste good even if you know not what you eating, yah?"

"You got me there. I eat hotdogs."

In the year I worked at Myers, the meat inspector only showed up once unannounced. While Roy stalled him up front, Adolf and I scrambled to hide the box of beef hearts, brains, and other viscera in the cooler. Now, here's a little challenge: Try not to think about the *secret ingredients* the next time you bite into a hotdog or polish sausage.

**\*\*\***

I convinced my parents to move from Nebraska to a small town twenty miles northeast of Fort Dodge. In Vincent, Iowa there was a small grocery store for sale. Since I was the only brother to have kids, I thought my parents would enjoy being around their grandchildren. Besides, they had worked in a grocery store before, and it wasn't by their choice that they still weren't. Lightning made their decision for them.

Vincent was a town of only 250 people. The grocery store had been closed for almost a year, and I thought the people would gladly patronize it if we opened it back up. We came to find out that ninety percent of the people worked in larger towns around Vincent, and bought their groceries there before they came back home. We tried everything we could think of to make it work—even opened up the back end of the store as a café serving breakfast and noon meals. Vincent had a large grain elevator with thirty employees working there. With just a bar to eat at, we thought the café would go over well. But there just weren't enough people shopping at our store to pay the bills.

We resorted to sending out letters telling the locals that we'd have to close up if they didn't start doing at least some of their shopping at our store. The Vincentites stepped up to the plate… for a couple of months; then went right back to their old habits. My parents and I decided we couldn't afford to keep losing money, and after two years of giving it our best shot it was time to throw in the apron. When we had the auction, I saw customers in the store I'd never seen the entire time we were open. It was amazing the amount of people who came out that day in order to bid on a case of canned vegetables for a buck.

***

While living in Vincent, Iowa I joined the Volunteer Fire Department & Ambulance service. I was required to undergo thirty hours of training. That was how I knew how to perform the Heimlich maneuver when Josh choked on the jaw breaker.

I had two memorable calls with the ambulance. The first time, radio dispatch informed us a man had cut his hand reaching under his lawn mower while it was still running. I couldn't imagine what he was thinking. En route, my instructions were to find any fingers that might have been cut off and lying in the grass. I looked all around the mower and in a nearby clump of grass but I found nothing. Another EMT thought to unwrap the towel around his hand, and he noticed that all the fingers were sliced but still attached by the skin.

The second time I was working at our grocery store when the call came in. I ran across the street and waited for the other volunteers to show up. Everyone was busy but one. Larry had one hundred hours of training, so he rode in the back while I drove the ambulance. This was my first time behind the wheel. We picked up a man who was having a heart attack and had to drive him the twenty miles to Fort Dodge Hospital. I had the lights flashing and sirens blaring as I entered the city. I was amazed when drivers didn't pull over with an ambulance coming. Was that page missing from the Iowa Driver's Manual? I had to drive the six miles from the edge of the city to the hospital on the left, or wrong side of the road, passing many vehicles who wouldn't yield right of way.

On the plus side, Larry and I were able to contribute to saving a man's life.

The ironic ending to this story is a few years after we sold the unpopular grocery store, a young couple bought the building and wanted to turn it into a knickknack shop. They decided to put new siding on the outside. When they tore off a couple of the old layers, they found a billboard-size Barnum and Bailey poster for a circus that came to the area in the 1930s. A man from Chicago heard about it, and was able to remove it in one piece with a special process. And here's the kicker: He paid the couple an ungodly amount of money for it.

After the grocery store fiasco, my parents moved to San Antonio, and I got that job I described earlier at Iowa Beef. You know, the short-lived one where I cut butt out of a cow. All I can say about it is I was willing to do anything to put food on the table for my family.

\*\*\*

Next was the door-to-door salesman job selling Electrolux vacuum cleaners, which you've already heard about. But I didn't tell you one of my better stories. I worked my way into a home around 11:30 in the morning and began my demonstration. The lady of the house was enthusiastic about the vacuum.

Her husband came home for lunch at noon and growled, "What the hell is this guy doing here?"

"He's demonstrating an Electrolux vacuum for me," she said, trying to reassure him about the product.

"You don't need no damn vacuum," he barked with a mean look on his face.

"Won't you please let him show it to you?" she said meekly.

My first thought was, *Start packing it back up.* But I figured as long as I wasn't going to get a sale, I might as well have some fun at his expense. He sat down in a recliner, folded his arms, and just glared at me.

I walked over to him. "Sir, is that your favorite chair?"

"Damn right it is," he sneered.

"Would you be so kind to stand up, so I can show you something?"

After he begrudgingly moved out of the chair, I proved to him that I had a brand-new clean cloth bag in the machine. I quickly vacuumed his lounger; then removed the bag and shook it over the chair. It left a pile of dirt over an inch high.

I said, "Sir, go ahead and sit back down."

He looked at me like I was crazy. "I can't with all that dirt there."

I took my hand and rubbed it back into his chair. "There, it is right back where it used to be. Now you can sit back down."

"I ain't sittin' with all that dirt there!" he snapped again.

"You did before I showed you what you were sitting on."

"You vacuum that up right now," he demanded.

I could tell by the look on his face that he wasn't finding it as funny as I was. I re-vacuumed his chair and casually proceeded to show him how good the machine worked on the carpet. I left clumps of dirt all around the living room proving to him their vacuum did suck, but not dirt. He remained quiet when I got out the shampooer and cleaned up half of the carpet to demonstrate the before and after. I could see by a transformation on his face that he was impressed.

He had to head back to work, but I heard him whisper to his wife, "Harriet, go ahead and buy both machines." I went from no sale to a thousand-dollar *ka-ching*! That was one of my favorite experiences as a door-to-door salesman. I wish I had a story about trading sex for a sale, but this is as good as it is going to get.

One other quick story. A bar in a town called Pocahontas was looking for a new vacuum to clean the place. I went there on a Saturday morning just before noon. I demonstrated the machine and the owner bought it after asking a couple questions that I answered to his satisfaction. During the demonstration, I noticed that the four men who were drinking at the bar were watching me with interest. When I finished writing up the sale to the bar owner, all four men were on their feet, asking me how they could get one. By midafternoon, each of them bought a vacuum for their wives. Lucky for me, that day I had five machines in my car. I always took plenty of vacuums along whenever I went canvassing, because one thing I learned early on: buying is a spontaneous decision. Plus, being a former Boy Scout, the motto is: "Be prepared."

While working for Electrolux, I was promoted to manager of the store in Waterloo, Iowa. I moved Karla and the kids over there—against her will, I should add. When I received my first paycheck, we still didn't have a checking account. Rather than depositing it, I went to a bank and cashed my check.

When I got home, Karla said in a snotty voice, "Did you get paid today?"

I just tossed $2,900 worth of twenty-dollar bills into the air. The look on her face was priceless as the money floated to the carpet.

As a manager, you had to maintain a 93% collections ratio in order to get your bonus. This meant from time to time I had to go knock on doors myself and collect the monthly payments. Rita, my district manager, who was in her mid fifties and around five-feet-four inches tall, stopped by the office with a list of delinquent accounts that we were going to collect on that day.

After knocking on several doors and getting some of the money, Rita said, "We've got Shirley Jones next on our list. She is four months past due. We might have to pick up her equipment if she doesn't pay us."

I thought, *This might be my first repo.*

We sat in Rita's Cadillac a few houses from where we'd heard that Shirley had just moved to, in the poor section of Waterloo. At 3:30, after school was out, we watched a young girl walk up to the house, and go in.

Rita smacked me on the thigh, "Let's go!"

Before I knew what was happening, Rita was out of the car and heading for the house. I hopped out and had to run to catch up to her. We arrived at the front door and Rita had me knock as she stood behind me. A big, black lady answered the door.

"Are you Shirley Jones?" I said nervously.

"Yes, I am," she replied. The next thing I knew, Rita, like a football linebacker, was shoving me from behind into the house.

Once in, I heard a deep, Barry White kind of voice saying, "What the mutha f##k you want?"

I slowly turned my head to the left and there on the couch was a massive black dude, with arms as big as cannons, glaring right at me. I opened my mouth but nothing came out.

Rita nonchalantly said, "We are with Electrolux and we're here to collect for the vacuum Shirley has. She is four months behind."

The man turned to Shirley and said, "Bitch, I been giving you money to pay for that f##king machine. What the f##k you been doing with the money?"

Now we were in the middle of a domestic fight.

After a five-minute shouting match, he turned back to Rita. "How much does the bitch owe?"

Rita said, "One hundred and twelve dollars will get her caught up."

"Bullshit, take the machine back," he snarled. "That'll teach her for spendin' my money."

Rita looked at Shirley. "We will need all of it."

Shirley went upstairs to get the vacuum cleaner. Meanwhile we were left downstairs with Big Brutus. I never said one word. I stood there motionless like I was frozen in time. I could feel a little pee running down my leg.

Shirley came back downstairs and said, "Here you go," handing Rita the vacuum, hose, and nozzle.

Rita didn't budge. "Where are the attachments? I'll need them too."

I'm thinking, *F##k the attachments, let's get the hell out of here while we still can.*

Shirley went back upstairs and within a couple of minutes she began throwing down the attachments. I felt like I was in one of those old western movies where they shoot at the guy's feet as I'm jumping in the air to get out of the way. I gathered them up, and out the door we went.

Back in the car I looked at Rita in disbelief. "Why did you ask for the attachments? I thought we'd done good by getting the machine."

Rita said, "As a manager, you will get charged back if you don't have the all the parts for the vacuum. I thought this'll be a good learning experience for you."

I wanted to say, *Rita, the only thing I learned is what it feels like to be scared shitless.*

So, there you have my best and worst days of the three and a half years I worked for Electrolux.

**✳✳✳**

I went from cleaning up Fort Dodge to keeping the wheels turning with Goodyear Tire and Rubber Company. I was paid by the hour so I knew from week to week what I was going to make. This took less of a toll on my marriage.

Goodyear was a company that believed in giving their employees plenty of training. They bought an old school house in Ohio. No matter where you lived in the country, you got your training there. I attended a three-week Retail Sales Manager Course, a four-week Store Manager Course, and a nine-week Commercial Tire Salesman Class. By the time I was done, I felt I could sell tires to a homeless man.

I started out in the company as a retail salesman. Four years later I took the store manager course, but turned down several opportunities in other Iowa cities, and some in other states, to stay close to my children. I knew I couldn't get Karla to move again. I found out the first time that her figurative umbilical cord only reaches 100 miles. While we were living in Waterloo, during my Electrolux manager job, her dad had gotten sick, and shortly after we returned, he died. She always blamed me for taking her away from her dad when he was ill. Karla was one for holding grudges, and that was one she never let go of.

Soon after, I was back in Ohio attending the Commercial Tire course. If you remember, it was during this stint that Karla asked me for a divorce.

After I completed the Commercial Tire course, my job was to deliver semi-truck tires to accounts in and around Fort Dodge. There were times that I had to bring back the large semi tires still on the rims. The combination of the two amounted to one hundred and fifty to two hundred pounds. I was no Arnold Swarzennegger. I had to lay one assembly on the ground, roll the next one on top of it, and flip it into the back of the pickup. As I said earlier, I didn't have a Tommy Lift on the tailgate; instead I had to use Rick Lift. There were many a time that I fell to the ground, writhing in back pain that brought tears to my eyes.

Three years later the manager's job opened up. I was sick of lugging truck tires with my bad back and I jumped at the chance. Besides, I got along great with my District Manager, Henry; especially after hours when we'd go to the strip clubs. One night in the Top Hat strip club, Henry and I were enjoying a couple of drinks and the dancers. A drunk man staggered by our table and bumped into Henry's back.

As Henry turned around, the drunk starred at him and said, "What're ya lookin' at ya bald mother f**ker?'

Before I knew what was happening, Henry hit the man. He rolled backwards over the table behind us and landed on the floor. The bartender threw him out of the bar and gave us free drinks. The dancers even came over and thanked Henry. The guy had been rude and obnoxious for most of the night. From that day on I called Henry, "Rocky".

Within six months, Henry was transferred to the Houston area, and I soon got a call.

"Hey, Rick," Henry said enticingly, "you gotta come down here to Texas and be my store manager."

"I don't know, Henry, I'll have to think…"

"They have golfing year-round down here, Rick…" he baited me, then upped the ante: "and Texas tittie bars put Iowa to shame."

It was tempting, but I knew that company people like him get transferred all the time. I figured as soon as I moved to Houston, he'd get relocated somewhere else, and I'm now stuck in Texas, hundreds of miles away from my kids.

After three years of managing the store, I met with Bob, the owner of Graham Tire, who said he was going to buy the Fort Dodge Goodyear Tire store, and he wanted me to stay on and run it. I agreed. The first year I made him good money. My store also won the Chamber of Commerce's very first Customer Service Award. I lost my commercial truck tire salesman and hired a friend of mine out of Des Moines. The second year the store lost around sixty-thousand dollars, and most of it was from the commercial side of the business.

Bob had hired Stu, an ex-Goodyear employee, to be his general manager. We didn't hit it off very well. He wanted to run some of Goodyear's old programs since that was all he knew. Being an ex-manager of the Goodyear Tire system, I was well aware of which ones didn't work, and I refused to use them. None of the other twelve managers liked Stu either. When he went from store to store, he didn't know how to read a profit and loss statement, Stu was helpless to fix the problems.

One day when Stu was in my office, I gave him an analogy: "If you were the general of an army, and your soldiers were the store managers, they'd find you dead with a bullet in the back of your head before the enemy ever had a chance to shoot you." Sometimes, and I think especially in this case, honesty was not the best policy.

Between my mouth, Stu, and my back-stabbing secretary (she secretly called Stu and tattled on me when I didn't do things his way), six months into my third year I was fired for not having the profit that Graham Tire wanted to see. At least that was the excuse I was given.

I collected unemployment for six months, and since it was the beginning of summer, I played golf every day. By November it was getting too cold to golf in Iowa. I took a job as the manager of a tire business in Webster City, twenty miles east of Ft. Dodge. The owner made the word "asshole" a compliment, but I needed the money. We got into shouting matches all the time. At one point, I couldn't raise my arms above my shoulders.

My doctor asked me, "Do you have any stress in your life?"

I said, "Do you know Dick Duke?"

He rolled his eyes and said, "You need to find another job."

I do have two good stories from working in Webster City that include my buddies, the State Patrol. The first one: I had picked up a fellow employee who lived at the Ft. Dodge Drug Rehabilitation Center. It was a cold, icy, snowy morning. On days like this, I always took the four-lane to work. I felt there was less chance of getting into an accident if all traffic was going the same direction as me. For some reason, I decided rather than follow the semi ahead of me, I'd pass it. I had pulled alongside of the eighteen-wheeler, when a white-out condition suddenly happened; and as I put on the brakes, I started to lose control of my car. I did my best to keep the car moving in a straight line until the rear end decided it wanted to lead.

After the second donut, I yelled to my passenger, " Hold on, we're going into the ditch."

Somehow, I was able to straighten the car back out, and continue heading in the right direction without hitting anything. My heart was racing. I looked over to the opposite side of the median and saw a State Patrolman heading the other direction and waving at me. I wasn't sure if he was impressed that I didn't crash (which kept him from having to fill out a report), or that he knew me?

An hour later, at work, the patrolman walked up to the counter and said, "Rick, I need to see your license."

I reached in my pocket, and as I was pulling it out, I looked up at him and said, "Sure thing, Cody, but what do you need it for?"

"I am going to write you a ticket for reckless driving," he explained.

"Reckless?" I nearly jumped out of my seat. "Hell, I kept the car out of the ditch, and didn't hit anything. In fact, I thought I did a damn good job."

Cody didn't say a word and kept on writing. When he was done, he handed me back my license and the ticket. I saw the fine was $1000.

I looked up at Cody, ready to scream, "What the fu…"

He burst out laughing, "When I saw it was you Rick, I decided to come here and pull a prank. I actually thought you did a hell of a job keeping your car on the road."

Since the tire shop supplied the State Patrol in the area with tires for their cruisers, I knew most of them; so, I was able to get away with responding, "You're an asshole, but you did scare the shit out of me at first." But I waited until he tore up the ticket, just to be safe.

The second time; I was on my way to work, and as I met a patrolman, he quickly turned around, hit his red lights, and pulled me over.

He came to my window and said, "I need to see your driver's license and registration please."

"What's up, officer?"

"I'm giving you a ticket for speeding."

"But sir, I wasn't speeding," I declared, then added, "do you know where I work?"

"Yes, I do. What does that have to do with this?"

"I hate my job, so I'm *never* in a hurry to get there. You have a better chance of catching me speeding on the way home, but never coming *to* work."

He began laughing, handed me back my license, and said, "I'll give you a warning this time."

Now, I don't know if I got out of the ticket because he understood, or that he'd never heard a line like that before, and gave me a break for originality.

My frustration with working for Dick Duke came to a boiling point. Three months later, Bob Graham finally wised up and fired Stu. He replaced him with one of the store managers, Kelly, who I got along with really well. I called Kelly up and got my old job back as a retail salesman with Graham Tire. Ironically, it was the first job that I had with Goodyear. I also handled the local truck tire businesses in Fort Dodge. So, in a way, I was doing two of the three jobs at the same time I had with Goodyear.

**\*\*\***

I was sitting at home watching TV one evening when my phone rang. It was the security company for Graham Tire. The lady on the line said, "The motion detector has gone off at Graham Tire and we need someone to go check it out."

I was really engrossed in the TV show but I said, "Okay, I'll go to the store and see what's going on." I hit RECORD so I could watch the show when I got home. I drove to Graham Tire which took me less than five minutes.

Even before I unlocked the front door, I could hear the alarm. It was loud, and reminded me of a school bell ringing incessantly. There was also a mechanical voice warning the perp: "Stop what you are doing! The police have been called."

I went over to the panel and put in my four pass code numbers which stopped the alarm. Within seconds the phone rang and this time it was a different lady at the security company.

"This is Rick from Graham Tire," I announced.

The lady said, "I need the password associated with the store"

I didn't feel like looking it up in the files. "I don't remember it."

"I need it or I will have to call the police," she said in a stern voice like a high school principal.

I couldn't believe it. "Look, do you think if I was robbing this place that I'd stop and answer the phone just to talk to you?"

"I need the password," she persisted.

"Once again," I said as if talking to a child, "I don't remember it."

"Well, I'm going to have to call the police then."

"Wow, you really believe that a thief would answer the phone!"

"Sir, I'm just following protocol," she huffed. " If you can't give me the password then I have to call the police."

"Then call the police." I hung up the phone. Less than four minutes later I saw two cop cars pull up with their lights flashing. Three officers got out of the two cars, pulled their guns and cautiously entered Graham Tire, where I was calmly waiting for them. One of the cops demanded," What's going on?"

I said, "I was home watching TV when the security company called and said the motion detector went off, and wanted me to come check it out. When I got here, I shut off the alarm, but since I couldn't remember the password, she called you guys."

Another officer said, "Do you work here?"

"Yes, I used *my* key to get in and shut off the alarm." I showed the men in blue the keys in my hand. I guess it would've been better if I'd put on a Graham Tire shirt before I came, but so far, they believed me.

One of them said, "Well as long as we're here, we might as well walk through the store and check it out." I gave them the *be my guest* gesture.

The biggest cop looked at me and said, "Why don't you go first since you know the way."

I thought to myself, *I go first. You got the guns. If you're too scared to lead the way you can at least give me one of your guns.* But I didn't say anything in case one of them had an itchy trigger finger and didn't like sarcasm.

I opened the door to the shop, walked all through it and into the back room with two of the brave officers right behind me. The third one stayed in the front office in case the thief came out of hiding and tried to make a run for it. Once we finished our walkaround, we all met back up front. After all the rigmarole, the cops were still eyeing me suspiciously. Like maybe I had stolen the key. It was only then I realized what I should've done the moment they walked in.

"Can I show you something?" I addressed them.

One of the cops nodded.

Very cautiously, I reached into my back pocked with my left hand, and removed my money clip with my driver's license. Simultaneously, with my right hand, I grabbed one of my business cards off my desk—then held the two of them up, side-by-side.

"Oh," the big cop grunted.

They holstered their guns and departed without another word.

I loved my job and couldn't have asked for a better group of guys to work with. I had a great relationship on and off the job with Mike, my boss, and Bill, the service manager. Two of the certified master auto technicians who worked in the shop I had hired when I was the manager with Goodyear. John, another salesman, and a golf buddy, has been my good friend for over twenty-five years. We could joke about things all day long and still put out the numbers the company was looking for. In all, I put in 39 years in the tire business. Now that I am retired, I look back at my successful career with a smile on my face.

## Chapter 19

# FRIENDS, ACQUAINTENCES & PEOPLE I'D LIKE TO FORGET

I have known several people in my life who I want to acknowledge. The first one is Alex, a middle-aged farmer who lived outside of Fort Dodge. Like all farmers in the area he raised corn and soybeans. Alex also grew a cash crop of marijuana. Alex had two friends who attended Iowa State University to become agronomists. Upon graduation, they were drafted into the military. One of them was stationed in Taiwan, and the other in Afghanistan. Upon completion of their service, they each smuggled pot from the two countries back to the United States.

Being agronomists, they were able to take the seeds, and cross pollinate them into one ass-kicking marijuana plant. Alex was given three-hundred seeds and he planted them smack in the middle of his cornfield. This way, when the marijuana grew to the adult stage, it was the exact same height as the corn, and thus invisible from passersby on the road. Each plant produced at least a half-pound of pot, which at the time was worth three hundred dollars. Alex delivered some of the finished product to his two benefactors, who now lived in Michigan. The rest was sold to and smoked by Alex's friends. I was one of the fortunate.

People always commented, "This is the best pot I've ever had."

Alex just shrugged. "Not bad for Iowa grown, huh?"

Alex continued with his cash crop for several years until the National Guard of Fort Dodge started doing weekend training exercises in helicopters, which included looking for pot plants growing in cornfields. Leave it up to the government to ruin a great enterprise. In addition to a hefty fine, and jail time, if caught, the farmer stood to lose possession of his farm. Alex didn't think the reward was worth the risk. For a while, Alex was stilling growing a plant or two here and there, but nothing like the original operation.

There's another story that involved Alex. We went down to Ames, Iowa to a football game between the Iowa State Cyclones and the Nebraska Cornhuskers. Of course, being a Husker fan, I was all dressed up in red. We got high on the way down and decided to eat before the game.

Alex said, "I know this perfect place called Duggan's Deli that serves great sandwiches. It's going to close after tonight for good because the owner is retiring."

Little did I know it had once been the #1 pre-game eating place for Cyclone fans. We went inside and everybody in the restaurant was wearing the Iowa State team's red and gold colors. I stood out like a fox in the hen house. Everyone was glaring at me, and probably thinking, "Who the hell let this frickin' guy in here?"

We got to the counter to place our orders. Alex said, "Gimme a pastrami on rye."

I was about to order when the owner came out of the kitchen and announced, "This will be the last sandwich to be served at Duggan's Deli."

Now, what are the odds that a huge Cornhusker fan as I am gets the very last sandwich at the most popular Cyclone eating place? I laughed for years every time I told this story to a cocky Iowa State fan who came into my store.

***

A fond story about Huskerland: Cliff and his wife Ryan came back to Nebraska for his fortieth-class reunion, and I hadn't seen him for a while so I took Patti over to Lincoln where we all met at Jeff's house. Since we were all big fans, we decided to go to the stadium. It was closed for the season, and we walked all around trying to find a door that'd get us in anyway. At one point we were even thinking of climbing over a fence. When we got to the last possible point of entry, Cliff grabbed the door handle and said, "Watch this," and it miraculously opened; although I think he was secretly surprised.

We ran out onto the field like we owned it. Patti took pictures of us in front of the goal posts and on the 50-yard line. We were on top of the world. Little did we know, security was watching us. In one of the tunnels there is red carpet that leads the football team from the locker room to the field. We had smiles as big as the stadium itself as we headed toward the locker room, but it was locked. Out of the corner of my eye I saw a uniformed guard coming at us. I tapped Cliff on the shoulder and said, "Security…run!"

Cliff and I zoomed past Jeff, Ryan, and Patti leaving them in our dust.

I heard the guard yell, "What are you guys doing in here?"

Jeff tried to explain, "Uh…We were just looking at the field."

"You are not allowed to be in here. It is a $500 fine."

By then Cliff and I had decided we'd better come back and help. It would've been hard to explain to people how we just left his wife and my girlfriend to be arrested for trespassing. But, I have to say, we did make a great getaway.

The guard asked, "How did you get in here?"

I answered, "The door was unlocked, so we just walked in. We didn't know there was a penalty for being on the field.

Cliff, Mr. Logic, added, "Why would the door be left open if there's a penalty for coming in? That's like, entrapment."

I continued, "I'm from Iowa and my brother here is from California. We are huge Husker fans. We just wanted to take some pictures, and give our women the Husker experience."

The guard said, "We've been watching you on a monitor ever since you walked onto the field."

He pointed to Cliff. "We thought you were the soccer coach at first, but after getting out the binoculars we could see you weren't.

"I must have some kind of generic face." Cliff shrugged. "I spend about ten percent of my life being mistaken for someone else… and everyone I meet thinks they've seen me somewhere before."

The guard shrugged and said, "Show me the door that was unlocked."

While we walked to the door, I continued spreading it on thick about being a big fan.

We showed him the door and he was surprised. "I checked all the doors first thing this morning—wonder how this one got missed?"

"We don't know, but as you can see it was open," Cliff pointed out, opening and closing it with ease a couple of times to prove he ain't lying.

At that point, the guard let his guard down, and became the nicest person you'd ever want to meet. (Between you and me, I think he was worried his job was on the line if word got out about that unlocked door.)

He put his hand on my shoulder and said, "Since you guys are fans, how'd you like to see the new Heisman room?"

"Yeah!" we all said at the same time.

"Well let's go. I'll give you the tour."

He escorted us around to the front of the stadium. He unlocked the door and we were in a room with all the National Championship Trophies, and the silver bowls filled with plastic oranges signifying the Orange Bowl victories. Our mouths opened wide as we felt like babes in Huskerland.

"Follow me," he said and led us to a little room. "Take a seat and I'll start the film."

He left and we looked around the room featuring three Heisman Trophies on display, as well as the three jerseys of the Huskers who have won the Heisman: #20 Johnny Rodgers in 1972, #30 Mike Rozier in 1983, and #7 Eric Crouch in 2001.

The lights went down and the sound of a projector started up. We looked at each other with excitement as the film came on introducing the athletes, showing their greatest plays and runs for about ten minutes.

The guard came in to get us and said, "You wanna take a few minutes and go into that room where all the other bowl games' memorabilia is on display?"

I can't remember who said it, but I heard *yes* and *wow* at the same time. We spent about thirty minutes in there before we left. In the end, we went from a $500 fine to a $500 tour.

*** 

As most of us were growing up, there's always *that* kid your parents tell you not hang around with. In my home town that bad boy was Dave Lubinski. It seemed he was always getting in trouble. Since Mom was the secretary for the school superintendent, she saw a lot of Dave in the office for one misdeed or another. But I think she was kidding when she told me the chair in front of the superintendent's desk had "Dave" engraved on it.

Since I was forbidden to be Dave's friend, I hung out with him from time to time without my parents' knowledge. After all, Dave owned the coolest car in town, a 1969 Plymouth Road Runner 440 cubic inch 6-pack engine with the hood scoop on it. The car could flat-out fly.

One fine Sunday afternoon while my parents were attending a church bake sale, I sat in the passenger seat while Dave and I were tooling down Highway 77. We found ourselves puttering behind a line of about eight slow moving cars--damn Midwestern Sunday drivers!

Dave goes, "Watch this!" (Note: If you've read Jeff Foxworthy, I'm sure you know that is the answer to the question, "What are a Redneck's last words?") Dave punched the gas pedal to the floor and began passing cars, one after another.

While white knuckling the dashboard, I glanced over at the speedometer and saw it quickly reach 120 mph—and this was up a half-mile incline! All of a sudden, we saw an 18-wheeler cresting the hill, coming right at us. Dave slammed on the brakes and as the car was sliding sideways, he somehow maneuvered it in between the sixth and seventh cars. My heart was pounding as rapidly as the Plymouth's rpms and it's a miracle I didn't drop a surprise in my shorts. I was both amazed and relieved that Dave pulled it off. It had to have cost him one of his nine lives. And I'm most surprised he never found his calling as a Nascar driver.

Every once in awhile we all fall into a pile of shit and come out smelling like a rose. Dave's moment came the night he decided to steal some top-of-the-line Pirelli radials from the local tire store. As you can imagine, Dave's car burned through a lot of tires—probably three sets a year. Anyway, it was after midnight when he chose to pull off the crime. Dave was walking out the back door he'd picked the lock on. He was making his second trip to his car with a tire in each hand. That's when Dave bumped into—literally—the waiting police. The silent alarm had busted him! The rose that came up for Dave was the sleepy-headed cop who wrote up the arrest warrant. On the ticket he put "April 31" as the court date. Since you can't very well show up on a day that doesn't exist, Dave caught a *bye* on that one.

✱✱✱

My friend Dan had a grandfather who invented the machine that takes tires off of the rims. We used several of them at Goodyear. When his grandpa died, he left Dan and his two brothers one million dollars to split between them. That is a lot of money for an eighteen-year-old to have. They bought cars, ATVs, and motorcycles, went on vacations, and did a lot of drugs until the money ran out.

Dan visited me at the recording studio from time to time. One day, in the middle of the winter, we were so stoned the music wasn't making any sense. I was having trouble using the 32-track mixing board. Usually, getting loaded made me more creative with music, but not this particular day.

Dan said, "I've got a great idea, let's go for a ride in my new car." Dan had just brought a 1976 Datsun 280-Z.

"Yeah, that oughta do the trick," I said in my drug-addled wisdom.

We hopped in and headed down the road. Next thing I know, Dan turned down a ramp that led onto the Des Moines River. It was so cold that week the river was frozen over, and there we were on the ice speeding down the river. As we went under the Kalo Bridge, people stopped their cars to look. Can you imagine the thoughts that must have been going through their heads as they saw us driving just like we were on the interstate?

Dan got the car up to fifty miles per hour then yanked on the emergency brake and cramped the wheel to the left. We started doing circles (aka donuts) five times before we came to a stop. That beat every county fair ride either us had ever been on. We were so high we couldn't be bothered with the possible consequences. First, the police could arrest us for reckless driving. Second, they could bust us for the copious amount of drugs we had in our possession. Third, and most important, the car could have fallen through the ice, meaning certain death. But all we could think of was, "Let's do it again!"

Dan and I worked together in a couple of jobs. The first, he was my boss when I sold Electrolux vacuums. I nicknamed him the "Gonna Man." I'd take a crew of new recruits to a town to show them the ropes knocking on doors selling vacuums.

Just as a bunch of us were leaving for the day, Dan always said, "I've got a little paperwork to do, then I'm *gonna* meet you there." After all these years, I'm still waiting for him. He never showed up once.

How's this for a twist: The second time we worked together, I was *his* boss, at Graham Tire, and he was *my* commercial truck tire salesman. The store quickly lost money after I hired him, and I was fired. Dan wasn't stealing, but a lot of the times he was selling at, or below cost. I think what happened was, he had the attitude, "Any sale is better than no sale." Thus, the expenses were much more than the profit he was bringing in. I'd been warned about hiring friends, but I was too stubborn to listen. I knew Dan had it in him to be a good salesman, and I needed to quickly fill the position. We're still friends, but we know better than to work together ever again.

**\*\*\***

Sonny was a lawyer. We met while jogging at the local YMCA. We'd run three miles a day. When you are young it is possible to run and still do drugs. I sold a lot of pot to Sonny. We became good friends, and eventually he was the lawyer in my divorce. Sonny quit doing drugs, and is a magistrate judge in an Iowa town. Kind of funny—now he is handing down sentences to people who're caught with drugs.

**\*\*\***

Jim, one of my coke "grammers" quit buying from me and began getting his stash from Dana. a heavy hitter in town. Dana was very well known in drug circles as a big player, dealing cocaine. Jim and Dana became great friends and, with the profits from the coke, bought a nightclub in a nearby town. They eventually sold the club and opened up several restaurants. Now, who says you can't have an illegal profession buy your way into legitimacy? I'm sure if people figure out this puzzle, they'll be very surprised. That is why I didn't mention the last names of the people involved, or the businesses, or what town it really happened in. I wanted to protect the guilty. But it did happen just as I described it.

**\*\*\***

I met Mark while bartending at Rustler's, the college bar. Mark liked to shoot pool and play foosball. He was also quite fond of alcohol and all kinds of drugs. Mark went on alcohol and drug binges that lasted for days. All of his friends and I were amazed that his wife put up with him as long as she did.

Mark was fired from a job when his boss came into the office unexpectedly one night to find Mark and a girl, naked as jaybirds, and having sex. I'm sure that wasn't the deciding factor, even though they were doing it in the boss's chair, but the lines of cocaine on the desk probably were the last coffin nail, as the saying goes.

Mark grew up in Omaha, making him a Cornhusker fan. Another reason we became friends. Mark and I decided to go to Lincoln to watch a game.

Mark said, "Could we take your car? Mine's not working too well."

"Sure, not a problem."

I wanted to drive anyway. That way I could lobby to visit my brother, Jeff, while we were there. When we were on the highway, Mark pulled out two containers. One had cocaine in it, and the other had what's called "peanuts"; which is what you get when cocaine is mixed with baking soda, then just enough distilled water is added to moisten and heat it with a lighter to harden, so it can be smoked.

"Which one do you want?" Mark held out one in each hand.

I frowned. "I might do a line or two, but I won't smoke it."

"Suit yourself." Mark pulled out his pipe and began to fill it.

Smoking cocaine gives you a faster and more intense rush than you get when you snort it. As soon as Mark finished a bowl, he'd begin the process of getting another one ready, which took about ten minutes. This went on the entire trip to Lincoln, and continued all night long in the hotel room we shared.

I tried to get some sleep, but I kept hearing Mark's lighter, and then the sound of him inhaling, and eventually coughing. When I woke up in the morning, the mirror was off the wall, and covered with a towel, the curtains were closed, and the rest of the towels were at the bottom of the door. Mark had his face pressed against the wallpaper.

"What in the hell are you doing?" I let out a chuckle.

"I'm looking for a camera in the pattern of the wall paper," Mark said, dead serious.

"Why is the mirror off the wall?"

"Some hotels have two-way mirrors…I'm not taking any chances."

I began to laugh. "If you took it off, why did you cover it?"

"I thought I could see someone looking at me."

I found out that smoking cocaine makes you very paranoid. I never tried hard drugs (acid, mescaline, or heroin)—I always wanted to be in control, rather than having the drug control me.

I don't know if Mark enjoyed the football game. He didn't have any sleep, and was out of peanuts. I'm sure that going through withdrawal was no fun. I remembered when I did cocaine, going up was great, but coming down absolutely sucked. That's why addicts are always looking for that higher high. He was on edge during the game, and just about got into a fight with the guy sitting in front of us who was rooting for the opposing team. One of the things about cocaine is when you are out of it, you crave more; and smoking it has to be even worse.

He really pissed me off on the way back home. As we were nearing Omaha, Mark pleaded, "Could we please make a quick stop? I really need to see a friend of mine."

He gave me directions to the parking lot of a warehouse.

Mark grabbed a bag from under the seat of my car and said, "Come on in with me."

I followed him inside to an office where a guy was sitting behind the desk. Mark shook his hand, and introduced me as a friend of his from Fort Dodge. After a short moment of pleasantries, Mark opened the bag and took out two ounces of cocaine. My eyes got big as manhole covers. I didn't know that I was driving with them in my car, or that it was in the hotel room while he was smoking. The only times that I like surprises is on my birthday, and at Christmas. I was always smart in my dealings, and this was absolute stupidity!

Even though Mark was out of peanuts for the game, he didn't break into the bags for two reasons: One, he couldn't sell both ounces if he had taken some out. Two, when you're smoking cocaine, snorting it is like going from Camel cigarettes to candy cigarettes. You have to do so much more to obtain the same buzz you're used to.

They cut some lines on the desk, and asked if I wanted any. I refused which I'm sure made his friend uncomfortable. At that moment I was sure he thought I was a narc. I could tell by the look on his face.

I said, "No thanks. I prefer to just smoke pot."

"Are you a cop, or something?" he yelled at me.

"No, I'm not." I said weakly, "I just don't feel like doing any."

Then he insisted that I do a line as he lifted up his shirt exposing a gun. Suddenly I was more than happy to do a line; or two, if he wanted me to. Besides, I didn't know him, or what he was capable of doing to me if I refused. Being an ex-dealer, I know the uncomfortable signs when there are three people in a room, and one could possibly be an informant. They finished conducting their business, and we left for home. On the way, Mark could see that I was very upset.

"Rick, I'm sorry," he said all nonchalant.

"What in the goddamn hell were you thinking? You should've told me you had all that cocaine on you. What if we got pulled over?" I was so pissed off I was spitting as I was yelling.

"I would've told the police it was all mine, and you didn't know anything about it."

"Yeah, if I was a cop, I'd buy that—ever heard the word 'accessory'," I glared at him. "It's my car, and we crossed state lines with it. I've been down this road before, and I can't afford to get busted again. Fuck you."

I looked straight ahead the rest of the way home, too mad to even look at him. In fact, if I thought he could've called someone and got a ride home I would've dropped him off on the side of the road.

Mark kept apologizing to me all the way home, but I was too pissed off to accept it. We are still friends today, but it took awhile before I could forgive him for his idiocy. Of course, whenever he throws a party at his house, I never miss the opportunity to tell the story while imitating him standing with his face two inches from the wallpaper, desperately searching for the hidden camera.

\*\*\*

Crazy Larry was a friend of Sammy's. He was about five-feet-five with hair hanging down to the middle of his back, and a beard just about as long. We met at Sammy's house during one of the many parties there. I never trusted him, and he gave me many reasons to feel that way. I learned to always bring my own bottle of rum to a party with Crazy Larry in attendance. He'd spike his bottle with several hits of LSD, then offer to make you a drink. I was smart enough to see the acid floating in the rum and always refused.

I was out to a bar one night, drunk as I could be. I wasn't sure if I could drive home. Believe me, there were several times I woke up in the morning and ran to my bedroom window to see if my car was in the driveway, having no recollection of driving home, or even getting into bed. This particular evening, I was in the same shape when in comes Crazy Larry.

I stumbled over to him and said, "You got any speed on you? I'm too drunk to drive, and I need some uppers to help get me home."

"Sure thing, Rick." He reached into his pocket and pulled out some white pills. "How many do ya want?"

"Better give me five or six, I'm pretty drunk."

"Okay, here you go," Larry said with a big smile.

I popped the pills in my mouth and washed them down with the rest of my rum and Coke.

"What's with the grin, Larry?" I asked.

"I just gave you some downers instead of speed," he cackled. "You better get home before they take effect."

"You asshole," I said, staggering out the door. I drove for a block, slept for an hour, drove for a block and a half, slept for an hour and a half, etc., all the way home.

Another time a friend from college came to my house with two good-looking girls who wanted to get high for their first time. I was out of pot at the time, but I knew Crazy Larry always had some. We drove to his house which was fifteen miles away, and out in the country. I took them all inside and explained the situation to Larry.

"I've got just what you need," he said with that maniacal chuckle of his, and went into his bedroom. He was in there for several minutes before he walked out with a joint that looked like he had slobbered all over it. I was trying to figure out why it was so wet. Whenever I rolled joints, I licked the paper just enough to stick together.

Crazy Larry said, "You'll have to wait a few minutes until it dries."

We all sat in his living room, but the girls were getting very uneasy with him and his off-color humor, and wanted to leave. The joint had dried, and out we went. On the way back to Fort Dodge we took turns inhaling the pot. I was getting extremely high, and the girls were flipping out. Being their first time, they didn't know what to expect, but they'd never experienced anything like this before in their lives. I could hardly see the colors of the stop lights as we came into town, and it was getting difficult to drive my van.

The girls were screaming, "Take us to our dorms! We're freaking out!"

"That's where I am headed," I said, trying to calm them down. I dropped them off and barely made it home myself to lie down and pass out.

A couple of days later I ran into Crazy Larry. "What the hell kind of pot was that? Everybody got seriously f'ed up on it."

"It was just regular pot…" he grinned like the Wicked Witch. "Then I rolled the joint in liquid morphine. I thought the girls would enjoy a good buzz for their first ride."

I shook my head. "I can't believe you did that to them. They were going totally out of their minds, wacko, all the way back to Fort Dodge."

Larry busted out laughing and walked away.

I was working at Goodyear one Saturday when Crazy Larry walked past the store.

I went to the door and yelled, "Hey, Larry, what're you doing?"

"Walking home—I lost my license," Crazy Larry cackled. He somehow found this humorous—or maybe C.L. laughed at everything, notwithstanding.

"I'm just about to close the store. I can give you a ride." Even though he was often a dick, didn't mean I had to be one. I knew he had moved into town, but I wasn't sure where he lived. He gave me the address and off we went.

On the way to his house, Larry said, "Lemme get you high for giving me a ride."

I accepted his offer even though I was somewhat leery from my last experience. I followed Larry up the walkway to his house, which only had six rooms in it, and I could smell the pot already. Once inside, I looked around and five of the rooms had large pot plants in them with expensive grow lights everywhere. All the windows had blankets covering them, so no one could see inside. I felt very uneasy. I didn't know whether to smoke a quick joint, then get out—or just do the latter.

"Aren't you afraid of getting caught?" I asked, surveying his indoor plantation.

"Fuck no," he chortled, "the police are stupid."

"What about the high electricity bills, and the *smell*?"

"Not worried about it." He shrugged casually.

I'd already got my buzz just standing there. "Well, now I know why they call you Crazy…Larry," I said and took off out the door.

✳✳✳

Fast Eddie was a member of the local biker gang. He lived a wild life, and had a look to match. I was introduced to him through the gang's Sergeant of Arms, Brian. Fast Eddie's claim to fame was his invention of the lighted bobber. He did a lot of night fishing and noticed it was hard to see if you had a fish on the line. He came up with the idea and had even built the prototype. His problem was getting his product mass produced by finding a company to license it.

Eddie traveled down to Memphis trying to find a buyer, and was close to making a deal, but he needed seed money to make it all happen. Eddie also sold cocaine in Fort Dodge. He was one of those big fish that kept the heat off of me. Fast Eddie didn't know he was being watched by the Feds. Eddie's connection was in Miami. He flew down there to set up the deal and bring the product back to Fort Dodge for distribution. Everything was going as planned until Eddie got to the Atlanta airport with his suitcases. He was immediately surrounded by ten agents with their guns aimed right at him. Busted with thirty pounds of cocaine! Eddie was sentenced to twenty years in federal prison, and the lighted bobber became someone else's invention.

***

Heavy, as he was called, was three hundred plus pounds. It was one of those times that the nickname perfectly fit the guy. Heavy was a big dealer in Fort Dodge. He sold all types of drugs to anyone who'd buy them, including young kids. I never approved of that, so I stayed away from him and his house.

One of Heavy's rules was if you were a female you had to give him a kiss and a hug when you entered his house. It either made him feel powerful, or he got his jollies that way. The few times I was around him, at someone's party, he was a bit too full of himself for my taste. I have no idea how he came into possession of it, but Heavy had a full-grown lion that he kept in his backyard.

As the story goes, one day the fire department responded to a neighbor's report of a cat stuck up in a tree. Can you imagine the look on the rescuer's face when he was expecting a defenseless kitty and came eye-to-eye with a "man-eating" lion? Allegedly, the guy screamed like a little girl. Between the complaints about the lion, and constant traffic of kids coming and going, he often had the police dropping in to say hello. I've never heard to this day if Heavy is still incarcerated, or a free man. I think the lion was donated to a zoo.

***

Frank was a singer and guitar player in a rock & roll band. He also was one of the owners of the recording studio I mentioned earlier. Frank and I hit it off right away and became good friends. I worked for hours on end with Frank recording his songs, and other bands that came into the studio. Frank was a perfectionist. He never wanted anything that had his name on it to leave the studio without it being absolutely perfect in his opinion, even if it took days or weeks to achieve.

Frank's father-in-law, Bob, was told by medical specialists that he had an aggressive cancer. Bob wasn't given long to live, but he was determined to beat the disease. Frank was not satisfied with the treatment regimen for cancer in the United States; he took his father-in-law to the Bahamas. A clinic there was practicing methods that weren't approved by the FDA—but the patients were living longer. After several weeks of treatments, they returned to the United States. Bob lived for five years beyond what the U.S. medical doctors had predicted.

Frank has become an advocate for research on nonconventional methods to treat cancer here in America. At times, Frank has been called a quack by various traditional doctors. Frank has an alternative medicine website, People Against Cancer.com. Frank has personally taken many dying patients to all parts of the world to help them find the right cancer treatment specifically for them. I could go on and on about Frank, but I hope to be able to write my next book about his struggles and successes if he will let me. Frank definitely has a great story to tell. More about Frank in a later chapter.

**\*\*\***

Little Willie, a five-foot three-inch black man, was the janitor at Iowa Central Community College in Fort Dodge. He was the one who had to clean up all the weekend puke on the dorm floors (though often it was weekdays, too.) Willie and I got to be good friends. He was easy to talk to. During one of our conversations, I found out that Willie owned a bar down in what is called The Flats. It is the predominately black section of Fort Dodge. Back in those days, the police drove straight through that section of town in their patrol cars and rarely got out. The only time they made an arrest was when the majority of the police force participated. They were afraid to attempt it with only one car.

"My bar stays open till four in the morning." Willie smiled and patted me on the back. "You oughta stop down some time."

One evening, after the rest of the bars closed at two, I felt I wasn't quite drunk enough yet, and decided to take Willie up on his offer. I thought, *What could go wrong? Willie will be there.*

I staggered into Willie's place and immediately noticed I was the only white person there. The bar wasn't very well lit. There were only a couple of lamps and the light coming off of the neon beer signs. Several regulars walked over and surrounded me. I felt like the white portion of an Oreo cookie.

The biggest of them gave me a little shove, "Wha-chu doin' here, boy?" The buzz I had when I walked in was gone. I went from staggering to shaking.

Have you ever had that feeling…that you are in the wrong place at the wrong time…and there never really is a right time? Well, welcome to my world. I looked in the direction of the bar and saw Willie. I shouted, "Willie, I could use some help here."

He recognized my voice and assured the fellows that I was cool. I walked over to the bar, sat down, ordered a rum and Coke.

I said to Willie, "Man, am I glad you're here. I think they were going to beat the shit out of me."

"They don't see many white folk in here, 'specially after two in the mornin'," Willie explained.

"You invited me down here the other day, so I decided to come check it out." I was so nervous I was practically shaking the ice out of my drink.

"Well, next time ya might wanna give me a heads-up you comin'," Willie reared back having a good laugh on me.

Even with my back turned I could feel the ice-cold stares bearing down on me. I thought, *If I don't get out of here soon there won't be a next time.* I downed my drink, thanked Willie for helping me, and headed for the door. The entire bar tracked me with their eyes as I crossed the room. I was praying that none of them were going to follow me to my car, and thank God they didn't. For the record, I've never been back. That first experience has lasted me a lifetime.

**✳✳✳**

When I first met Jack, he was a Goodyear mechanic. Jack wasn't the most hygienic person I've known in my life. He was known to show up for work in the same wrinkled uniform he had worn and even slept in all week long. And it was often covered with dog hairs from the mutts that shared his couch where he generally passed out for the night. Yes, Jack loved his booze. Sometimes I thought he only worked to be able to afford his alcohol. All the same, we hit it off from day one and have remained friends all these years.

Sometimes, Jack and I met an hour early in the morning at Goodyear to get high before everyone else showed up for work. We usually smoked behind the store. One morning it was too cold, so we decided to catch a buzz in the backroom where flat tires are repaired. Just as we were polishing off the roach, the door to the backroom flung open.

I thought, *Who the hell is coming to work this early?*

I turned around and saw a brown uniform with a shiny badge on it. Standing in the doorway was a State Patrolman. I was having flashbacks of my past experiences with the law…handcuffs…and I figured I'd be losing my job. As luck would have it, Jack was also smoking a cigarette in between hits on the joint. I shoved Jack as hard as I could toward the patrolman. The distance was about thirty feet from the door to where we were. Jack quickly realized what I was doing. He began puffing on the cigarette as fast as he could to mask the smell of the pot.

Jack put an arm around the cop's shoulder and guided him up to the front like they were best buddies. "Hey, Bill, how's it going?" I heard Jack say. " You weren't supposed to drop your cruiser off until seven-thirty."

By then I'd opened the large overhead door, grabbed an empty clipboard, and was furiously fanning the smoke out. After that episode Jack and I agreed never again to tempt fate by toking at work.

The last time I was in Ohio for Goodyear training, Jack was going to pick me up at the Des Moines airport upon my return.

Midmorning, I boarded the airplane from Cleveland to my layover in Chicago. About thirty minutes into the flight, I noticed the plane had banked a hard turn to the right, which was my side of the plane…I could see the ground out the window almost straight below.

The captain came on the intercom: "We are experiencing a problem, and I have decided to turn the plane around and to go back to Cleveland. There is nothing to worry about."

Ten minutes later, when I looked out my window again, I noticed that all I could see was Lake Michigan. Before, I'd seen towns and fields. I thought, *If there's nothing to worry about then why are we taking the water route back to Cleveland?"*

Once we'd landed, and were taxiing on the runway, the captain's voice came over the speakers again: "I want to let everyone know the reason we came back to Cleveland is because we lost power in the number one engine. We are going to have a mechanic look at it and we should be back up in the air as soon as possible."

I looked around me. Most of the other people were getting off to try to find another plane to take them to Chicago. I agreed it sounded like a good idea, but by the time I got to the ticket counter, I found out all current flights were booked solid, and it'd be two hours before I could get another flight. This meant I'd miss my connecting flight to Des Moines.

I went back to my original gate and asked, "How much longer do you think it will take to fix the engine?"

The female ticket agent smiled at me and said, "Not much. I think they got the problem fixed. You can get back on the plane and take your seat if you want."

Back in my seat, I looked around and noticed that only twelve other people were on the plane. That was a far cry from full capacity an hour ago.

The captain's voice came over the speakers: "Ladies and gentlemen, we should be taking off in approximately thirty-five minutes. We had an oil sending unit go out on the engine and a new one is being installed. Thank you for your patience."

After the repair was completed, once again we took off for Chicago. Upon landing, I sprinted through the airport, dodging people and leaping over anything that got in my way. I was completely out of breath when I reached the gate, and I noticed the door to the boarding ramp was closed.

I pleaded to the attendant behind the counter, "Am I too late for flight 1080 to Des Moines?"

"See that plane taking off?" She pointed out the window to a dot that was disappearing in the sky. "That's flight 1080."

I let out a sigh of defeat. "When is the next one for Des Moines?"

She hit a bunch of keys on her computer, then looked up at me and said, "The only remaining flight today for Des Moines is at 8:45 tonight."

"That's five hours from now! What am I going to do?" I threw my hands up in despair. "It wasn't my fault I missed this one, the plane I was on was late because of engine trouble."

"I'm sorry, sir," she said with that practiced airport nonchalance, "there is nothing I can do about that. Do you want me to book you on flight 1565 for Des Moines or not?"

"I have no choice," I said irritably, "but I have another problem."

"Yes?"

"I have a friend picking me up in Des Moines who has no idea I am not on that plane."

"What's his name?"

"Jack Smith."

She held up a reassuring finger, "I will call the Des Moines United Airlines desk and make sure they give him the message."

"Thank you." *Wow,* I thought, *they actually do care.*

Now I had five hours to kill in the airport. I bought a *Chicago Tribune* Sunday paper that was as thick as an unabridged dictionary. I sat down and read every page of it from one end to the other. I was able to kill about two hours. The rest of the time I just observed people as they passed in front of me.

People watching is a great pastime, especially when they have no idea you're doing it. A game I like to play is asking myself, *If someone in this airport was a hijacker, which person would it be?* Then I cross my fingers they don't board *my* plane.

When I finally arrived in Des Moines, Jack walked up to me a bit bleary eyed and said, "I stood at the gate and watched as ever' one got off the plane, but none of 'em was you. I even waited an extra ten minutes. But when I saw the captain and his crew leave, I knew something's wrong. I go to the ticket desk and ask if you're on the flight. I 'bout shit my pants when they ask me if I'm Jack Smith. I said yeah, and she says you missed yer flight but yer on the next one landin' in five hours."

Since Jack had a long wait for me, he decided he'd pass the time in the lounge. Let me tell you, at five dollars per mixed drink, I had one hell of a bar tab to pay. I helped Jack to his car with one arm, while dragging my luggage with the other. Soon as his butt hit the seat, he passed out cold, and I ended up driving us home. To this day, Jack has no memory whatsoever of "picking me up" at the airport.

***

Timothy was in my broadcasting class in college. He was six feet tall with a baby face and black as coal. Timothy and I became great friends. I could tell him racial jokes, he'd tell me redneck jokes, and neither of us were ever offended. In fact, no matter at whose expense we'd laugh our asses off. He grew up in Sioux City, Iowa which is thirty-five miles north of my hometown. While at Iowa Central, I usually went home once a month. I'd give Timothy a ride to Sioux City on Friday night and pick him back up on Sunday. It wasn't the route I usually took since it was a bit out of my way, but I didn't mind.

We had to take a test to get our broadcasting licenses. Our choice for a testing office was Omaha or Minneapolis. Timothy and I decided on Omaha since I knew my way around there. Rather than getting up and making the long drive early in the morning, we drove to Lyons and spent the night. I took Timothy out to the Branding Iron bar knowing that while he'd be accepted there, he'd turn a lot of heads. Blacks are not a common sight in rural Lyons, Nebraska. Besides, I wanted to have one of those laughs at his expense. I think Timothy felt like I did when I was at Willie's bar. Although he was never approached by any rednecks, he sure drew a lot of stares.

I told him, "Don't worry. They may have cowboy hats on, but I don't see any ropes."

He didn't find it as funny as I did.

After college, Timothy got married to a wonderful woman, and has three children. Like me, he also didn't pursue a career in broadcasting. Instead, he has worked for the post office in Fort Dodge for thirty years. I run into him once in a while and we still laugh about our trip to Lyons.

To all my friends, I want to thank you for being there when I needed you. As far as the acquaintances go, I'm glad that I never got closer to any of you than I had to. It is said that you can tell a lot about a person by their friends. And, as far as I am concerned, that makes me a very blessed person. I have the fortune to be associated with buddies like Paul, Marv, and Bryan who'd give you the shirt off their backs and fifty cents of their last dollar.

# Chapter 20

# DAD

I got a call from Mom in November of 1988. I could immediately tell from the waver in her voice it was news I didn't want to hear. She said, "Your dad and I just got back from the doctor and he's been diagnosed with cancer."

I knew this day would come. When Dad was in his forties, he always carried a Butane lighter in his pocket. It broke and spilled the fluid down the side of his right leg, leaving a terrible looking blister. He put salve on it for years, but to no avail. I later learned that one of the signs of cancer is a sore that doesn't heal.

I told Mom, "I'll check to find a flight out and be down there as soon as possible."

I was in San Antonio two days later to visit Dad. We went to play golf together. I wanted to be able to do that with Dad while he still could. Dad took me to a course on the Air Force base. I thought it strange playing golf as military airplanes zoomed overhead. I hit a shot that landed by a pond. I went to find my lost ball and saw a ten-foot brown snake heading in my direction. I was screaming like a little girl as I ran back to the golf cart. I absolutely hate snakes of all kinds. That was one of those times I was happy to take a two-stroke penalty for a lost ball. I thought the golf might help take Dad's mind off of the cancer. After seeing the snake, I forgot about his cancer for a while. We had a great time bonding while I was there, but I had to go back to Iowa for my job.

"I will be back down here as soon as I can," I told Dad, "I love you."

Once back in Fort Dodge, I went to see Frank, the friend of mine from the recording studio days. Frank was one of the owners of the studio and a member of the band, The Hawks, that recorded there.

If you remember from the previous chapter, Frank's father-in-law was diagnosed with cancer and given a short time to live. Frank and his wife Denise were determined that there had to be other alternatives than chemotherapy and radiation. Their decision to take her dad to a hospital in the Bahamas that offered alternative treatment, resulted in five extra quality years.

Frank gave up a promising rock 'n roll career to dedicate his life to finding ways to beat cancer. It has been thirty years since he began his quest.

I was going to head back to San Antonio in January of 1989 for a meeting with Mom, Dad, my brother Cliff, the doctors, and my brother Jeff by phone, since he couldn't make it, to determine Dad's strategy to fight the disease. I wanted some knowledge before heading back down there and I knew I needed to talk to Frank first.

Frank taught me so much in the two hours I was at his house. He had me write down questions to ask the doctors so I could report back to him on Dad's condition.

I left the next day for Texas. The meeting was scheduled for two days later. It gave Cliff and me some quality time to spend with Dad. We did several things together like visiting the San Antonio River Walk and the Japanese Flower Garden. Mom and Dad had lived there for ten years but had never been to them. I don't know if Dad really felt up to going, but he was a real trooper and came along.

We went to the VA hospital; Dad was there for more tests, and the rest of us for our meeting. The doctors were trying to assure us that everything possible was being done. I'm sure that most of the time when people hear "cancer" from a doctor, you go numb and into a daze, and you don't listen to what else they say.

Immediately, I started in with my questions, "What kind of cancer does Dad have? Is it small or large cell? What stage is he in? What is your recommended method of fighting the disease? Is it curable, and if not, how much time does he have?"

The VA doctors turned to each other with a *Who the hell is this guy?* look on their faces. They thought they could waltz in to the room and give their normal cancer spiel on what they were going to do and then leave. Now they had to answer intelligent questions.

One of the doctors responded, "Your dad has oat cell carcinoma."

I said, "That is the better one to have, isn't it?"

"It is easier to treat," the doctor said, "and he is in stage two."

Frank told me that there were four stages, so two was better than three or four in my mind.

"We plan on starting him on chemotherapy," the doctor went on, "then doses of radiation."

Thanks to Frank, I knew chemo was basically injecting poison into the system, and it is a crap shoot of what it kills more of: the cancer, or the good cells.

I wasn't thrilled with the course of action, but we didn't have the money for alternative methods. That's why Dad was in a VA hospital to begin with, instead of Sloan Kettering.

I looked the doctor square in the eye to let him know I meant it when I said, "Don't give us the run around—give it to us straight." And we all held our breaths.

The doctor looked down at his chart and said, "Because the cancer is in his brain and lungs, we believe he has six months to live."

That was the bombshell. Even though you know one day it is inevitable, nobody wants to hear how long their parent has to live.

The doctor continued, "I have to ask…in the end do you want us to put Lou on a ventilator to keep him alive?"

"No…" I turned to my family, then back to the doctor, "we've agreed on this, and we don't want him to feel any pain."

After the meeting was over, we took Dad back to the house and discussed our options. Dad agreed to do whatever the doctor recommended. He was willing to fight the disease and even held out hope to win. Heck, he didn't let a heart attack get him down, and he wasn't going to let cancer beat him either.

I flew out the next day to Fort Dodge and immediately drove to Frank's house to give him the update.

Frank said, "I know you can't afford alternative methods, so what the doctors are recommending is probably the best way to go."

I went home, called Mom to tell her what Frank had said, and suggested they proceed with the doctor recommended plan of action.

I want to take this time in the book to say, "Thank you, Frank, for all of your help and mentoring. I hope you know that I couldn't have gotten through this ordeal without your advice and expertise. You were really there for me in my time of need."

My kids wanted to go down with me to see their grandpa before he died. I talked them out of it. I wanted them to have the memories of Dad when he was healthy, and not emaciated and in constant pain. I didn't enjoy watching him get rapidly worse, and I wasn't going to expose my children to that. I knew it probably wasn't fair, but I thought it was for the best.

When I went back to Texas a month later, Dad had lost even more weight. He went from 165 to 120 pounds. His face was all sunken in, with purple X marks on his head for the radiation points. When he ate food, he'd get sick. So, he didn't eat much, which explained the weight loss.

We decided to get Dad outside for some fresh air, and went to a golf driving range. Dad said he wanted to see me hit some balls. I didn't mind, but I wished he had the strength to hit them too. Alas, he was way too weak for that. This was the man who taught me the game and now he couldn't hit the ball.

I tried to smile when I'd hear Dad say in his weak voice, "Good shot Rick."

I was hurting inside, but I didn't want Dad to see my pain, or the tears in my eyes. I was glad that I had sunglasses on. I wanted to make Dad happy, and if it meant watching me smack golf balls, then that was what I was going to do.

I knew deep inside that Dad didn't have a lot of time left to spend with me. It was hard living seventeen hours away and knowing that I had to go back to my job. I was lucky to have an understanding boss who was more than glad to give me the time I needed.

After I got back home, I called Dad every night to talk to him, and to say every time before I hung up, "I love you, Dad." I didn't hear it from him growing up, but he was going to hear it from me.

I also told Dad, "I hope you were not disappointed in me, and feel that I let you down. If so, I want to tell you that I am very sorry."

In his weakened voice he said, "I have never thought that, in fact, I'm very proud of you."

I wanted to clear that up in my mind, so I didn't have to live the rest of my life wondering if I'd let Dad down because of my drug years. I know that a parent doesn't want their child taking —and much worse selling —drugs. Whether they admit it or not, I'm sure that my drug involvement hurt my parents to some degree and I'll have to live with that for the rest of my life.

A couple of years earlier I renewed my faith in God. I went to church classes and learned things about the Bible that I didn't learn in Sunday school. I read a passage about asking the Lord for forgiveness for your sins. I sent it to Dad to read at night, hoping it'd make him feel better. I also thought Dad needed to make amends with God, before his final day on earth, for all of his breaker-one-nine interruptions during church services. Dad wasn't a religious person at all, and I knew he could use some extra help to make peace with his God. I prayed to God every night, asking Him that Dad would be cured of the cancer; but if that was not part of God's plan, then please take him quickly, so he doesn't have to suffer.

Three weeks later, Mom called me and said, "Your dad was taken to the hospital and it doesn't look good."

Dad was admitted complaining of severe stomach pains. I remember for years Dad downing Bromo Seltzer almost every day. The doctors opened Dad up and found that his intestines had been completely ravaged by the cancer. The decision was made to close him back up and to just administer morphine for the pain.

The primary doctor told Mom, "Lou has no stomach left and he will probably not live through the day."

Mom called me from the hospital and gave me the bad news.

I called Jeff and said, "Dad is dying, I'm going to fly down. Are you able to get away?"

Jeff said, "Yes, but I don't have the money to fly. I'll have to drive down there."

I knew Jeff's car wasn't good enough for the drive, and mine wasn't much better. My wonderful boss overheard the conversation and said, "Take mine and drive careful."

I called Jeff back and said, "I'm on my way to Nebraska to pick you up."

I then phoned Mom, "I'm headed for Lincoln to get Jeff. We'll take turns driving, so we should be there by noon tomorrow."

"Okay, but please drive careful," she said.

Jeff lived four hours away. I drove like a man possessed and made it in three hours. I didn't have a cell phone back then, so I couldn't get updates as I was driving.

Once I got to Jeff's house, I called Mom, and through tears she said, "You don't need to hurry, Dad is gone, so take your time coming down."

Dad died at 5:00 PM April 24, 1989.

Of the six months Dad was given to live, he made it six weeks and then went quickly, and without severe, ongoing pain. I guess in that one respect, my prayers were answered.

I remember I almost dropped the receiver out of my hand. I knew Dad was going to die sooner than later, but hearing the words from Mom's mouth still sent shock waves through me. I wanted so bad to be there before it happened, so I could tell him goodbye and that I loved him one last time.

I turned to Jeff. "Dad has died."

Jeff was also in stunned disbelief. We got in the car and drove all night until we arrived at our parent's house. After lots of crying and hugging each other, Mom could see that we needed some rest before other relatives and friends started arriving. I lay down for a couple of hours, but I really couldn't sleep.

When I got up, Cliff had arrived. We knew that the arrangements had to be made. Mom, Cliff, Jeff, and I got in the car and drove to the funeral home. Since Dad was a veteran, he had the right to be buried at Sam Houston Cemetery.

We toured the funeral home looking at different casket options. That was an eerie feeling. It makes you think about your own mortality. You picture your kids having to go through the same ordeal when you die.

We couldn't afford their casket and burial program. The funeral director suggested cremation and showed us some urns. I suppose it's sad that money had to come into play, but unfortunately when you don't have it, there is no choice.

The next day, at one in the afternoon, we held hands and prayed as Dad was being cremated.

At the funeral service, a picture of Dad, the urn, and an American Flag sat on a table at the front of the church. This was my first funeral without seeing a casket there. It seemed really odd. I tried to be strong until the song *How Great Thou Art* was played. I choked up and couldn't sing the words.

In some people's mind Dad may have been considered a strong disciplinarian, but he taught his sons the importance of honesty and showing respect, and that has made me a better man, for which I'm very grateful today. I know that was how he was raised by his parents. Did I fear him when he got angry? Yes, but most of the time we, as kids, created the anger, and got the punishment we deserved. Would I want to change my childhood? Not at all, I am very proud to be his son. Did he always make perfect choices—like turning down that cement truck partnership in Los Angeles—no but he never once complained about what might have been. Although growing up in California and being a surfer dude would've been my preferred lifestyle.

Even though I knew Dad was in a better place and that his pain and suffering was over, it was still hard to imagine I'd never see him again. I do want to take this time to say, "Dad, I LOVE YOU and MISS YOU VERY MUCH!"

I've learned that cancer plays no favorites; it doesn't care about the color of your skin, if you're rich or poor, or your religion; cancer will take you if and when it wants to. You can fight it, but the majority of us will lose the battle. Hopefully, in the near future someone will come up with a cure. Too many people have had to see what this horrible disease can do to loved ones.

One of the hidden treasures in Fort Dodge is the Paula J. Barber Hospice Home. It is a comfort to know that when your time, or a loved one's, is near there is a place you can go to and die with dignity and peace. Unfortunately, my dad died in the VA hospital where at that time their only compassion was administrating morphine.

Hospice is considered the model for quality, compassionate care for people facing a life-limiting illness. Hospice provides expert medical care, pain and symptom management, as well as emotional and spiritual support tailored to meet the patient's needs and wishes, including the surviving family members. Death is one of the most important events in our life although most of us never take the time to plan for that day. Hospice is there to teach us how to appreciate the journey toward death in the same way that we treasure and plan for other significant events in our life.

Each year, while I was working at Graham Tire, we hosted a benefit for a nonprofit organization. Following my tour of Baber Hospice, I approached my boss, and said, "I know who we should raise funds for this year."

Mike agreed and when the two-day event was over, Graham Tire employees had raised $8,000 for the Home.

At Paula J. Barber Hospice Home, the staff and volunteers will go out of their way to make every last request a possibility. I think it takes a special kind of person with a huge heart who can witness death almost every day, and have to wake up tomorrow with a positive attitude. I know I couldn't do it. These extraordinary people cannot be paid enough for what they have to deal with. I'm sure in some cases they become very attached to the dying. In fact, the youngest person to go through the Hospice Home was a five-year-old boy, Jacob, who succumbed to cancer. That had to be tough to watch him die. Jacob was an Iowa Hawkeye fan. The volunteers decorated his room in the school colors, black and gold, for him. They even got him an autographed ball from all members of the football team. He had a smile from ear to ear. I was told he said that getting the ball was his happiest day ever. He had a twin brother who was there all day long playing and laughing with him until the end. If that doesn't touch your heart…you don't have one.

*Melanie and me, circa 2011*

## Chapter 21

# WHO KNEW?

On an ordinary day in March of 2011, I went to work as usual. One of the first things I do after I arrive is check my emails. I was disgusted by the excessive "spam" I was staring at. Just as I was about to gang delete them, one jumped off the screen at me. All it said was "RE: question." It made no sense to me; and it was as if a higher power made me click on it.

This is what I read: "Hello, I am not sure I have the correct person, so please forgive me if I am wrong. I was born in September of 1972, and recently found out my mother's name was Marsha Jones. I attempted to make contact, but I found out she passed away thirteen years ago. Upon speaking with a few people, the name Rick Carle was mentioned as the possibility of being my birth father. Again, I apologize if you are not him.

I was hoping you may be able to give me some background information, and I'd love to talk to you. I do understand if this may be hard, or if you have closed this chapter in your life. It took me about ten years to get to this point of reaching out in an attempt to contact my birth family. I hope to hear from you. If I have the wrong person, or if you are not interested in getting a hold of me at this time, please let me know. Thank you for your time--Melanie"

I fell off my chair-- not metaphorically—I was sitting on edge and slid off about midpoint through the letter. Part of me was absolutely elated, and another part felt ashamed that I hadn't looked for her. I got back in the saddle and read it two more times. I couldn't believe after all these years she'd found me. I then printed it out and began formulating my thoughts on how I'd respond. I wasn't sure how much information to give her. But I was extremely happy with a smile as large as Alaska on my face, as I read her email again and again and again. I felt on top of the world at that moment.

I wrote back: "I am your birth father and Marsha is your mother. It's too bad that Marsha died of ovarian cancer. I know she would've wanted to see you and to get to know you. I thought this day would never come in my lifetime. I'm truly overwhelmed that you found me. I want to know all about you. Where you grew up? Where you live now? How was your childhood? When were you told that you were adopted?" I had so many questions for her and I couldn't wait to hear the answers. We emailed each other a few more times. I finally worked up the nerve to ask if it'd be okay to call her. Melanie said yes and forwarded her number.

The first night we talked for at least an hour. I was nervous and I could tell she was too. There were even a couple of times that we both sat in silence. Once we got past that, questions and answers were flying back and forth between both of us. I told Melanie about Marsha and me, and how events played out beyond my control that led to her being given up for adoption.

Melanie said, "It's okay, Rick, I've never been mad at you or Marsha. I was told by my parents at a very early age that I was adopted, and they helped me understand the situation."

To my utter shock, she grew up in Omaha until she was twenty. I don't know how many times I went to see either my brother Jeff, or Husker games in Lincoln, and drove right past Omaha. I found out she is married, has three girls, and is living in Southern California about two hours south of Los Angeles. That meant I now have four kids and ten grandkids. I had to keep pinching myself to make sure I wasn't dreaming.

We sent pictures to each other and couldn't believe the similarity in our faces. There was no doubt. I made copies and distributed them amongst my kids, Mom, and brothers. They saw the same resemblance that I did. In fact, Cliff said, If Mom would've had a daughter she'd look just like Melanie."

Melanie had made plans in July to fly back to Omaha to visit her parents, and was hoping we could meet. Rather than me going to Omaha, I convinced her to drive to Fort Dodge. It made the most sense. All of my kids and grandkids live here, and she could meet them all at one time. She met me at Graham Tire. We hugged for a long time; then she followed me out to Katie's house.

A perhaps interesting sidebar: The week before Melanie arrived, a couple of my kids were nervous and having second thoughts. My house is too small and I wanted to have the get-together at one of theirs. They suggested having it at a park. I found out after much inquiring they figured that if things didn't go well, they could make an excuse and leave. It's hard to do that if the party is at your house.

I said to my kids the night before she arrived, "Please see this from my side. Melanie was taken away from me all those years ago, and I didn't have a say in the matter. The Jones's ran the show and I wasn't even allowed an opinion. I have carried the burden with me a long time that I didn't fight harder for her—even though her adoption was a forgone conclusion. This is my chance to make amends. But I can't do it without your help."

Once Melanie arrived, my kids floored me with a complete 180-degree turnaround and welcomed her into the family with open arms. They began chatting away like long lost friends. In fact, it was hard for me to get a word in. We talked and talked for hours, and took boatloads of group pictures—you'd have thought the paparazzi were there.

Just before Melanie got in her car to leave for Omaha, I gave her a huge hug and said, "You have lifted thirty-eight years of guilt off my shoulders."

It brought tears to my eyes when she said, "Your welcome…" then the magic word, "Dad."

## Chapter 22

# LIGHTNING STRIKES TWICE

I n the Spring of 2022, Melanie called and told me about this site she was on called 23 And Me. You buy a kit, then spit in the enclosed tube, seal it up, and send it back to have your DNA analyzed. It can tell you about your ancestry, other DNA relatives you have, diseases that might run in your family, and more. She got on the site because her mother (my first girlfriend, Marsha) had died in her early forties from ovarian cancer. Melanie had wondered if any of those cancer traits, or other genetics, were possibly passed on to her. Luckily for her they haven't been so far. But she did find out that she has a one hundred percent match for a brother. She asked, "Could my mom have had a son?"

I said, "No, I don't think so. I know that when she remarried, she had two daughters…" but then I remembered: "When I was in college, a girl came to my dorm room, said she was pregnant, and claimed I was the father."

So, here's the story: I'm in my dorm room, smoking pot like I do practically every day. I hear a knock at the door. I open it a crack, and to my surprise there is a pretty blonde looking at me, somewhat harshly. And she's holding a legal-size document in her hand.

I say," Can I help you?"

She responds, "Do you remember me?"

I answer, "You look a little familiar. But no, I don't remember you."

She says, "We met at a keg party three months ago. And we had sex."

"We did? Boy I must have been really wasted. Because I sure don't remember that."

"Now I'm pregnant," she stated, "and you're the father."

When I was a young boy, I used to stutter once in a while. All I could muster out of my mouth was, "*Uba-dah, uba-dah, uba-dah.*"

She says, "Don't worry, I don't want anything to do with you. And I don't want you to have anything to do with the baby." Then she hands me the document and says, "This takes away any rights that you have as the father. All you need to do is sign it, and we are done with each other."

I was so stoned, and stunned; I didn't even read it. I took the pen she was holding out to me and signed it. And I never saw her again. Over the years I guess I just put that moment in the far-reaches of my mind.

Melanie suggested that I sign up for 23 And Me and give them my DNA. I told her I would, and in a few weeks I got back my results. It showed that in addition to the kids I had fathered with Karla, I also had a daughter named Melanie, which I already knew, and a *son* named Clayton, who were one hundred percent perfect matches. Clayton lived in Fargo, North Dakota. He was given up for adoption in Minnesota. I looked him up on Facebook and his picture was a dead-ringer for my older brother, Cliff.

Melanie had talked to him a few times. I decided to reach out, and sent Clayton a message on Facebook. He quickly responded and was interested in knowing more. He also wanted to find his birth mom and wondered if I had any information.

Unfortunately, it had been almost fifty years ago, and I couldn't remember her name, or give him anything concrete. Now, you have to remember, at that time it was the seventies. I've always said that when I moved to Fort Dodge to go to college, I didn't know anybody. When I started meeting the group of people who became my friends and acquaintances, they weren't book hounds, or A-students. If they had been, I might have ended up a doctor, or a lawyer. Instead, they smoked pot, drank alcohol, and on weekends went to keg and wapatooli parties. In my defense, that is why I ended up the way I did. I'm blaming it on my friends. Just like when I was a little boy—it's not my fault.

In case you were wondering what a wapatooli party is, let me explain. You get a 5-gallon bucket and pour in orange, lemon, and pineapple juice. You fill it up the rest of the way with bottles of vodka, rum, tequila, Everclear, and whatever other alcohol you have on hand. Then slice up apples, oranges, lemons, and any other fruit that is handy and toss them in. Add ice. Mix it all together and after a couple cupfuls and a few hits of pot, you'll have a decent buzz on that will last the entire night.

At these parties it was common to hook up with someone and engage in meaningless sex. Many times, the next day you'd be lucky to remember her first name, or even what she looked like. Depending how big both of your buzzes were, you might not even remember having sex. But the two of you did wake up naked, so you must have. Bottom line: Trying to remember a girl's name fifty years ago was next to impossible.

I got Clayton's phone number so we could try to figure this out together. I told him that I'd go to Iowa Central Community College here in Fort Dodge, and look through the 1974 and 1975 yearbooks to view all of the female student's faces, and see if hers would ring a bell. Once again, my memory bank struck out. Too many years of drugs and alcohol had taken its toll. But I did write down the names of possible girls that I might have dated. Of course, they had to be the 3 B's: Blonde, Beautiful, Bodacious. That was my type back then. After looking at approximately one hundred pictures, I narrowed it down to about fifteen possibilities, and sent the names to him. Clayton checked the names against the adoption records in different counties in Minnesota. He came up empty.

Clayton then hired a private detective who specialized in finding the parents of adopted children. Low and behold he was successful. Turns out his birth mom also lives in Fort Dodge. And I couldn't believe it…she lives a few blocks from me. Clayton reached out to her, and she was happy to hear from him. They met halfway between Fargo and Fort Dodge. His mom and I have not contacted each other after finding out about Clayton. I'm sure right now she is focusing on bonding with her son. But who knows, there might come a day when the three of us have what will definitely be a bizarre "family reunion". It's strange. All my life I thought I had three children. It blows my mind to know that I am actually the father of five kids!

## Chapter 23

# IT'S BEEN A GOODYEAR

When I was working for Graham Tire, I heard about a contest the Goodyear Tire Company was sponsoring. To enter, you had to write about a sales event you were having that promoted Goodyear tires. You were also required to take pictures, and send it all to Goodyear's racing department. I decided to use one of Graham Tire's annual silent auctions that we held for a local nonprofit organization. I chose the Paula Baber Hospice House, a place for terminal patients to spend their final days. I said it earlier, but it bears repeating: I've always been in complete awe of the people who work there. Besides family, the nurses and volunteers are the last person the terminal patient interacts with before they leave this earth. The staff takes care of end-of-life patients helping them feel as comfortable as possible; sadly, watch them die, and then do it all over the next day, and the next day. They are truly heroes in my book!

Instead of sending a bunch of 8 x 10 glossy photos with a paragraph on the back explaining each event picture, I put all of it on a DVD, complete with the song *Smoke on the Water* by Deep Purple, in the background.

The nationwide contest had two winners. Graham Tire was one of them. Four employees, Denny, Jason, Nick and myself were flown from Fort Dodge to Miami for the final Nascar race in November of 2010 at Homestead. This was after 9/11, so nobody was allowed to bring any bottles over three ounces in their carry-on bags. Nick didn't get that memo. The TSA ran his bag through the X-ray machine and they must have seen something fishy. They took his bag aside and searched it. The TSA confiscated a 64-ounce bottle of shampoo, and another one with conditioner. Nick was informed that the *illegal hair products* would be here when he got back. We gave him the nickname "GQ" because Nick always had to have his shirt and pants just right. His head needed to have every hair perfectly in place. And he would only use his specially-formulated shampoo and conditioner. He figured the hotel wouldn't have his brand, so he brought them with. He should've put them in smaller containers. Then again, he probably would've run out on the first day.

When we got off the airplane, we were greeted by a chauffeur holding a "GRAHAM TIRE" sign, who led us to a stretch limousine that was stocked with alcohol. We were driven to the Miami Hilton hotel near the beach. After we got settled in, we decided to go for a walk to see the sights, and to find a drug store so Nick could buy his special brand of shampoo and conditioner. We were cruising the boardwalk when Jason yelled, "Wow! Look at that!"

We snapped our necks around thinking we were about to see some beautiful, tanned, voluptuous babe in a skimpy bikini.

Instead, Jason was pointing to a 300-pound, leathery-skinned, elderly man, riding a bicycle and wearing nothing but a thong. His humongous butt cheeks hung off both sides of the seat. The only thing the bicyclist and our imaginary babe had in common was the tan.

Denny grumbled, "Why the hell did you want us to see that?"

Jason laughed. "You have to admit that is something you'd *never* see in Fort Dodge."

We all thought, *"Thank God."*

Jason had no idea that image would forever be burned in my memory.

Jack, our local Goodyear rep, also got to go, but he flew out of Des Moines. He had a very pricey Nikon D300-35 mm camera with various size lenses for any close-up shot he needed. Jack constantly snapped pictures of our entire trip.

As part of the prize, the next day, two H3 Hummer vehicles picked us up at the hotel and took us to the Florida Everglades. We visited an alligator farm stocked with 15-foot gators. They were lying next to a small lake, just sunning themselves. We were encouraged to go over and touch them since, the guide assured us, they were sleeping. None of us lost any fingers, or arms, or legs, so thankfully the guide was telling the truth. We also got to hold a 3-foot baby alligator. And for lunch we even tasted fried alligator. You know I gotta say it: I thought it tasted like chicken.

That night we were taken to Randazzo's Little Italy, a five-star Italian restaurant. The owner told us he was going to personally make whatever we ordered. The portions were so huge we could've fed a family of six with each of our plates. Jack ordered spaghetti and meatballs. His four meatballs were the size of baseballs.

The next day was race day. We were each given what is called a "Hot Pass" that we wore around our necks. It meant that we could go practically anywhere we wanted. We were in on the Driver's Meeting where they were given instructions for the race. Afterwards, I walked at least 50 yards side-by-side with Jeff Gordon, a five-time Nascar champion. I had a pen and paper in my hand, and asked him several times for his autograph. With all of his years of driving the loud cars I figured he must be hard of hearing. He never responded, and kept walking to his trailer completely ignoring me. Now I know why many people hate Jeff Gordon, he acted like an a-hole.

Another bighead was Dale Earnhardt Jr. When the meeting was over, he practically ran out of the room and back to his trailer, not even acknowledging one fan. Yet when you first arrived at the track, out front there were three big trailers selling his memorabilia. If his fans only saw what I did, they might change their minds about him, and think twice about spending their money on his stuff. I used to be a big fan, since he was the son of one of the greatest drivers ever. Not anymore. In fact, when the race was over, I observed him jumping out of his car, and once again darting to his trailer to avoid any fans.

Fifty yards away, I saw about 30 people in a circle, and went over to investigate, thinking maybe I could get an autograph from a driver who didn't have an over-sized ego. But the crowd wasn't surrounding another driver--it was Brett Michaels, the lead singer from the band Poison. He was there to perform on stage after the race. In just a few minutes, I was able to get his autograph, which for me was better than Jeff Gordon's, any day of the week.

We went to the garages to see the crews getting the cars tuned up before the race. During the race, we even watched the crews in the garage area put back together a car that had side-swiped a wall on one of the turns. We were amazed when in mere seconds they took off a wrecked bumper, and side panel, and installed new ones. Within about 5 minutes, the car looked good as new. I really came to appreciate the incredible job the crews do.

As we were walking around the infield, Jason yelled, "Follow me!"

We were wondering what sick thing he was going to show us now. But to our surprise, he led us to the Miami Dolphin Cheerleaders, who were posing for photos in their bathing suits. This time Jack put his Nikon on automatic and fired off about a thousand shots. Meanwhile, the rest of us got their autographs. And once again, that beats the hell out of a Jeff Gordon autograph, any day of the week.

We got to walk around the track to experience the feel of the turns, and even signed one of the walls with a Magic Marker. So, unless they have repainted the walls, my signature is still on the final turn.

Our passes even allowed us to get within 20 feet of the pit crews to watch them change tires during the race. After witnessing the amazing speed of the crews switching out several tires, we decided to sit in the Goodyear suite, which had plenty of alcohol and a huge food buffet. They gave us noise-cancelling headphones to block out loud cars as they raced by the grandstand. And we were able to listen to various drivers when they were talking to their crew boss, and the spotters warning them about an accident that was up ahead. I even met several of the race car owners like Ray Childress and Joe Gibbs.

The winner of the race was Jimmy Johnson. And by winning, he secured his 5th Nascar Cup Series Championship. Jimmy won two more championships before he retired, which tied him with Richard Petty and Dale Earnhardt for seven total cup series championships.

When the race was over, we all piled into a Goodyear chartered bus. There was around 30 of us on board. Most of the people were Goodyear executives, and the other four winners of the contest. We were given a police escort by four patrolmen on motorcycles. Whenever we approached an intersection, the officers pulled ahead and stopped the cars from all directions until we'd passed by. You could see the looks on the drivers' faces. They were wondering what famous people could be on the bus that they had to wait for. I'm proud to say, among those supposed celebrities were four employees from Graham Tire in Fort Dodge, Iowa.

I'd never been to a Nascar race before. I watched it on TV only if Dale Earnhardt Sr. was racing that day. But wow, what a way to lose your virginity at your first ever Nascar race!

That night, we decided to eat in the hotel's restaurant. We were finishing our meal when a hefty guy walked by the table. Jack said, "Hey… isn't that Greg Olson?"

Besides a Husker, I am also a big Chicago Bears fan. In fact, that night I was wearing a Bears' T-shirt to supper. I snapped my head around and exclaimed, "Where?"

Jack pointed. "The guy in the blue shirt, walking out of the restaurant."

I grabbed my camera, chased him down, and caught up to him at the elevator. Indeed, it was Greg Olson, the Bear's starting tight end. I'd recognize him anywhere. I nervously said, "Uh, Greg, can I get a picture with you? I'm a big fan."

I figured he was probably thinking, *"I just finished eating, I'm going to my room to rest, and this jerk stops me for a picture. What do I have to do to get away from people like him?"*

But when he turned around and saw my Bear's T-shirt, he grinned. "Sure, you can have a picture." This was before selfies and I got a random tourist to take the shot.

So, now I have a photo of myself and Greg Olson, with the elevator door as the backdrop, in a frame, hanging next to the Husker handkerchief in my man cave.

I went back to tell the guys about it in the restaurant. They couldn't believe I ran him down for a picture. But most football fans know that we're willing to do all kinds of crazy things in the name of sports.

✳✳✳

For the last part of our prize, all of the store employees were invited to the Iowa Speedway in Knoxville, Iowa on a Sunday, to drive a *real* Nascar. First, we watched a video; then we got suited up one at a time, put a helmet on, climbed into a race car, and were seat-belted in. Next, we drove eight laps around the track following one of the trainers in his car. The back of his car had special lights on it. If you saw a flashing yellow light, he wanted you to speed up. Flashing red meant: "Slow down idiot! You're on my ass."

We were also given the option (for $49.95) to have our laps around the track videotaped from inside the car. The video shows what we were seeing while driving. I knew this was a once-in-a-lifetime opportunity, so I ponied up the cash. How cool! I have played the video for friends, my kids, and grandkids. Grandpa the race car driver. Put that on your bucket list!

✳✳✳

The following year, I read in Goodyear's newsletter that they were having the contest again. I entered it with a different event this time. And what do you know? The Fort Dodge store won. Again!

301

This year's contest prize was appallingly different. For one thing, it was for only two people. And, instead of in Homestead, it was the first race of the year at the famous Daytona Speedway. After hearing about last year's race, six of the employees were dancing on tip-toes to go. Mike, the manager, wanted to make sure the selection of the two lucky employees was fair. I thought there should only be one other employee besides me, since I put the entire winning package together all by myself. Mike didn't see it that way. He took a pack of playing cards and ripped seven of them in half. He then handed each of us one half, and the other half was put in a bowl. Mike mixed them up, then announced, "When I pull out half a card, the person with the matching half goes. Fair enough?"

We all shook our heads, even though I was still thinking, *I should get an automatic pass!*

He pulled out the six of diamonds. Denny hooted and hollered. Next, Mike pulled out the two of spades. It was all quiet. Everybody was looking at each other. I looked down at my half and to my surprise, it matched the half I was holding. Luck was in my corner. Or so I thought…

Denny and I flew to Daytona in February of 2012. Things turned out a bit different this time. Goodyear had gone cheap. There was no chauffeur and stretch limousine waiting for us. We were given instructions before we left to locate a shuttle bus to take us to the Holiday Inn (and no Hilton) where we'd be staying. At the hotel, after checking in, Denny and I were given an information packet. Inside was the itinerary for our weekend. The hotel was paid for, but all other expenses were on us. The first contest had been an all-expense paid trip. This was "Sorry, you're on your own, folks."

The first night, Denny and I were tired from the flight, and we decided to eat in the hotel restaurant. We were browsing at the menu and noticed the least expensive item was a bowl of mac-and-cheese for $15.95. A hamburgers and chips was $21.95. Denny remarked, "It's a good thing you and I were the winners. All the other guys from work live week to week. They wouldn't have brought much money with them thinking Goodyear was paying for everything upfront. After two or three of these pricey meals they'd be broke."

Friday was a "Do it yourself" day. We walked around and found a rag-tag carnival with a few things to do, if you had lots of money to spend. So it was just sight-seeing for us that day. Friday night we splurged on a hamburger and fries for $27.95. Soda was extra. According to our packets, Saturday and Sunday shuttle buses were going at different times to and from the race track.

On Saturday we decided to go to the track. It was cloudy and starting to sprinkle when we arrived. We were given passes again, so we could check out the garages, and the infield. We heard Richard Kramer, the president of Goodyear, was at the garage where all of the Goodyear tires are mounted on rims for the race cars. We hightailed it to the garage, but security wouldn't let us in while Richard Kramer was inside.

Denny proclaimed, "We have passes. We're going in."

We got about ten feet inside before one of the president's refrigerator-size bodyguards told us to scram. We took our sweet time leaving, backing up slowly and craning our necks, trying to get a glimpse of the president and his entourage. The bodyguard finally shooed us out the door. We hung around a good distance away until the VIP and his retinue left. Denny wanted to see for himself the tires being mounted, since that was his main job at Graham Tire.

Right when we left the garage, rain started pouring down hard. I even saw a few cats and dogs. We ran from one garage to another, getting soaking wet, glancing at the race cars, until we got to the shuttle that took us back to the hotel.

On Sunday, we arrived to a light rain at the race track. The loudspeakers announced that radar was showing a possible clearing and the race might go on. That clearing never materialized. Once again, we got completely drenched.

We found a large building with a huge Goodyear Tire sign on it. Denny and I went inside. It was the Goodyear suite. Like last year it was stocked with alcohol and had a nice spread of food. We were stopped by a Goodyear rep and asked who we were. We showed him our passes. He told us we could dry off inside, and help ourselves to food and drinks. We stuffed ourselves like food was going out of style because it rained all the rest of the day.

The race was postponed to Monday, but that was the day we were scheduled to fly back to Iowa. I got ahold of Jack, the Goodyear rep who was in charge of our trip again this year.

Jack informed us that if we wanted to stay, we'd have to pay for the extra night in the hotel, and any difference in the airfare. Once again, what a U-turn from our first experience. It was hard to sit down with the Goodyear shaft up our butts.

Denny and I decided to stick to our original plans, and we flew back on Monday. Our flight took us from Florida to Texas, and then to Iowa. During our layover in Texas, the race had started. We found a TV in the airport to watch what we could before we boarded our final leg home. We were amazed to see there was a small delay in the race due to a passing rain cloud. Then these large jet dryers were brought on to dry the track, so the race could continue. When the cars were back on the track taking a couple warm-up laps, one of the drivers, Juan Pablo Montoya, on turn number three, hit one of the jet dryers, causing a huge explosion. Of course the crash looked much smaller on an airport TV compared to being there in person. In all, it was great to be at the legendary Daytona Speedway, but Denny and I could only imagine what it would've been like to see an actual race there.

Once we were back to Graham Tire, I dug out the Goodyear Racing rep's business card. I called and told her all about our terrible experience at Daytona. She said she'd make it up to us. She'd send us two tickets to any race that we wanted to go to, but we had to pay our own way to get there.

Denny and I chose a race in Kansas City, Missouri. It was only four hours away by car. When the tickets arrived, I decided I didn't want to go. I gave my ticket to Denny, so he and his wife could go together. They had a great time with plenty of sunshine. Goodyear never held the contest again. I guess when a small store in Fort Dodge wins in back-to-back years, it's time to shut the contest down.

*Me, Jeff & Cliff, 1989*

## Chapter 24

# PARTING THOUGHTS

I try to live my life today to the fullest. I share my knowledge and experiences with my children and grandkids. And I can't express in words how lucky I am.

As I write this, I am now retired from Graham Tire. I worked thirty-nine years in the tire business. I have proven that you can turn your life around from drugs and make something positive out of it. As I have said, I worked with a great group of guys, which made it easy to get up in the morning and go to work. I'm looking forward to enjoying my retirement that will include a lot of fishing and playing golf.

I feel healthy myself thanks to eating the right kinds of foods, fruits and vegetables, and I exercise every day. I have God in my life. He has been with me when I probably didn't deserve him. I don't preach my belief to others; I just live it for myself. My life, good and bad, is between God and me. In the end, it will be He who judges me, not anyone else on this earth. Just for the record, I didn't get religion after I quit doing drugs. I've always believed in a Higher Power. I don't want you, the reader, to think that I had a revelation, or that I quit for religious reasons. I quit simply because it was the smart thing to do.

Who knows, I might even get married again? That will be a tough decision though since I've been divorced for over thirty years. I didn't have what you'd call a happy marriage. But if it wasn't for Karla, I wouldn't have my pride and joy...aka my kids and grandkids. I'm sure there is a good woman out there somewhere, around a corner I haven't yet turned, who wants the same things I want in life, and there we'll be.

With getting older, I sometimes find myself getting stuck, wanting to have everything my own way. I have to live with the good and bad decisions that I made in my life. When I look into my past, do I wish that I had not experimented with and sold drugs? The answer is yes! But I can't change the past; all I can do is make the life I have ahead of me a better one. I do hope, after bringing my skeletons out of the closet, that the statutes of limitations have run out, or else I am screwed.

When you lead a second life as I did, you don't want normal, everyday people to know who you are. You just want to get through the day as stoned as possible without attracting any attention upon yourself. If I was high and in a grocery or convenience store, I'd purposely avoid anyone who didn't know I did drugs.

Dealing drugs is not a life I'd recommend *anyone* should get into. You are constantly looking over your shoulder. I rarely got a good night's sleep. Since most drug busts happen in the middle of the night, I constantly had the vision in my head of the battering ram knocking down my door, and the DEA boys rushing in with their guns drawn, then slapping on the handcuffs. No money that you make will ever replace that fear, or the stomach ulcers.

To quote one of Michael Jackson's songs: *I'm starting with the man in the mirror. I'm asking him to change his ways. If you want to make the world a better place, take a look at yourself and make the change.* It is possible for anyone to quit their bad habits. All you have to do is put your mind to it, be strong, stay positive, and don't let anything get in the way of achieving your goal.

My advice for anyone reading this book is to live your life to the fullest for today and to save for tomorrow. Life is too short to let it get you down. Do your best to remain positive and not dwell on the negatives. The next time you find yourself hating your life, remember: It's all about perspective. I have a friend who has sex at least once a day, exercises twice a day, reads two books a week, and yet complains how much he hates prison.

Make a budget for yourself and stick to it. Experience all that you can and share your blessings with people who are less fortunate. Respect is earned, not given. Be courteous to people; it doesn't hurt to say *Thank you, You're welcome,* or *I'm sorry.*

Some people who are unhappy with their lives think suicide is the quick and easy way out. They think suicide will put a stop the pain. Unfortunately, they don't consider how it will affect others. Your friends and family will be hurt in ways you cannot imagine. Don't be afraid to ask for help. You might be surprised by all the hands that are willing to be held out for you.

I got a call from Josh's wife once when they were having a terrible fight. She told me he was going to kill himself. I drove over to their house to find that he'd just left on foot. I was driving around the neighborhood looking for him when I heard a gunshot. My heart immediately went to my throat. I couldn't even swallow.

I was shaking and having a hard time holding on to the steering wheel. I actually had to stop the car, find my breath, and wipe away my tears. Part of me wanted to go where the shot came from and the other didn't want to see the aftermath.

For a parent, this fear of losing a child that way will tear you apart and break you down to the lowest point you've ever been in your lifetime. Several things were going through my head. *What could I have done? Why would he do this? Why didn't he wait until I got there so I could talk him out of it?*

It turned out one of the neighbors had just fired a gun into the air. The timing couldn't have been worse. I continued driving around looking for Josh; finally, my cell phone rang to let me know he'd shown up back at the house.

I gave him a big hug and said, "I heard a gunshot and thought you'd killed yourself."

Josh said, "I heard it too. I thought about it, but changed my mind."

"Promise me in the future if you ever get to that point in your life, you'll call me first," I pleaded.

"I will, Dad."

Then I told Josh, "No matter what you do, I will always love you."

✳✳✳

Try treating everyone you know or meet, friends and even not-so friends, like you were never going to see them again, and give them all the love and respect that is inside you. Do it without any thought of reward, and your life will never be the same, and you yourself will feel so wonderful! Furthermore, always tell the truth. When you lie it takes a long time to gain back the trust you lost. It's easy to keep the facts straight when they are the real ones.

I wish that someone would've taken the time to give me this advice when I was younger. I've told my kids this and I plan to share the advice with all of my grandkids.

Time waits for no one. Treasure every moment…it will mean even more when you can share your time and life with someone special!

Here's something I read—sorry I can't remember the source—that made me stop and think about what I do with my time:

1.  To realize the value of a family member, or a friend: Lose One!
2.  To realize the value of one second: Ask a person who survived an accident.
3.  To realize the value of nine months: Ask a mother who gave birth to a stillborn.
4.  To realize the value of one year: Ask a student who failed his final exam.
5.  To realize the value of a lifetime: Waste yours on drug, alcohol, or a gambling addiction.

I'm not the most religious man, or the most intelligent, but I am smart enough to know that all goodness on Earth comes through God. Without Him in my life I am nobody. Each time I pass the First Evangical Free Church, where I sometimes attend, I put my hands together and ask God to forgive me for my sins, and to please watch over my kids and grandchildren.

At church one Sunday, the pastor said, "We are not human beings going through a temporary spiritual experience; rather we are spiritual beings going through a temporary human experience." That statement made sense to me, especially if there is life after death.

Before I get to the end of this book, I'd like to take a moment to ask my family, kids, and friends for forgiveness. Being forgiven is not about forgetting. It is letting go of the past mistakes or old grudges and seeing the good in the person today.

I know that when they read this book, some of them will be shocked. They might have had some ideas that I smoked pot, but the revelation about dealing drugs may hurt them. If that is the case then I want to say, especially to my kids; Joe, Katie, and Josh that I AM VERY SORRY, and PLEASE FORGIVE ME for what I have done. I also want to tell them, I LOVE YOU.

I don't say it as often as I should, but I hope they know that I do love them with all of my heart. I've promised them I'll do a better job of telling them! I feel that I should've done more with them when they were younger. I sometimes put the drugs ahead of them. Maybe if I'd helped them become more interested in sports, or other social interests, Joe and Josh wouldn't have had to go through what they did. It was MY FAULT, and it should've been my responsibility as a parent. If I had just one wish, I'd like to go back into the past, and spend more time doing things with my kids, and less time doing drugs. I owe them that!

I tried to at least partially make it up by taking them and their spouses for an all-expense paid week to Las Vegas. Before you think it, yes, I know that a one-time trip can't make up for lost time, but I hope the effort was appreciated all the same. I've also instituted a once-a-month family get-together for supper at my house.

Cliff, my oldest brother, waited until he was fifty-seven years old to find the right woman for him. Cliff married the beautiful

Ryan S. Sands; they live in Los Angeles, California. Cliff is a writer and an editor. I have to thank him for his wit and wisdom, and for helping me with both books. Without your help there is no way I could have done this! Now I know the reason why I've always looked up to you!

Jeff, my second oldest brother, has a heart as big as the state of Alaska. He lives with his wife Theresa in Bancroft, Nebraska. Interestingly, in the house TC grew up in. Jeff and TC have been married for 40 years. That blows my mind only because of my track record with women. Jeff and TC are now retired and just kicking back on the farm. Being a huge Nebraska Cornhusker fan, I used to to see them once or twice a year, when they lived in Lincoln, to share a game or two at the stadium.

✱✱✱

In case I didn't make it clear earlier, I'm a huge Nebraska Cornhusker fan. GO BIG RED! Yes, I'm one of those crazy football fans you hear about. Even with all the years I've lived in Iowa, I'm still a true Nebraska fan, and will be forever. Let me explain. On game day I eat the same breakfast (two eggs scrambled, hash browns, and wheat toast) in the same restaurant, in the same booth. If someone is in "my" booth, I'll wait for them to leave. Some of the items I own are: A Tom Osborne autographed football, A red Nebraska #1 golf club, A red and white Nebraska Cornhusker windmill in my front yard, so I always know which way the wind is blowing. I put Cornhusker grips on all of my golf clubs. I painted my golf cart red and white. I bought and installed a twenty-five foot flagpole so I could have a large Big Red flag flapping in the wind on game days. I even painted my house red and white which really gave the neighbors a reason to wonder about me. At Christmas,

I take a long string of red lights and form the letter N on the side of my house. One of my neighbors asked me if it stood for "Noel". I had to set him straight. I have a light switch that says "Up with Nebraska and Down with Oklahoma". I bet not many people have a Big Red toilet seat. Well, I do! I have Cornhusker lamps, coffee mugs, tumblers, gloves, Christmas decorations, and the protector case on my phone. I have a Scott Frost autographed picture that is worth less today than the day I got it, since he had one of the worst records of any coach at Nebraska. I'd probably sell the picture if anyone is interested.

During football season, every Friday for lunch, I made a tailgate meal for the guys at Graham Tire. I made dishes from Chicken Fried Rice, to pulled pork sandwiches with cheesy potatoes, to roast beef sandwiches with au jus sauce for dipping. I did this for six years, cooking something different every week during the season. The guys really enjoyed it since one of the things I learned from my mom is how to cook. They'd be about to fill up their plates, but I'd hold up a hand and try to get them to say "Go Big Red" first. However, most of them were either Iowa Hawkeye, or Iowa State Cyclone fans, and wouldn't have any part of it.

I'd say to them, "You're getting a free meal, humor me."

Every once in a while, one of them mumbled it under his breath.

I found a way to somewhat get even. I'd take the cellophane wrapper off of a pack of cigarettes and place it upside down, so it will stand up by itself. Then, I'd say to an Iowa fan, "Look in there and tell me what you see?"

He'd respond, "I don't see anything."

I'd come back with, "Exactly. That is the Iowa national championship trophy case, and it is empty. Nebraska has five."

I wear an identical Nebraska T-shirt, Nebraska socks and shorts every game day. I even wear black underwear which is for the "Black Shirt" defense. Now, if Nebraska wins that Saturday, I wear the very same clothes the following Saturday for good luck. If they lose, then I put on a different set of Husker clothes until they win again. With the years of Scott Frost as the head coach, (his record was 16 wins and 21 losses) it was a good thing that I have lots of Nebraska clothes to wear. During his time as coach, I even bought a plaque that reads: "Grant me humility. I'm a Husker fan." With all the years of success that include five national championships, it is so f'ing tough to go through a losing season. That's why I take it hard every time the Cornhuskers lose. By now you are probably thinking this guy is either superstitious, or just plain nuts. Most of my friends and coworkers lean toward nuts. I don't care. And I'll say it again: GO BIG RED!

On Saturday October 29, 1994 Nebraska was #3 in the rankings until they lost to number two Colorado on that day. From where I sat, in my plush Husker quarterbacking chair, the officials made several bad calls. One in particular was a punt return by Colorado that scored a touchdown and eventually won them the game. It was blatantly obvious when you watched the replay that the refs missed one of the Colorado players clipping a Nebraska player in the back, who otherwise would've made the tackle. If the refs had thrown the flag and called the penalty, more than likely Nebraska would've won the game and moved up to #1 in the rankings.

One of the officials from the Big Eight was Dean Cramer. He was a retired coach from Fort Dodge. I knew Dean, and that following Monday I went to the YMCA to work out on my noon hour, hoping to run into Dean, who usually went there around the same time as me. Sure enough, I found him by his locker.

I had brought a rag with me from Goodyear, and threw it on the floor right by his feet. "Do you know what that is?" I scoffed. "It is a flag. And you should've thrown one for that clipping call you missed during Colorado's punt return for a touchdown."

After his surprise wore off, he calmly said, "It wasn't a clip."

"The hell it wasn't," I growled.

Dean replied, "Us refs always watch the game film on Sunday to critique ourselves. We saw the play you're talking about. We even replayed it several times." He shrugged. "Sorry Rick, it was not a clip."

"Well then you need to get a new pair of glasses, because you were wrong," I said with a grin.

Dean knew that I was just messing with him, and we shook hands.

A few days later I was at the YMCA again and Dean saw me. He said, "Hey Rick, I got something for you."

I raised an eyebrow. "Oh yeah?"

He handed me a handkerchief. I wasn't sure what it was until I unfolded it. Dean had given me the Game of the Century Part II handkerchief that the Nebraska fans were waving at Memorial Stadium for the Nebraska v. Oklahoma game in 1987. He had refed that game.

Dean said, "Maybe this will make up for how you feel about the clipping non-call."

I couldn't believe it. I took it home and framed it. I still have it in my Nebraska man cave in my basement. What a class guy Dean was. Oh, by the way, GO BIG RED!

\*\*\*

Joe, my oldest son, lives in Fort Dodge with his lovely wife Melissa. They've been married for 22 years. Joe and Missy have two wonderful children; Michael who is my oldest grandchild, and Makayla who is my oldest granddaughter. Both of them are very good at the Wii and computer games. Michael is the bar manager at the Sports Page restaurant. Makayla is a manager at the local McDonald's. I'm very proud of both of them. Joe is an avid Iowa Hawkeye fan and without my blessing he has brainwashed Michael and Makayla to think the way he does. Joe is the manager for the local Napa Auto store, while Missy is a department head at Target.

Katie, my daughter, lives in Coalville, Iowa five miles from Fort Dodge with her husband Jeff. They have been married for over 15 years. I've said many times that if I could've handpicked a husband for Katie it would've been Jeff. A dad is always fearful what a daughter can attract and bring home. Katie, you did a wonderful job. Katie and Jeff have two children, Addison and Emma. Addison is truly a sweetheart. She cracked me up with her innocence, and the unexpected things she does. For instance, whenever I pushed her on the swing when she was a little girl, she automatically started singing, "Ol' MacDonald had a farm…" Over a year ago, to pass the time, I sang that to her the first time I pushed her on her new swing set. It amazes me that she still remembers. Or, I'm sitting next to her on the couch, and out of the blue she'll chirp, "Grandpa, I love you!" That makes me want to laugh and cry at the same time.

Emma is the cutest little girl. When grandpa has problems doing something on his iPhone, he can hand it to her, and she will fix it in a minute. I wanted the app Spotify to listen to while I work out and wasn't sure how to download it. Emma said, "Grandpa give me your phone." She had it all set up for me in no time.

Katie is a nurse working for the Webster County Health Department, and Jeff is a foreman for a construction company in Fort Dodge. They decided to get a horse for Addie; but when you get a horse for one, to be fair you have to get a horse for the other. The second horse was too big for Emma. They decided to get her a smaller one and keep the first one for Jeff to ride. This way the girls didn't have to ride by themselves. Addie enters barrel races with her horse. She has won several competitions and was awarded silver belt buckles. They have also found how expensive horses can be. It didn't take the girls very long to figure out that cleaning up horse poop is more of a chore than dog droppings. I remind them, the bigger the animal the bigger the pile. For some reason they don't see the humor in it.

Josh, my youngest son, lives in Fort Dodge. Josh has three children; Kolten, Gavynn, and Brayden. At times the boys can be a handful, especially after watching a WWF wrestling match. Then they like to mix it up, which I'm sure most young boys do; but they are great kids. I've have taken each of them golfing with me. They like to go so they can drive grandpa's golf cart, but I also let them use a putter when I get to the green. Josh buys and sells rare coins. Kolten has moved to Ankeny and got himself a tech job. Both Gavyn and Brayden are employed at Caseys. When the boys were younger, and got into trouble, they were yelled at. Now I don't yell, rather I use the old grandpa wisdom on them.

Even though I've had my good and bad moments with my kids, I'd never trade them for anyone else. They are my special treasures. I'm so proud of each and every one! I am so lucky that they, and the grandkids, live so close to me, so I can see them whenever I want to. I am trying my hardest to make up for lost time.

With all the drugs that I did, all the bad decisions I made, I was still able to restart my life—and if you are in some kind of a predicament, I know that you can too. But you can't accomplish anything if you don't try. If this book helps someone else for the better, then my life was a success. That is all I can wish for.

Please give those you love a great big hug when they least expect it. Let those you love know it and tell them often. You can't say it enough. I didn't hear it as much as I would've liked, and that is why I don't say it as much as I should. Please don't let that happen to you, or the ones you love.

You only get so many chances in life to make the right choices. Think hard before you make your decisions. How will it affect your future, and the ones who love you? Will it be for the better, or will it be a disappointment? When you're not sure, ask for help. The dumbest question is the one that is not asked. Don't be ashamed, embarrassed, or think you are too good to help those in need. You'll be surprised how good it will make you feel. Do charity, or volunteer work. Be a mentor in someone's life.

We have the power to rid the world of racism, poverty, bigotry, hunger, cancer, and war to name a few, yet we choose not to. It all starts with the person you see when you look in the mirror each day.

Instead of seeing someone as a stranger, look at them as a friend you haven't met yet. We can change the world and make it a place where we all get along and live together in harmony and peace by just this simple action: Love thy neighbor!

**\*\*\***

I couldn't close this book without the following: A big "THANK YOU" goes out to all of the soldiers, past and present. If it wasn't for your service and sacrifice, we couldn't enjoy the freedoms Americans have.

The next time you think your life is tough, try looking through the eyes of a soldier in combat who just lost his arms, or legs, or sight due to a roadside bomb. Being in a foxhole and having your buddy shot and killed right next to you; and just when you think you are getting over it, another friend dies right in front of you. Our lives can never be as tough as what a soldier goes through. They deserve our utmost respect.

Go out of your way the next time you see a soldier in uniform and tell them you appreciate his or her sacrifice, and without it your life wouldn't be the same. I have witnessed firsthand the look on their faces, and it is priceless! You will make the soldier feel good about what they are doing, and it will make you feel good as well! Look at all the countries where life isn't free, and how they live. Be thankful you live in a free country. Most of all may GOD BLESS YOU, America, and those dear to you!

***

I've been asked why I wrote this book. I tell people, "We all have a skeleton or two in the closet. I just decided one day to open the door and write about whatever tumbles out." I didn't hold a thing back, even with the fear of the friends and relatives reading this and changing their opinions of me.

My life for better or worse is one that I have to accept. I'm glad that I was smart enough to finally make the necessary changes, and to make it one that I and those closest to me can be proud of. I try not to dwell on the past even though it has molded me into a better person. The present is all that I can truly control. What I do from here on is up to me. As I am getting older, I know that the choices I will make are going to be the right ones. I am living proof that anything in life is possible if you want it bad enough.

***

You have read in previous chapters about my outlaw years. I'm now going to introduce you to the leading citizen. While I was working at Graham Tire, the Fort Dodge Growth Alliance, which is a fancy name for the Chamber of Commerce, started a leadership program. The goal was to get young citizens involved in becoming the future leaders in Fort Dodge. The class was nine months long and met one day a month for the entire day.

The first day of the program was held at the Vincent House. The purpose was to learn about the history of Fort Dodge. The significance of the Vincent House is it was the first house in the country to use wall board instead of wood lath and plaster. Three men in Fort Dodge invented the wall board system. They were Ringland, Meservey, and Vincent. All three men became very rich for their time. When they died, they were buried in Fort Dodge's Historic Oakland Cemetery. Fort Dodge at one time had the most skyscrapers per capita west of Chicago. At that time a skyscraper had to be five stories or more.

***

Each month the leadership program went to different places to learn about the business. One day we visited the United States Gypsum Mill and drove down over one thousand feet into the pit to see the large excavators dig into the ground to take out limestone.

I heard an amusing story about a gypsum mill in Fort Dodge. George Hull, a cigar maker by trade, was into science and Darwin's theory of evolution. George believed that giants once roamed the earth. At a revival meeting George made a bet with Reverend Turk on the existence of giants, and he lost. Hull was pissed off and wanted his revenge.

In 1868, Hull and H.B. Martin hired some men to quarry out an 11-foot tall block of gypsum from a Fort Dodge gypsum mill. The men were told it was intended for a monument to Abraham Lincoln in New York. The block of gypsum was sent to Edward Burghardt, a German stonecutter, in Chicago. Edward hired two sculptors to help him create a "giant". All three were sworn to secrecy. When completed, the fake giant was over ten feet tall and weighed almost three thousand pounds. The men used several stains and acids so the giant appeared weathered and thousands of years old.

Hull transported the giant by train to his cousin William Newell's farm in New York state. It cost Hull $2600 for the hoax or $53,000 in today's money. One evening in November of 1868 the giant was buried on Newell's farm. A year later Newell hired two men to dig a well, and on October, 16, 1869 they found the so-called "Cardiff Giant". Newell charged the public fifty cents for a fifteen-minute viewing session. More than three hundred people a day were coming to his farm. People either thought the giant was a petrified man or a prehistoric statue. Hull sold his part-interest for $26,000 or $493,000 in today's cash. PT Barnum tried to buy it for $50,000 but was turned down. Barnum hired a man to make a plaster replica that he put in his show. Barnum claimed that his giant was the real one and the Cardiff Giant was a fake.

On December, 10, 1969 George Hull came clean to the press telling them everything about his hoax. Today there is a replica of the Cardiff Giant at the Fort Museum in Fort Dodge.

\*\*\*

This is for all you who grew up with dreams of being a policeman, fireman, nurse, doctor, etc., and it didn't work out for you. Or whose parents wanted you to follow in their footsteps by becoming a lawyer, or take over the family business, and you decided to do something else. So did I: Be yourself, not what someone else wants you to be. My dad was a meatcutter and owned a grocery store. He then bought a café after the grocery store burned down. I had no interest in following in his footsteps since the knarly surfing dude in California didn't pan out.

I saw the Clint Eastwood movie *Play Misty for Me* and after that I wanted to be a disc jockey. I moved from my childhood Nebraska home to Iowa to attend Iowa Central Community College in Fort Dodge to achieve my dream. After two years in the program, it turned out that a disc jockey was not in my future. I can assure you my childhood dreams were not cutting assholes out of cows at Iowa Beef, or selling Electrolux vacuum cleaners door-to-door and getting hundreds of doors slammed in my face. But those were the jobs I did. You may be thinking to yourself that those jobs are a long way from a disc jockey, and you're right. But, in my defense, I was married with children. Al Bundy sold shoes. I sold vacuum cleaners. And those jobs kept a roof over my kid's heads and food in their bellies.

At age 30, I began my career as a Retail Sales Manager with the Goodyear Tire, and then Graham Tire. I worked for four years in a tire store in Webster City, Iowa. In all I worked thirty-nine years selling tires and thirty-five of them in the same store in Fort Dodge. I got in my car each morning and said, "Take me to work." My car knew right where to go. If it could've driven itself, it would have. I only lived six blocks from work.

I was able to pay eighteen years of child support, pay off my house, and own several cars. Plus retire with no bills. The moral to my story is your life may not end up the way you had originally dreamed it would, but if you can find a job that makes you happy, pays your bills, and allows you to retire comfortably, your life will still be a success, and you'll be okay in how your life turned out.

Success is not what your parents or other people think of you; it's what's between your two ears that matters. Don't be afraid to stand up for what you want and believe is right for you. You are the one who has to live with yourself every day, and look in the mirror and be proud of what you're looking at. As the saying goes, "Just be the best you can be."

I got it in my head a long time ago that I don't care what other people think of me. After I got a girl pregnant at the age of seventeen, and was caught selling drugs at the age of eighteen, several adults in my hometown told me that I'd never amount to anything. Well, they were wrong! I am a happy man with very few regrets.

I have great children and wonderful grandkids who always make me happy, which proves to me my success in life. I'd rather hear "Grandpa I love you" than "You did a great job selling tires" any day. That is my success story!

You can go out and make your own. Whatever you decide is entirely up to you and no one else. Thank God we live in America where we are free to make choices. In your life, you will make good choices and bad ones, but they are your choices. Sometimes we have to pay the consequences for the bad choices we make. But that's life. Live yours to the fullest and enjoy each day, because you never know when your last one is coming.

When you retire, be sure you have some hobbies in order to stay busy. All the time you hear about people who retire and die six months later. They did nothing all day but sit on the couch and watch mindless TV. I go to the gym at least five days a week, and do up to four miles on an elliptical machine. I'm building up my cardio. Three times a week I work out on all the of weight machines to build up my muscle mass. I might even hit my golf shots twenty yards farther than before. I am working on this second edition of my book, and putting together the annual Oakland Cemetery Walk. I love retirement! Best job I have ever had.

***

While I was writing this final chapter, I went down to San Antonio to help my mom achieve one of her dreams. She wanted to be living in her house when she reached 100 years old—and then some. At age 99, Mom had fallen a couple of times and unfortunately broke *both* of her hips. I stayed there for seven weeks, helping Mom go through rehab. During that time, she had a wonderful 100th birthday party with many friends and all three sons.

Hayward had onset of dementia; Mom was still sharp as a tack, but struggled to get around, even with a walker. My brothers and I began floating the idea that they needed to go into assisted living, so that after we went back home, we'd have the peace of mind they were being well taken care of; because they clearly could no longer cook and clean for themselves. And a year-round live-in nurse was out of the question ($16,000 / mo.). Still, against all reason, they fought tooth and nail about staying in their house.

I stayed an extra—what was one of the longest—months of my life, trying every day to prevail upon the two hunkered-down parents. At the eleventh hour, I finally convinced them they needed to go. Hayward's son found a place called Country Life—and it *was* out in the country—20 miles outside San Antonio. But the facility was cozy and the staff was wonderful.

But wouldn't you know it, their rebelliousness continued there. Both Mom and Hayward argued with the staff, refusing to take baths; some days staging a "sit in" and wouldn't leave their room so the cleaning crew could do their job (John and Yoko would've been proud). I was fielding calls from the manager almost every other day and my brothers and I were worried it wasn't going to work out.

Then, about three months in, Hayward started pitching the idea to Mom of a "jail break". He somehow came up with this *delusion* that they were going to go live in a trailer on his son's nearby property. It was one of my greatest joys when Mom called me and said, "Please talk to Hayward for me. I don't want to go live in a trailer. I like it here."

On October 2, 2024, our mother went to heaven to be with our dad and brother Rodney. The morning after she died, as I was driving to the gym, a beautiful sunrise filled the sky with many vibrant colors. I saw it as a message from my mom saying, *Don't worry, Rick, I'm okay.*

\*\*\*

I wanted to share my life with you, the reader, because I thought it was a good life, with ups and downs. There were funny and sad times. It may be a life for people to learn from—even if for what *not* to do. I love to laugh, and I hope this book has brought some laughter to you. It's a proven fact that laughter will add years to your life.

If you have enjoyed this book, please pass it on to someone who is going through a rough time in their life. It could be a divorce, bankruptcy, unemployment, someone who is using and struggling with drug addiction. It is my hope they'll see that if they make up their mind to give themselves a second chance, they'll have a decent shot at changing their life, as I did. Trust me, with a positive attitude, and taking one small step at a time in the right direction, tomorrow will be a better day than today.

I've become involved with local politics following my retirement. Almost every month I wrote a letter to the editor of my hometown paper, *The Messenger*, expressing my views. I found that I am not as shy as I used to be with my thoughts on the government. In fact, I've sat on sit on five boards which have provided me with my second chance to give back to the community:

Webster County Historical Society
Habitat For Humanity
Almost Home Animal Rescue Society
Friends of Oakland Cemetery
Ft. Dodge Historical Preservation Commission

Ironically, perhaps, the last two are funded by the government. I went from hiding from the government to being a part of it. Years ago, I would've bet any amount of money that would never happen. In the seventies I was a big-time drug dealer and today I am good friends with the Chief of Police, a local DCI agent, attorneys, and judges who if I had been caught and arrested would've thrown me in jail in a heartbeat.

I have to credit author Glenn Beck for bringing me out of that shell, and for giving me the inspiration to write this book. I read his book *The Christmas Sweater*, then immediately sat down over two weekends and wrote the first draft of my manuscript.

I can't believe how much better it feels to give than to take, take, take. For so many years all I cared about was, *What's in it for me?* I couldn't have cared less about humane shelters, hospice homes, preserving the history of Fort Dodge, or the Oakland Cemetery.

Now I get to experience the gratification of volunteering; being able to see the difference I've made on these committees. I can't tell you the pride I feel before attending a city function; looking in the mirror and there's Rick Carle in his dove grey business suit. When just as easily, I could be wearing an orange prison-issued jumpsuit.

Go figure.

www.ingramcontent.com/pod-product-compliance
Lightning Source LLC
Chambersburg PA
CBHW060447290526
45791CB00001B/17